# Equity Valuation and Analysis

W9-BIR-871

## Fourth Edition

**Russell Lundholm**
University of British Columbia

**Richard Sloan**
University of Southern California

Equity Valuation and Analysis. Fourth Edition.

Copyright ©2017 by Russell Lundholm and Richard Sloan
All rights reserved.

Cover design by Evelyn Giron.

6" x 9" (15.24 x 22.86 cm)
Black & White on White paper
ISBN-13: 978-1548118921
ISBN-10: 1548118923

No part of this publication may be reproduced or distributed in any form or by any means, or stored in a database or retrieval system, without the prior written consent of the authors, including, but not limited to, in any network or other electronic storage or transmission, or broadcast for distance learning.

The Internet addresses listed in this text were accurate at the time of publication. The inclusion of a website does not indicate an endorsement by the authors and the authors do not guarantee the accuracy of the information presented at these sites.

# Table of Contents

# Chapter 12
# Some Complications

# Index

# Preface

## WHY THIS BOOK?

We wrote this book because we saw a void between the abstract theoretical treatment of equity valuation and the practical problem of valuing an actual company using real-world data. We give serious treatment to the underlying theory of financial analysis and valuation, but our main goal is to be able to arrive at a pragmatic answer to the important question, "what is this company really worth?" To answer this question, we adopt a different approach from other textbooks. The key differences can be summarized as follows:

1. Our focus is on generating good financial statement forecasts.
2. We provide detailed practical guidance on how to obtain and analyze relevant real-world data.
3. We demystify the mechanics of equity valuation.

Our overriding theme is that good forecasts of the future financial statements are the key input to a good valuation. Most other aspects of the valuation process are mechanical and can be programmed into a computer. In fact, this text refers often to *eVal*, a fancy Excel workbook that provides a template for these many mechanical tasks (and *eVal* is freely available at http://www.lundholmandsloan.com). As with many other textbooks, we discuss topics like business strategy analysis, accounting analysis, financial ratio analysis, and so forth. However, we always do so with a clear view to how these analyses help us to generate better financial statement forecasts.

We also provide plenty of advice on where to go to obtain the most relevant raw data. Armed with such a rich source of data, we are able to provide you with plenty of practical examples and limitless opportunities for you to practice doing your own analyses.

A final goal of this book is to demystify the valuation process. In the past, we have seen students become lost in a sea of valuation formulas and inconsistent spreadsheet models. For example, students get confused as to whether they should use a DDM, DCF, or RIM valuation formula and whether they need to use the CAPM, APT, or MFM to estimate their WACC (and to how many decimal places). They become obsessed with learning acronyms and formulas but flounder when asked to provide a plausible valuation for an actual company. We demonstrate that these different formulas are easily reconciled and refocus students on developing the best set of financial forecasts to plug into these formulas. This reinforces our main point that the key to good valuations is good forecasts.

# THE *eVal* WORKBOOK

We created this workbook because we realized that students were spending way too much time building and debugging their valuation spreadsheets and, consequently, way too little time thinking about the forecasts that they put into their spreadsheets. The tail was definitely wagging the dog. They also couldn't talk to one another because each student tackled the spreadsheet problem differently—it could take hours just to figure out why Jill's value estimate differed from Jack's value estimate. By building one "mother-of-all spreadsheet valuation workbooks" and making it completely transparent and customizable, we turned our students' attention back to the real problem at hand, which is forecasting the future financial statements. Thus, *eVal* was born. As we used the early version of the workbook with students, we discovered that we could use *eVal* to organize the entire financial analysis, forecasting, and valuation process. All the pieces of the puzzle could finally be kept in one place. We found that once we had familiarized students with *eVal*; we could effectively teach complex valuation cases that would previously have been overwhelming.

The *eVal* workbook helps in doing valuation and it helps in *learning* valuation. There are many software products and Web services today that take a few forecast inputs from you and then spit out a valuation, as if by magic, but how they arrived at the result is hidden in a black box. In contrast, this book and the *eVal* workbook that accompanies it are designed to be completely transparent at every stage of the valuation process. The software displays the valuation implications of your forecasts in both discounted cash flow models and residual income models, and it shows exactly how the flows of value from these models are linked to your financial statement forecasts.

No matter how proud we are of *eVal*, we have to acknowledge that it has one important limitation. *eVal* employs a standardized set of financial statement data and ratios. The text emphasizes the limitations of using standardized data. While *eVal* is a useful pedagogical tool for learning equity analysis and valuation, professional analyst's typically build their models and communicate with management and investors using the company's 'as-reported' financial statement data. The textbook explains the difference between standardized data and as-reported data and we encourage students to aspire to build their own models using the as-reported financial statement data. The 'Analyzing Apple' case provides practice in doing so.

## HOW DOES ALL THIS HELP YOU?

The theory of financial analysis and valuation is more compelling when linked to real-world examples. The abstract theory of financial statements, ratios, and valuation formulas can be covered in a few boring lectures. What makes this topic exciting is seeing how an organized approach to studying a real company leaves you so much better informed about the firm's future. Is Apple really worth more than any other public company in the world? The answer is probably yes, once you understand its free cash flow generating ability. Under

Armor is scorching a new trail in the sports apparel market and sporting growth rates and valuation multiples that leave competitors like Gap in the dust. Is it really the superstar stock that Wall Street analysts and bankers claim it to be? A careful analysis suggests that, unless we all start wearing Under Armor to work, its valuation is likely unsustainable. Tesla wants to produce and sell hundreds of thousands of cars in the future, but can it generate enough cash from existing sales to fund the production of all these new cars? A careful study of their cash flows shows that they will almost certainly be borrowing lots of money to build all these cars. Financial statements, accounting rules, financial ratios, and valuation models are all pretty dull beasts on their own, but if we can use them to answer questions such as these, we can really bring them to life. By blending the theory of equity analysis with practical application, we feel that students learn both more effectively.

## ONLINE RESOURCES

Our website at http://www.lundholmandsloan.com provides a number of additional online resources. These resources include quizzes, cases, standardized financial data, webcasts, slides and updated links. These resources complement the textbook and warrant a brief introduction.

At the end of each chapter, we provide links to recommended online quizzes and cases. The quizzes typically have relatively straightforward answers and are designed to help students apply the concepts discussed in the chapter. Solutions to the quizzes are also provided online so that students can check their own answers. The cases are designed for classroom discussion and student evaluation and tend to be more open-ended than the quizzes. Most of the quizzes and cases require students to analyze real-world companies. These quizzes and cases are an integral part of the learning experience.

Many of the quizzes and cases are revisited in consecutive chapters. One chapter will address business strategy analysis; the next will address accounting analysis, and so on. We recommend that you pick a subset of the quizzes and cases and follow them throughout the textbook. It is hard to do a meaningful job of evaluating a firm's financial ratios if you haven't first analyzed its strategy and accounting policies. Several of the cases are tailored directly to the *eVal* workbook, and financial data for these cases are included in *eVal*'s final sheet.

A challenge in writing cases on real-world companies is the determination of the information to include along with each case. Traditionally, case writers have carefully selected just the most relevant information for inclusion in the case. Unfortunately, this approach has two disadvantages. First, the case writer is robbing the student of the opportunity to learn one of the most important skills in equity analysis: identifying the relevant information. Second, to the extent that the case writer omits relevant information, the richness of the case is compromised. We adopt a new approach to this problem by posting a broader set of information along with each quiz and case on our website. Each quiz comes with its own online booklet of financial information and each case contains links out to its own set of financial information. Students must take responsibility for locating the relevant information. For example, we may provide a 100-page Form 10-K along, and the student must be able to navigate the 10-K and extract the relevant information. We think that the ability to extract relevant information is one of the most important skills of a real-world equity analyst, and our cases provide students with the opportunity to develop this skill. But think twice before hitting the 'Print' button!

One task that you will encounter when analyzing a company outside our list of cases is getting the historical financial statements into your valuation model. Our *eVal* workbook uses a standardized financial statement format and the final sheet in *eVal* provides standardized data for many of our cases. You simply cut and paste the relevant block of standardized data from the data sheet to the financial statements sheet in *eVal*. Our website also provides standardized *eVal* data for the S&P 500, updated in spring each year. Finally, we provide another workbook, titled 'datamaker.xls' that takes data from various financial data providers and translates them into the standardized block of data that can be cut-and-paste into *eVal*. This step might require some customization by the user, as the formats used by data providers are constantly changing.

While all this standardized data sounds very convenient, we stress that it has important limitations. As you read through the textbook, you will learn about these limitations and the associated advantages of using the 'as-reported' financial statement data directly from a company's financial filings. The standardized data provide a common language, and are therefore useful from a pedagogical perspective. This language, however, lacks the richness of the as-reported financials. Moreover, management and professional analysts communicate using the 'as-reported' language. If you really want to be an expert on a company, you will have to learn and build your models using the language of the 'as-reported' financials.

The website also contains links to a series of webcasts and associated slides that summarize the material in this book. The webcasts are useful for review and to reinforce important concepts. Each chapter of the text contains a set of relevant links and an updated set of all the links is provided on the website. If a link in the book no longer works, try the associated link on the website. If that doesn't work, please contact us and we will update the link on the website.

Finally, if you are a full-time instructor, we also have a top-secret set of instructional materials, including suggested course outlines, case teaching notes and slides. Contact us for details, but be ready to present your bona fide instructor credentials!

# ACKNOWLEDGMENTS

Before getting down to business, we would like to thank everyone who has helped us in the preparation of all four editions. Patricia Dechow and Kai Petainen have been involved throughout and have provided valuable and timely feedback. We would also like to thank the following list of people for excellent input: Noel Addy, Mississippi State University; Ervin Black, Brigham Young University; Michael Butak, Boise State University; Mike Calegari, Santa Clara University; Ted Christensen, University of Georgia; Bryan Church, Georgia Institute of Technology; Ilia Dichev, Emory University; Paul Hribar, University of Iowa; Amy Hutton, Boston College; Bruce Johnson, University of Iowa; Reuven Lehavy, University of Michigan; Joshua Livnat, New York University; Sarah McVay, University of Washington; Steve Monahan, INSEAD; Panos Patatoukas, University of California at Berkeley, Michael Sandretto, University of Illinois; Akhtar Siddique, Georgetown University; Richard Simonds, Michigan State University; Stephen Sloan; Sarah Tasker, University of California at Berkeley; and Peter Wysocki, University of Miami. Finally, we'd like to thank our significant others, friends, students, colleagues, families, pets, and everyone else who had to put up with us while we worked on this project.

"To Tricia and Patricia"

CHAPTER ONE

# Introduction

## 1.1 GETTING STARTED

The basic objective of this book is to provide you with the skills to efficiently allocate financial resources among different businesses. There are many situations where these skills can be useful. Perhaps the one that first comes to mind is buying and selling stocks. But there are many other such situations, including private equity investing, corporate acquisitions and internal capital budgeting. This book and the associated online tools will provide you with a systematic framework for valuing businesses and making sound resource allocation decisions. There are many books written on this topic. Our approach is to provide a close marriage between theory and practice. The aim is to provide you with both a firm grounding in valuation theory and a good understanding of the techniques that have evolved to facilitate practical application of the theory. The end result is that you should be able to either confidently make a sound financial decision, or you should be able to clearly articulate why you are unable to do so.

Valuing businesses necessarily involves uncertainty. We give plenty of guidance on what constitutes a reasonable forecast in an uncertain world. We also point out many sources of data that are available to aid you in constructing your forecasts. We are living in the middle of an information explosion. The Internet puts an ever-increasing array of financial data at our fingertips. In the spirit of practical advice, we will suggest places to find the best, juiciest tidbits of information and how to incorporate them into your analysis. All this work will reduce the uncertainty in your forecasts, but plenty will still remain. No one knows exactly how the future will unfold; uncertainty is the nature of the beast.

This introductory chapter outlines our equity analysis and valuation framework. We begin with an overview of the nature of business activities. Next, we provide a brief discussion of equity valuation theory. We then explain the critical importance of the financial statements in the practical application of equity valuation theory. Finally, we outline the steps in our systematic approach to equity valuation. This textbook contains the relevant theory. To provide you with practice in applying the theory, we provide a set of supporting cases and quizzes on our website. We close the chapter with more details on these supporting materials.

## 1.2 OVERVIEW OF BUSINESS ACTIVITIES

Equity securities represent ownership claims in the business activities of profit-seeking entities. The valuation of an equity security must therefore begin with a thorough analysis of the entity's underlying business activities. Business activities can be divided into three broad categories to facilitate analysis: *operating activities, investing activities,* and *financing activities.* Each category is briefly described below.

## Operating Activities

Businesses typically generate profit for their owners by providing customers with goods and services in return for cash or other consideration. As long as the consideration received exceeds the costs incurred in providing the goods and services, profit is generated. *Operating activities* are those activities that are directly related to the provision of goods and services to customers. For example, in a restaurant business, the purchase, preparation, and serving of food to customers are all examples of operating activities. Washing the dishes and cleaning the restrooms are also operating activities, since these are part of the package of services that a restaurant provides to its customers. The operating activities are the primary means through which the owners of the business hope to make a profit.

## Investing Activities

Nearly all businesses must make investments in productive capacity before they can begin to provide goods and services to their customers. For example, a restaurant business requires a restaurant building, furniture, and cooking equipment. Purchases and sales of resources that provide productive capacity are referred to as *investing activities.* We define investing activities with respect to the nature of the goods and services that the firm is in the business of providing. If the firm is in the business of retailing cooking equipment, then the purchase of an oven is an operating activity. However, if the firm is in the business of providing restaurant meals, then the purchase of an oven is an investing activity, because it provides the productive capacity required to provide meals.

   Why bother to distinguish between operating activities and investing activities? Investing activities involve resource commitments that are expected to provide benefits over long periods of time. Investments take place in anticipation of future operating activities and the profits from operating activities must be sufficient to provide a competitive return on investment for the investments to have been worthwhile. Because the resources acquired in investing activities provide benefits for long periods of time, it can take many years to find out how profitable these investments have been. In addition, the investing activities that a company makes today may be used to support future operating activities that differ from the current operating activities (e.g., entering a new line of business). It is therefore useful to separate our analysis of the performance of a business's current operating activities from its investments in productive capacity to support future operating activities. In the long run, however, operating and investing activities are closely linked.

Operating activities are made possible by past investing activities, and the profits from operating activities should be evaluated in relation to the cost of the investing activities that made them possible.

### Financing Activities

In order to acquire the resources necessary to engage in operating and investing activities, businesses require financing. The owners of the business provide the initial financing in the hope that the business will provide them with a competitive return on their investment. In a corporation, these owners are the holders of the common equity securities. If a business is financed solely by its equity holders, and immediately distributes the net cash flows generated by its operating and investing activities back to its equity holders, its *financing activities* consist of these simple cash flows between the equity holders and the business. In practice, however, there are many other sources of financing. For example, a business can issue debt, preferred stock, and warrants, to name just a few alternatives. In addition, a business need not immediately distribute all the cash generated by its operating and investing activities. Instead, the business may choose to invest this cash in financial assets, such as bank accounts, treasury bonds or financial securities issued by other businesses. Financing activities incorporate all such transactions.

Financing activities are distinct from operating and investing activities. A firm can finance a given set of operating and investing activities many different ways without affecting the nature of the underlying operating and investing activities. But this does not mean that the firm cannot add value through financing activities. Financing activities create the opportunity for the owners of the business to leverage the return from their operating and investing activities, to minimize taxes and transactions costs, and to exploit inefficiencies in capital markets. Investment bankers and corporate lawyers specialize in advising businesses on their financing activities, and the large fees that they charge speak to the potential value that can be created.

## 1.3 OVERVIEW OF EQUITY VALUATION THEORY

The basic theory of equity valuation is straightforward and well established. Equity securities are financial instruments, and, as such, their value is equal to net present value of the future cash distributions that they are expected to generate. These cash distributions traditionally have taken the form of cash dividend payments, and so the value of equity often is expressed as the net present value of the expected future dividend payments, as shown in the following equation:

$$P_0 = \sum_{t=1}^{\infty} \frac{Cash\ Dividend_t}{(1+r)^t}\ , where$$

$P_0$ is the value of the common equity at time 0,

Cash Dividend$_t$ = expected amount of cash dividends to be paid in period $t$, and $r$ is the discount rate.

This valuation model is widely known as the dividend-discounting model. Dividends, however, are not the only way that cash can be distributed to equity holders. Stock repurchases have become increasingly popular. While dividends represent routine cash payments made on a pro rata basis to all equity holders, stock repurchases involve the business buying back its own stock from specific equity holders. Nevertheless, both transactions involve distributing cash from the business to its equity holders. Another consideration in the valuation of equity securities is that companies often seek new cash infusions through the issuance of additional equity securities. These equity issuances can be thought of as negative cash distributions that should be netted against the positive cash distributions associated with dividends and stock repurchases in order to determine the net cash distributions to equity holders. So the dividend-discounting model is more precisely expressed as:

$$P_0 = \sum_{t=1}^{\infty} \frac{Cash\ Dividend_t + Stock\ Repurchases_t - Equity\ Issuances_t}{(1+r)^t}\ , where$$

Stock Repurchases$_t$ = expected amount of cash to be paid out via stock repurchases in period $t$, and

Equity Issuances$_t$ = expected amount of cash to be raised via equity issuances in period $t$.

Throughout the remainder of the text, we will avoid this mouthful and simply refer to the numerator as "net distributions to equity holders."

What determines the amount and timing of distributions to equity holders? Since equity holders are the owners of the business, they have the residual claim on the net cash flows available from a business's operating, investing, and non-equity financing activities. In practice, distributions to equity holders are made at the discretion of management, based on a variety of factors. The major factors are

- How much cash did the business's operating activities generate?
- How much cash was used for investing activities in order to maintain or expand the scale and scope of the business's operating activities?
- How much cash is required to make scheduled payments to providers

of non-equity capital, such as interest and principal payments on loans?
- How much cash should be retained in the business in the form of financial assets to provide for future cash flow needs?

In the long run, the cash flows generated by a business's operating activities are the key driver of distributions to equity holders. However, the other factors listed above can make the amount and timing of a business's operating cash flows very different from the amount and timing of the distributions to its equity holders.

In summary, while the basic theory of equity valuation is quite straightforward, the devil is in forecasting the future distributions to equity holders. There are many different equity valuation formulas floating around academia and practice. These formulas implicitly use different variables to forecast future distributions to equity holders. For example, practitioners are fond of substituting variables like earnings, "EBITDA," and "NOPAT" for distributions to equity holders. We will talk more about these variables later in the book. For now, we simply note that these substitutions can be justifiable if done in a way that maintains consistency with the underlying dividend discounting model. However, practitioners all too often throw caution to the wind and come up with formulas that require heroic assumptions to reconcile with sound valuation theory.

# 1.4 THE ROLE OF FINANCIAL STATEMENTS

The financial statements are the primary device for bridging the gap between theory and practice in equity valuation. Some finance texts criticize financial statements and their underlying accounting principles on the basis that they do an imperfect job at measuring value. However, these criticisms represent a basic misunderstanding of the role of financial statements in equity valuation. Financial statements are not designed to directly estimate equity value, and accounting book values rarely match market values. Instead, the role of the financial statements is to provide a detailed description of the financial consequences of a firm's historical business activities. In other words, the financial statements summarize the past operating, investing, and financing activities of a firm, and show how these activities affect the past, present, and (in certain very limited cases) expected future cash flows. With a few special exceptions, the primary purpose of the financial statements is not to directly forecast the future cash flows.

Given that the financial statements do not directly forecast how future business activities will affect future cash flows, what is their role in equity valuation? Their role is twofold:

- They provide the language for translating forecasts of future business activities into forecasts of future cash flows.

- By describing the cash flow implications of past business activities, they provide a good starting point for forecasting the cash flow implications of future business activities.

The first role of the financial statements in valuation is to provide a language for describing how a firm's future business activities will affect its future cash flows. We cannot forecast cash flows in a vacuum. The role of the financial statements is to identify and categorize the activities of a firm that have cash flow implications. A set of financial statements tells us how the various operating, investing, and financing activities of a firm combine to produce cash flows. In order to forecast a firm's future cash flows, we first need a set of financial statements that capture the various intended operating, investing, and financing activities of the firm. We can then begin the process of forecasting the cash flow implications of these activities. For instance, by forecasting sales and accounts receivable, we can derive a forecast of the cash collections from customers. By constructing a complete set of forecast financial statements, we can systematically derive the cash distributions to equity holders.

The second role of the financial statements is to provide historical data on the cash flow implications of a firm's past business activities that may prove useful in forecasting its future cash flows. Many firms engage in similar business activities for multiple periods. Over time, these business activities are subject to change. Nevertheless, these changes are rarely so drastic as to make the results of past business activities completely irrelevant to the prediction of the future. Thus, the most common forecasting procedure is to start with the past financial statements and then modify those statements based on changes that are anticipated to occur in the future. The effectiveness of this procedure varies widely. For firms in mature industries with established products and stable customer demand, past results can be a very good predictor of future results and the past financial statements will be very relevant in estimating firm value. In contrast, for start-up firms in emerging industries with evolving products and growing customer demand, past results can be a poor predictor of future results. Past results also will be a poor predictor of future results for firms making significant acquisitions or significant changes to their business activities. But we have to start somewhere, and the past is usually the best place to start when forecasting the future.

## 1.5 THREE STEPS OF EQUITY VALUATION

The discussion thus far indicates that the equity valuation process can be broken down into three distinct steps, which are illustrated in Figure 1.1. *Understanding the past* is the first step. This analysis must go beyond simply looking at the firm's past financial results. You need to understand the firm's financial results in the context of its business strategy and the industry and economy in which it operates, and you need to look for clues about planned changes in future business activities. The second step involves using our analysis of the past in *forecasting the future*. This step is structured around forecasting the future financial statements, from which we will derive our estimates of future cash distributions to equity holders. The third step comprises *valuation*. In this step, we convert our estimates of future distributions to equity holders into a single estimate of firm value. In the rest of this section, we summarize how the remaining chapters in this book guide you through these three steps.

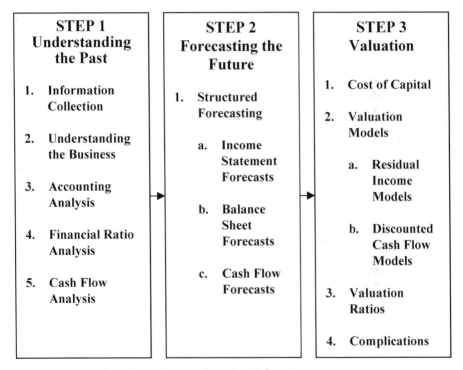

**FIGURE 1.1: The Three Steps of Equity Valuation**

## Understanding the Past

The first step involves examining relevant information about the business. This step begins with the systematic collection of pertinent information, which we refer to in Figure 1.1 as *information collection*. If the equity security is publicly traded on a major exchange in the United States, then the usual starting point for information collection is the firm's financial filings with the Securities and Exchange Commission (SEC). However, there are a myriad of other information sources that should be investigated, ranging from company press releases to industry and macroeconomic data. Today, much of this information is available via the touch of a screen. We provide a more detailed discussion of the most important information sources in Chapter 2.

Once the pertinent information has been gathered, we begin the process of analyzing this information. We first need to *understand the business*. This process is primarily qualitative in nature and is aimed at developing a detailed understanding of the business activities in which the firm is engaged. What does the business make, how is it made, and who buys it? Who are the main competitors, what are the industry characteristics, and how is the industry related to the general economy? We also want to identify the elements of a firm's business strategy that are expected to make it more successful than its competitors. Just as investors strive to find securities that will provide abnormally high investment returns, company managers strive to find real investment opportunities that will provide abnormally high profits. Competition among managers limits the availability of such investment opportunities. Your business analysis should leave you with a clear understanding of the firm's business plan, and some opinions about whether this plan represents a viable strategy for generating abnormally high profits. We cover the basics of business analysis in Chapter 3.

Armed with a thorough understanding of the business, we can start to scrutinize the historical financial statements. This step is called *accounting analysis*. The objective here is to develop a thorough understanding of how the economic consequences of the firm's business activities are reflected in the financial statements. The financial statements report on the periodic financial position and operating performance of a business. Over long periods of time (i.e., many years), the cash flows from a firm's operating and investing activities become known with perfect certainty, and so the economic consequences are easy to measure. But over short periods of time (i.e., a quarter or a year), the periodic cash flows can have little relation to the long-run economic consequences. This problem arises because a firm's operating and investing cycles often span many years. Firms often produce and hold inventory over several months, invest in assets that will provide benefits over several years and reward employees with retirement benefits that will be paid after several decades. As a result, the net cash flows to a firm over short periods of time provide a very noisy signal of the long-run cash flow consequences of a firm's business activities.

This is where accrual accounting comes to our aid. The primary objective of accrual accounting is to provide a better indication of the long-run cash consequences of a firm's short-run business activities. For instance, investing in a productive asset is not merely a cash outflow; the accrual accounting system tracks the store of future benefits that this investment represents by recording an asset on the balance sheet. But, while the accrual accounting process undoubtedly creates useful information, it is also fraught with distortions. Some distortions are a direct consequence of following generally accepted accounting rules, while others may be intentionally created through managerial manipulation of the rules. Accounting analysis is concerned with understanding a firm's accrual accounting choices and their implications for the interpretation of the associated financial statements. Accounting analysis will help you understand the key strengths and weaknesses of a firm's financial statements, identify where management may have attempted to mislead you, and help you draw informed conclusions about the economic consequences of the firm's past business activities. Accounting analysis is the subject of Chapter 4.

Once you have a solid understanding of a firm's financial statements, you are set to use the financial statements to evaluate the financial performance of the firm. Chapter 5 develops a systematic *financial ratio analysis* framework to facilitate this task. This analysis shows us how the components of a firm's financial statements interact to produce overall financial performance. What margin does the firm earn on its sales? How much investment is required to generate the sales? How aggressively does the firm use debt financing? This analysis enables us to quickly identify the key drivers of financial performance and spot any irregularities. When combined with accounting analysis, financial ratio analysis provides the basis for evaluating the economic consequences of a firm's past business activities and the success of its business strategy.

Ratio analysis focuses almost exclusively on a firm's accrual accounting statements—the income statement and the balance sheet. However, in order to remain solvent, fund new business opportunities, and ultimately make cash flow distributions, a firm also must carefully manage its cash. A firm's cash flows are detailed in its statement of cash flows, and the analysis of this information is the topic of Chapter 6. *Cash flow analysis* is concerned with understanding the cash flows from a firm's operating, investing, and financing activities. A sound business strategy should anticipate the cash flows associated with each activity and make sure that they articulate. Also, firm value is ultimately dependent on the distribution of cash flows to equity holders. Unfortunately, some firms choose to invest surplus cash flows in wasteful ways rather than making timely distributions to equity holders. These and other related issues are explained in Chapter 6.

## Forecasting the Future

Once you understand the past, you are ready to forecast the future. The tasks involved in this step are summarized in the second box of Figure 1.1. Our goal in this step is to forecast the future financial statements. Recall from our earlier discussion that the financial statements represent the language for converting forecasts of future business activities into forecasts of future cash flows. In Chapter 7 we introduce *structured forecasting*—the systematic way that we go about developing forecasts. Rather than attempting to directly forecast the amount for each line item of the financial statements, we frame the forecasting problem using the same types of ratios that you studied in Chapter 5. You express your forecasts about the firm's operating, investing, and financing activities by developing forecasts of these ratios, and then derive the implied values for the underlying financial statement line items.

In Chapter 8 we give you more specific guidance on *detailed forecast construction*. The process begins with the very first line on the income statement, the "Sales" forecast. Most firms have business models that center around providing goods and services to customers in return for sales revenue. For these firms, the sales forecast is the single most important forecast; it represents the starting point for most other forecasts. For example, most of the remaining lines in the income statement capture the costs that are incurred in the firm's operating activities, and many of these costs depend on the level of business activity, as summarized by the sales forecast. But the costs also depend on the efficiency with which the business is run and the prices at which the inputs for the business (such as materials and labor) are purchased, so forecasting these costs is not as simple as taking a fixed percentage of sales.

Income statement forecasts concern operating activities. Balance sheet forecasts concern the impact of the operating, investing, and financing activities on the resources and obligations of a firm. The forecasting of the balance sheet can be divided into two distinct tasks. First, we must forecast the resources and obligations necessary to sustain the forecasted operating activities from our income statement. Operating activities typically require investments in working capital (e.g., inventory) and long-term capital (e.g., property, plant, and equipment) and can also result in obligations (e.g., accounts payable and pension benefits for employees). The forecasted amount of operating resources and obligations depends on both the forecasted level of operating activity and the efficiency with which the firm is forecasted to conduct its operations. The second distinct task is to forecast the resources and obligations associated with the firm's financing activities. Most firms hold some financial resources (e.g., cash and marketable securities) and use some non-equity financing (e.g., debt and preferred stock). The forecasting of the individual financial resources and obligations on the balance sheet involves determining the amount and mix of financing that is used to support the firm's operating and investing activities.

The next task is to create cash flow forecasts. As discussed earlier, the financial statements provide the language we use to describe the economic consequences of business activities. Ultimately, these economic consequences are represented by cash flows and the statement of cash flows reports these cash consequences. Contained within the cash flow forecasts are forecasts of the net cash distributions to equity holders, the key inputs for equity valuation, so this is a critical step. Fortunately, cash flow forecasting is quite straightforward. As you may recall from your introductory accounting classes, we can derive a statement of cash flows from an income statement, along with the associated beginning and ending balance sheets. So, we simply use our income statements and balance sheet forecasts to construct our cash flow forecasts.

The forecasted financial statements are often referred to as "pro forma" financial statements ("pro forma" is Latin for "a matter of form"). The last step is to apply the same ratio analysis and cash flow analysis that we discussed in

Chapter 5 to the pro forma financial statements. This final step provides a reality check on the plausibility of our forecasts. For example, we may find that our forecasting assumptions imply a level of profitability for a firm that far exceeds the historical industry average. Such performance may be justified through some unique feature of the firm's business strategy. But in the absence of a compelling justification, we should revise the forecasting assumptions to bring profitability back to plausible levels. Similarly, our pro forma cash flow analysis may reveal that our forecasting assumptions imply that a firm must raise substantial additional capital. If the firm has no plans to raise new capital, or would have difficulty accessing capital markets on the forecasted terms, we should revise our forecasting assumptions accordingly.

## Valuation

With your forecasts of the future fundamentals under your belt, you are ready for step number three, valuation. The tasks involved in this step are summarized in the third box of Figure 1.1. First you need to decide on the necessary valuation parameters. The most important of these is the discount rate, or *cost of capital*, which enters the denominator of our equity valuation model. Unfortunately, there is much disagreement concerning the selection of an appropriate cost of capital. In Chapter 9, we discuss popular techniques for estimating the cost of capital and provide some broad guidelines for handling this issue.

A second issue in constructing the valuation models is whether we choose to discount the cash distributions directly to equity holders using the cost of equity capital, or whether we discount cash flows to all providers of capital (i.e., common equity plus preferred stock and debt) using a weighted average cost of capital, and then subtract the value of the non-equity capital to derive equity value. We will show you how to do the valuation both ways, both should give the same answer, and the choice between the two approaches is largely a matter of taste. Chapter 10 provides a detailed explanation of the valuation gymnastics involved in these alternative *valuation models*.

The remaining steps in equity valuation are primarily computational. The good news here is that these can be handled by a standardized set of formulas in a spreadsheet. We provide an Excel-based workbook called _eVal_ to do all of this work for you. _eVal_ provides computations using both a *residual income valuation model* (RIM) and a *discounted free cash flow model* (DCF). Why do we need two valuations? Well, we don't, and it turns out that both of these valuations will give you exactly the same answer. These are simply two different algebraic formulations of our basic valuation theory. Regardless of the formula used, it is your forecast of the future financial statements, along with your valuation parameters, that ultimately determine equity value. The only issue here is whether you would like to look at computations based on earnings or cash flows. By providing you with both sets of computations, you will be able to effectively communicate your equity valuation work to aficionados of either model.

Financial analysts often communicate their beliefs about the value of a firm in terms of *valuation ratios*. Some of these are quite straightforward, such as the price-to-earnings ratio, defined as the market price divided by EPS. Others are much more complex, like the PEG ratio (don't ask). In Chapter 11 we discuss some of these ratios, what they represent, and how they can be used as a starting point for identifying potentially mispriced stocks. These ratios are commonly used heuristics, but they are just that; they are no substitute for a comprehensive valuation analysis.

The final step in the equity valuation process is to consider some *complications*. If you are lucky, none of these complications will apply to your valuation. Unfortunately, one or more of these monsters often rear their ugly heads. We mention them here briefly only to alert you to their existence; Chapter 12 provides more detailed coverage.

The first complication concerns negative equity values. Real world stock prices cannot be negative, but valuation models can be constructed that generate negative equity values. If you find yourself with a negative equity valuation, then you should read Chapter 12. A second and related complication concerns the abandonment option. If you come up with a positive equity valuation, but your sensitivity analysis reveals that negative valuations are also reasonably likely, then you need to consider the abandonment option.

A third complication arises when we introduce the possibility that a firm may create or destroy value through transactions in its own mispriced securities. For example, if a firm's stock is overpriced relative to its intrinsic value, it can create value for its existing equity holders by issuing additional shares of the overpriced stock. Thus, not only do we have to correctly determine the intrinsic value of a firm's operating and investing activities, but we also have to forecast how much additional value will be created or destroyed through the firm's financing activities.

A final and related complication concerns contingent equity claims. Contingent equity claims provide holders with the option, but not the obligation, to purchase shares of common stock for a pre-specified exercise price. Firms issue contingent claims on their equity for a variety of reasons. For example, firms often compensate employees using employee stock options. Because the holders of contingent claims only have to exercise their claims when it is profitable for them to do so, the claims themselves will have value as long as there is some probability of a profitable future exercise. These claims can therefore result in new equity securities being issued for consideration less than fair value.

## 1.6 CLOSING COMMENTS

We close each chapter with a list of relevant quizzes, cases, links and references. The quizzes and cases may be found on our <u>website</u>. The quizzes are essentially cases with straightforward questions that are designed to help you practice the concepts introduced in each chapters Solutions to the quizzes are provided on the website. The cases are more comprehensive and open-ended in nature and are designed for in-class discussion and assessment. Accordingly, we do not provide case solutions on the website. Many of the quizzes and cases consist of multiple parts that are listed in consecutive chapters of the book. These quizzes and cases follow a single company through the entire analysis and valuation process. We encourage you to pick a handful of these quizzes and cases and follow them throughout the text.

Linked material is underlined in the text, and the associated URLs are provided at the end of each chapter. One linked resource that we have already mentioned above is the *eVal* workbook. This workbook provides a series of worksheets that guide you through the valuation process. We will use *eVal* throughout this book to illustrate many of the computations used in the equity analysis and valuation process. We also provide a case called Building *eVal* that helps you to understand this valuation workbook. The *eVal* workbook, however, has a serious drawback. Like all 'canned' valuation workbooks, it uses a standardized financial statement format that is okay for most companies, but not really ideal for any company.

We will discuss the perils of standardized data in more detail in Chapter 2. For now, we simply note that while we will use *eVal* to illustrate the equity analysis and valuation process, you should strive to build your own bespoke valuation model that reflects the financial statements of the company you are analyzing. The quizzes and cases will give you plenty of practice in doing so. One case that we will emphasize here is the Analyzing Apple case. This case appears at the end of most chapters and guides you through the process of building your own equity analysis and valuation workbook using Apple's 'as-reported' financial statements. Whenever you see this case listed at the end of a chapter, we encourage you to start with this one.

## 1.7 QUIZZES, CASES, LINKS AND REFERENCES

### Links
• *eVal* Valuation Workbook:
http://www.lundholmandsloan.com/software.html
• Lundholm and Sloan website: www.lundholmandsloan.com
• Building *eVal* Case:
http://www.lundholmandsloan.com/Case%20Materials/20.%20Building%20eVal/Case.pdf
• Analyzing Apple Case:
http://www.lundholmandsloan.com/New%20Cases%20and%20Materials/Apple%20Real%20Time/Case.pdf

CHAPTER TWO

# Information Collection

## 2.1 INTRODUCTION

The heart of a good valuation is a good forecast, and a forecast is only as good as the information that is used to construct it. So the more relevant information you collect, the more accurate your forecasts will be. You may be thinking that information collection is time consuming and costly, and that our "more is better" advice ignores this aspect of the trade-off. But our advice comes from years of experience watching students and practitioners underinvest in information collection. The chapters that follow talk in more detail about how to interpret information. This chapter focuses on describing the most important sources of information and also explains the critical difference between the 'as reported' financial statements provided by the companies themselves and the 'standardized' financial statements provided by most financial data services.

We begin by identifying the key sources of company-specific data. For public companies with securities trading on exchanges in the United States, filings with the Securities and Exchange Commission (SEC) are the most important source of company-specific information. We identify the most important filings and describe their contents. We then discuss other data sources, such as company web sites, company press releases, news stories, and analysts' reports. Next, we identify and briefly discuss sources of industry and macroeconomic information.

Throughout this chapter, we will give you links to sources of information on the Internet. We hyperlink the site in the text and, at the end of the chapter, provide list of all the URLs. Please remember that these sources are continually being revised and some of the links provided may be dead or stale. We maintain an updated version of these links on our <u>website.</u>

## 2.2 COMPANY INFORMATION

You should spend most of your time collecting company-specific information. Over half of the variation in a typical stock's price is company-specific and unrelated to market or industry information. This analysis will typically start with the mandatory financial filings and then extend to discretionary company disclosures (e.g., press releases) and information provided by third parties (e.g., sell-side analyst reports).

| Filing | Description |
|---|---|
| Form 10-K | This is the annual report filed by most companies. It provides a comprehensive overview of the company's business (see Figure 2.2 for details). Depending on company size, it must be filed within 60 days of the close of the fiscal year. |
| Form 10-Q | This is the quarterly financial report filed by most companies. It includes unaudited financial statements and provides a continuing view of the company's financial position during the year. Depending on company size, it must be filed within 35 days of the close of the quarter. |
| Form 8-K | This is the "current report" that is used to report the occurrence of any material events or corporate changes that are of importance to investors and have not been previously reported. |
| Proxy Statement (Form DEF 14A) | The proxy statement provides official notification to designated classes of shareholders of matters to be brought to a vote at a shareholders' meeting. |
| Form 13F | This is the quarterly report filed by institutional investors managing over $100 million. It lists the name and amount of each security held at the end of each quarter. |
| Schedule 13D | This filing is required by 5 percent (or more) equity owners within 10 days of the acquisition event. |
| Schedule 13E | These are filings required by persons engaging in "going private" transactions in the company's stock or by companies engaging in tender offers for their own securities. |
| Schedule 13G | This is similar to Schedule 13D but is only available in special cases where control of the issuer is not compromised. |
| Schedule 14D | These are filings required pursuant to a tender offer. |
| Form 3, Form 4, and Form 5 | These are statements of ownership filings required by directors, officers, and 10 percent owners. Form 3 is the initial ownership filing, Form 4 is for changes in ownership, and Form 5 is a special annual filing. |
| Registration Statements (Forms S-1 and S-3) | These are filings that are used to register securities before they are offered to investors. The most common registration filings are Forms S-1 and S-3. |
| Prospectus (Rule 424) | This document is made available to investors in a security offering. It comes in varieties 424A, 424B1, 424B2, 424B3, 424B4, 424B5, 424B6, and 424B7. |

**FIGURE 2.1: Guide to Common SEC Filings**

## SEC Filings

Public companies issuing securities in the United States are required to file a number of detailed financial reports with the Security and Exchange Commission (SEC), which in turn makes these reports available to the public via EDGAR. These SEC filings represent the most important source of company-specific information and provide the natural starting point for the collection of company data. A summary of the most important SEC filings is provided in Figure 2.1. A comprehensive listing of SEC forms is available on the SEC's website (yes, all 300 of them!).

Listed first in Figure 2.1 is the annual Form 10-K, usually the most relevant SEC filing for our purposes. Domestic publicly traded companies are required to file this form within 60 to 90 days of their fiscal year end, depending on their size. If you were going to read only one document about the company before starting your valuation, this would be the one. This can be quite a lengthy document, but it follows a standardized format and familiarizing yourself with this format will improve your ability to efficiently process the contents.

The basic format of a Form 10-K is summarized in Figure 2.2. The first item, the description of the business, provides a detailed discussion of the company's business activities. Companies are required to provide a long list of information on things such as the principal products sold, sources and availability of raw materials, key patents, trademarks and licenses, seasonalities, key customers, competitive conditions, government regulations, and risk factors associated with the business. The SEC designed this item to be a thorough and objective overview of a company's business activities, and is a great starting point for getting to know a company.

The next three items in the Form 10-K provide information about other aspects of the company that the SEC decided were worth singling out. Item 2 requires a description of the property of the company, Item 3 requires a description of any material pending legal proceedings against the company, and Item 4 requires a description of any matters submitted during the fourth quarter to a vote of security holders. You should scan this information for anything important, but there isn't usually too much here. Item 5 requires summary information concerning recent stock price and dividend activity and Item 6 provides summary financial data for the last five years. You can obtain the information in Items 5 and 6 in more detail from other sources, but since it provides a convenient summary, you may want to scan through it.

Item 7 contains management's discussion and analysis of the firm's financial condition, results of operations, off-balance-sheet arrangements, contractual obligations, and critical accounting policies. Referred to as the "MD&A," this is a "must read." The discussion and analysis of financial condition requires management to identify any factors that might cause the company's liquidity to change. It also requires a description of the company's material capital expenditure commitments, the purpose of such commitments, and the anticipated sources of funding for the commitments. Finally, the company is

| Item | Description |
|------|-------------|
| Cover Page | Lists company name, fiscal year end, state of incorporation, each class of publicly traded securities, and other information. |
| Item 1—Business | Identifies principal products and services of the company, principal markets and methods of distribution, and other key attributes and risks of the business. |
| Item 2—Properties | Location and character of key properties. |
| Item 3—Legal Proceedings | Brief description of material pending legal proceedings. |
| Item 4—Submission of Matters to Vote | Information relating to the convening of a meeting of shareholders, whether annual or special, and the matters voted upon. |
| Item 5—Market for Common Stock | Principal market in which common stock is traded; high and low quarterly stock prices for the last two years; number of stockholders; dividends paid during the last two years; future dividend plans. |
| Item 6—Selected Financial Data | Five-year summary of selected financial data, including net sales and operating revenue, income from continuing operations, total assets, and long-term obligations. |
| Item 7—Management's Discussion and Analysis | Discussion of results of operations, liquidity, capital resources, off-balance-sheet arrangements, and contractual obligations. Discussion should include trends, significant events and uncertainties, causes of material changes, effects of inflation and changing prices, and critical accounting policies. |
| Item 7A—Disclosures about Market Risk | Provides qualitative and quantitative disclosures about market risk (e.g., interest rate, exchange rate, and commodity price risk). Requirements apply to financial instruments and commodity instruments. |
| Item 8—Financial Statements and Supplementary Data | Two-year audited balance sheets, three-year audited statements of income and three-year audited statements of cash flows, along with supporting notes and schedules. |
| Item 9—Changes in and Disagreements with Accountants | Description of any changes in and disagreements with independent auditors on any matter of accounting principles or practices, financial statement disclosure, or auditing scope of procedure. |
| Item 9A—Controls and Procedures | Opinion of top management and auditors regarding the effectiveness of the company's internal controls and procedures over financial reporting |

**FIGURE 2.2: Items of Disclosure Contained in Form 10-K**

required to discuss any pending changes in the company's capital structure. The discussion and analysis of results of operations requires management to walk the reader through the line items in the company's income statement, identifying any unusual or nonrecurring items and explaining any significant changes during the last two years. The discussions concerning off-balance-sheet arrangements, contractual obligations, and critical accounting policies are relatively recent additions in response to the accounting scandals at Enron and WorldCom. These discussions can be useful for identifying potential problem areas in the company's financial reports. But if a company is really "cooking the books," it is unlikely to tell you exactly how it is doing it right here. Lastly, because much of the material in the MD&A is forward-looking, it normally finishes with a long list of all the risk factors that add uncertainty to these forecasts. As you can see, the management discussion and analysis requires management to divulge a wealth of information that is useful in forecasting. Moreover, the company's auditor is required to review the information in the MD&A. So read the MD&A carefully and completely.

Following the MD&A is Item 7A, requiring disclosures about the company's exposure to certain market risks, such as interest rate risk and currency risk. This item provides useful information for financial services companies and other companies holding large amounts of financial instruments or engaging in significant hedging activities. Next is the all-important Item 8. Item 8 contains the company's financial statements and supplementary data. This item includes annual balance sheets for the last two years and annual income statements, statements of stockholders' equity and statements of cash flows for the past three years. This section must also include a detailed description of significant accounting policies, detailed supporting notes and schedules, and the external auditor's opinion on the financial statements. The analysis of these financial statements is one of our most important tasks, and is the subject of Chapters 4, 5, and 6.

Item 9 contains information about changes in and disagreements with the independent auditors on accounting practices and financial disclosures. If the company's auditor either resigned or had a major accounting disagreement with management in the past two years, you will find out here. Most of the time you will find nothing in this section, but you should always check it out just to be sure. It usually takes a serious disagreement for the company and auditors to get to the point of hanging out their dirty laundry in Item 9. A relatively recent addition to Form 10-K is Item 9A. This item was added by the Sarbanes-Oxley Act and basically requires the senior management and auditors to attest to the effectiveness of the company's controls over its financial reporting system.

To summarize, Form 10-K is the most important SEC filing and your starting point for analyzing a company. The most important parts of Form 10-K are the description of business in Item 1, the MD&A in Item 7, and the financial statements in Item 8. The main drawback of Form 10-K is that it is only made available once a year. Our main interest in the other SEC filings in Figure 2.1 is to gain access to more timely information.

The second filing listed in Figure 2.1 is the Form 10-Q filing. This is the quarterly version of Form 10-K. It must be filed within 40 to 45 days of the end of the quarter, for each of the first three quarters of the fiscal year (the annual 10-K filing handles the fourth quarter). These filings are not as detailed as the 10-K and do not give you the description of the business and much of the other information that comes with the 10-K. But, obviously, they are more current. They typically contain a summary version of the MD&A and abbreviated, unaudited financial statements. You should plan on reviewing all Form 10-Qs filed since the most recently available Form 10-K. You also should make sure that you are familiar with the information in the most recent 10-K before attempting to read the intervening 10-Qs, since the 10-K provides the necessary background to understand the information in the 10-Q.

The third filing listed in Figure 2.1 is the Form 8-K filing. This filing is used to report significant current events on a timely basis. Examples of events that warrant a Form 8-K filing include a change in control of a company, the acquisition or disposition of a significant portion of the company's business operations, bankruptcy, change in auditors, and the resignation of key directors or officers. Most companies also announce their quarterly earnings via newswires significantly in advance of filing their 10-Ks and 10-Qs and they are required to file the text of these announcements on Form 8-K. These earnings announcements provide timely updates on financial performance, but you should remember that they are voluntary disclosures by management that are only loosely regulated and often emphasize non-GAAP definitions of earnings that are made up by management to make performance look better. The Form 8-K filing must generally be made within four business days of the event being reported.

There are lots of other forms that a firm must file with the SEC; the most common ones fill out the remainder of Figure 2.1. Most of these other filings aren't as relevant for our purposes as the 10-K, 10-Q, and 8-K, but here are a few of the more interesting ones. Whenever shareholders are required to vote on something (which is usually at least once a year), the firm must file a proxy statement. This statement gives the lowdown on management compensation. So if you think management is skimming too much off the top, this is the place to see just how much they are taking. There are a few different filings related to proxy statements, but the most common one is filed under the designation DEF 14A. Also, insider trades (i.e., trades by management in the company's stock) are reported on Forms 3, 4, and 5. Note that these forms are filed directly by the managers themselves, rather than under the name of the company. Finally, if a company issues new securities, it will typically file a Form S-3 to register the securities and a Form 424B3 for the final prospectus.

All of the above filings can be accessed directly from the EDGAR database on the SEC's Web site. It can sometimes be a challenge to find the exact filing that you are looking for. Companies frequently file one form and then later file an amendment to the form (appending a "/A" to the form name). They also incorporate information in a required filing by referencing another filing. But be persistent, especially when seeking the 10-K and 10-Q. They should be out there somewhere.

## Company Web Site

You can learn much about a company's business by surfing its Web site. Most companies have a dedicated investor relations section of their Web site providing financial information about the company. In fact, the development of the Internet and the passage of Regulation FD (Fair Disclosure) by the SEC have proved to be a boon to small investors. Regulation FD was introduced by the SEC in 2000 and basically prohibits companies from selectively disclosing nonpublic information to a few individuals, such as portfolio managers or Wall Street analysts. In order to comply, most companies immediately put any information that they disclose to other investors onto their website.

One "must read" in the company Web site is the press release section. Company press releases often provide more timely information than periodic SEC filings. However, you also should remember that any financial information in these press releases is not subject to the same standards as the company's financial statements on Forms 10-K and 10-Q. Good examples are press releases related to quarterly earnings announcements. These press releases are made days or even weeks ahead of the corresponding Form 10-Q filing. However, companies often make up their own 'pro-forma' measures of earnings in their press releases and typically emphasize good information and downplay bad information. So always read these press releases with a grain of salt. Another document that you will often find on the Web site is the annual report to shareholders. Be careful not to confuse the firm's annual report with its official Form 10-K filing. There are fewer required disclosures in the annual report than in the 10-K and, for many companies, the annual report is little more than a marketing document. You will see lots of fancy graphs and images of happy employees and customers all designed to convince you that the company is financially healthy, very profitable, an exemplary corporate citizen, and especially kind to animals and small children.

If you check out the company's Web site shortly after an earnings announcement, you will frequently find an audio file that replays the conference call that management had with analysts to discuss the most recent quarter's results and perhaps also a transcript of the call. These can be a rich source of information, but can be short-lived; some companies remove them from the Web site after a week or two. After listening to a few of these, you will notice that they tend to be short sighted and long winded. Most analysts are primarily interested in forecasting the next quarter's results, and most CEOs are counseled to refrain from expressing opinions about the future.

## Financial Press

The company isn't the only one talking. A very active financial press ferrets about hoping to uncover interesting, and sometimes scandalous, facts about the company. Companies are reluctant to highlight their own questionable accounting practices, but the financial press will not hesitate to do so. And the company will not generally compare itself to other firms in the same industry, but a good news article frequently does this. The only word of warning we offer is that writers for the financial press are paid to write exciting stories that people will be drawn to read; being accurate is desirable but not paramount. Frequently the financial press is the first to call attention to a firm's questionable accounting practices, but, in our experience, only about half the time does the accounting really turn out to be bad.

Most of the major financial portals on the Web have links to recent news stories, along with the firm's press releases. The Yahoo! Finance portal provides access to a particularly wide range of sources.  Other free sites that we recommend include Reuters and MSN Money. If you want to join the professionals, then a real-time subscription to Bloomberg or the Dow Jones News Service will give you timely and comprehensive access to both financial news and sports scores.

Lots of regional newspapers also write about companies in their own backyard, and the major news services may not pick up these stories. One way to be sure you haven't missed something big—and we hesitate to recommend this—is to check out the investment message boards and blogs for views on the company. Seeking Alpha, Yahoo, Motley Fool, and several other sites sponsor blogs and message boards where investors exchange views about particular stocks along with insults about one another's intelligence. The analysis offered by the average user of these sites is suspect, but you can benefit from the board's collective eyes and ears. If a great story about the company appeared in a local newspaper, or some other source you have overlooked, the odds are high that somebody on the message board has posted something about it. Look for message titles with headlines like "Did anyone else see the article on Hurricane Corporation in the Miami Herald?"

## Analyst Research Reports

One final source for company-specific information is the research distributed by analysts working for the independent research firms and the research departments of brokerage houses. Analysts working for brokerage houses are referred to as sell-side analysts to distinguish them from the buy-side analysts who work directly for institutional investors. Buy-side research is used directly by the investor and is not typically made available to the public. Sell-side research is primarily produced for brokerage clients, and a number of services now collect and redistribute these research reports. A popular service is Thomson One. This is a subscription-based service that is offered through many business school libraries.

Sell-side research reports generally provide very precise and confident forecasts based on a rudimentary analysis of a company. Our experience suggests that students and other neophyte investors are often taken in by the apparent confidence with which these reports are written and their association with prestigious investment houses. Historically, however, the recommendations and price targets contained in these reports have been unreliable and overly optimistic. Moreover, sell-side analysts rarely charge a direct fee for the research they issue to clients. Instead, they generate revenue from two indirect sources. First, they help their brokerage business to generate brokerage commissions by attracting clients and encouraging them to trade. Second, the analysts often work for brokerage houses that are affiliated with investment banks. By issuing positive research on current and potential investment banking clients, sell-side analysts help to generate investment-banking business. As you can imagine, the fact that sell-side analysts generate revenue through these indirect sources poses a conflict of interest. A strategy we recommend is to zero in on the research report of the analyst issuing the least favorable recommendation on a stock. This way, you are more likely to find insightful analysis rather than sales hype.

Given the limitations of sell-side research discussed above, we encourage you to read this research with a healthy dose of skepticism. However, sell-side research does have its redeeming features. First, sell-side analysts tend to be industry specialists. A sell-side research report may give you some deep industry insights that you missed in your own industry analysis. Second, sell-side analysts are usually up to date on recent company news and guidance, so their reports are a good place to check that you have all the latest company-specific information. Third, sell-side research almost always contains earnings forecasts for the next year or so. One of the strongest catalysts for a stock price change is an earnings surprise, whereby a company announces earnings that differ from the consensus forecast of sell-side analysts. A number of services collect sell-side analysts' forecasts and compile consensus earnings estimates from these forecasts (the consensus earnings estimate is simply the mean or median estimate of the analysts following the stock). A leading service is Thomson Reuters and it is available through the Yahoo! Finance portal.

There are also numerous independent research firms that sell their analyst research reports. Since our goal is to do our own analysis, we do not recommend relying too heavily on such reports.

## 2.3 MACROECONOMIC AND INDUSTRY DATA

Careful analysis of company-level data is where you are most likely to generate the best insights. However, a good understanding of the industry and macroeconomy is also useful for interpreting the past and forecasting the future. We have had many experiences where students have become excited about stocks that look "cheap" relative to past fundamentals, only to learn that the students have overlooked some key macroeconomic shifts. Examples include "cheap" oil services stocks in periods immediately following dramatic declines in the price of crude oil and "cheap" banking and home construction stocks in periods immediately following dramatic rises in interest rates. You don't have to be a guru macroeconomist to do sound equity analysis and valuation. But you do need to have a good idea of the macroeconomic factors that impact the company you are analyzing. And you should track the consensus view of where these macroeconomic factors are heading. Macroeconomic and industry analysis is covered in Chapter 3. In this section, we tell you where to collect the necessary data for your analysis.

## The Global and Domestic Economy

A taxonomy for conducting macroeconomic and industry analysis is provided in Figure 2.3. At the broadest level, we have the global economy. As domestic economies become increasingly integrated, domestic economies are increasingly linked to the global economy. Global economic trends are measured by summing the trends in domestic economies. Countries with the largest domestic economies, such as the United States, Japan, and China, tend to dominate global economic trends. However, economic crises in smaller countries, such as those in the Europe and Asia, can have a material impact on the global economy. There are a number of Web sites tracking the global economy. We recommend the economy.com website provided by Moody's Analytics.

Armed with data on the global economy, you should next collect data on the domestic economy. The operations of most businesses are concentrated in a particular country and the health of this country's domestic economy is a key driver of profitability. Our discussion focuses on the U.S. economy. There is a wealth of free data available on the domestic U.S. economy, most of it made available courtesy of the U.S. government. A good starting point is the monthly economic indicators publication prepared by the Council of Economic Advisors for the Joint Economic Committee. If this report is too bland, sites such as Briefing.com provide monthly summaries.

Finally, you should keep track of major economic announcements by following an economic calendar of events. Briefing.com provides a good free economic calendar that includes descriptions, forecasts, and additional links for many economic statistics. We'll give you a framework for interpreting all of this macroeconomic data in Chapter 3.

## Sectors and Industries

Economic sectors and industries are the next two levels in our taxonomy. Before we can discuss sources of data for analysis at these levels, we need to define what we mean by "sector" and "industry." An economic sector consists of a group of industries that engage in related activities. For example, "consumer goods" defines an economic sector consisting of firms that manufacture goods for consumers. Examples of industries included in this sector are automotive and tobacco. The production technologies are very different across these two industries, but it is their common customer base that places them in the same economic sector.

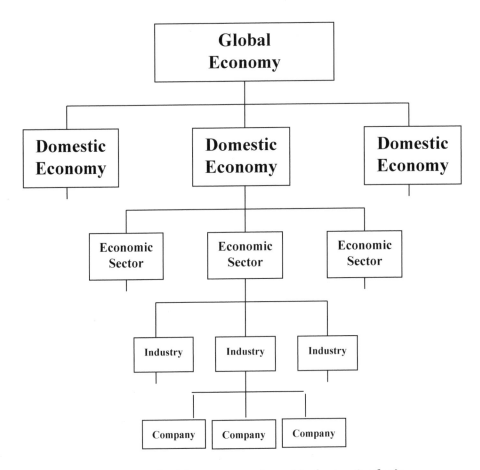

**FIGURE 2.3: Taxonomy for Macroeconomic and Industry Analysis**

Within each sector are many industries. Industries are defined by the nature of the good or service that is provided by the business. Firms in the same industry provide similar goods and services and will typically use similar inputs and production technologies. Because of these similarities, common analysis techniques can be applied to firms in the same industry. Also, because firms in the same industry typically compete for market share, analysis of the competitive structure of input and output markets is usually conducted at the industry level.

| Code | Sector | Subcode | Industry Group |
|------|--------|---------|----------------|
| 10 | Energy | 1010 | Energy |
| 15 | Materials | 1510 | Materials |
| 20 | Industrials | 2010 | Capital Goods |
|    |             | 2020 | Commercial & Professional Services |
|    |             | 2030 | Transportation |
| 25 | Consumer Discretionary | 2510 | Automobiles and Components |
|    |             | 2520 | Consumer Durables and Apparel |
|    |             | 2530 | Consumer Services |
|    |             | 2540 | Media |
|    |             | 2550 | Retailing |
| 30 | Consumer Staples | 3010 | Food & Staples Retailing |
|    |             | 3020 | Food, Beverage & Tobacco |
|    |             | 3030 | Household & Personal Products |
| 35 | Health Care | 3510 | Health Care Equipment & Services |
|    |             | 3520 | Pharmaceuticals, Biotechnology & Life Sciences |
| 40 | Financials | 4010 | Banks |
|    |             | 4020 | Diversified Financials |
|    |             | 4030 | Insurance |
| 45 | Information Technology | 4510 | Software & Services |
|    |             | 4520 | Technology Hardware & Equipment |
|    |             | 4530 | Semiconductors & Semiconductor Equipment |
| 50 | Telecommunication Services | 5010 | Telecommunication Services |
| 55 | Utilities | 5510 | Utilities |
| 60 | Real Estate | 6010 | Real Estate |

**FIGURE 2.4: Overview of the Global Industry Classification (GICS) System**

There are several competing classification systems for allocating firms to sectors and industries. While the similarities between systems outnumber the differences, it is important to use a single classification system consistently; otherwise, you can end up double-counting some companies and missing others altogether. We will use the S&P/MSCI Global Industry Classification Standard (GICS) system in this book. This is one of the more commonly used and comprehensive classification systems. It starts with 11 economic sectors, and then progressively divides them into 24 industry groups, 68 industries and 157 sub-industries. Figure 2.4 provides an overview of the GICS system. The system is based on an 8 digit GICS code, with the first two digits identifying the economic sector, the next two digits the industry group, the next two digits the industry and the final 2 digits the sub-industry. Figure 2.4 shows the economic sectors and industry groups. The complete GICS system includes the additional 157 sub-industries. One place where you can find a company's GICS sector and industry without requiring a subscription is the Fidelity.com website. Simply select 'News & Research' and 'Stocks', load the company of your choice and scroll down to the company profile where the GICS sector and industry is listed.

The best starting point to begin analyzing a new industry is the pertinent Standard & Poor's Industry Survey. These surveys are available through web-based subscriptions to S&P, available through many business school libraries. There is also a wealth of industry-specific information available on the web. One such source is Hoovers.com, which provides a wealth of industry information using its own classification system.

In closing this section, we offer a final word of advice. The list of information given above may seem quite daunting. You may be asking, "*Do I really need to gather and read all of this every time I want to value a company?*" The answer is probably *Yes* if this is the first time you have ever studied a business and you know nothing about it, the economy, or the industry in which it operates. But a more typical situation is that you already have a good knowledge of general macroeconomic trends and may have good industry knowledge from following other companies operating in the same industry. With experience, you also should more quickly identify what is relevant and what is irrelevant, thus zeroing in on the company-specific information most relevant to forecasting.

## 2.4 THE PITFALLS OF STANDARDIZED DATA

We close this chapter by discussing the pitfalls of using standardized financial statement data. The first step in building a valuation model is to enter the company's historical financial statement data into a spreadsheet. This data is the foundation on which you will build your valuation model. The usual starting points are the historical income statements and balance sheets. This data can be readily obtained from a company's most recent annual financial statements. Unfortunately, most companies do not make their financial statement data available in spreadsheet format. This means that you have to either manually enter the data yourself or use one of the many services that collect companies' financial statement data and allow you to download it into spreadsheet format. Examples of such services include Bloomberg, FactSet and WRDS. Many of these services are available to students through university-wide subscriptions.

Using one of these services sounds like the easiest way to go. Unfortunately, there is a big catch to the financial statement data provided by these services. In order to allow systematic coding and comparisons of the data, these services typically take the data reported by the company and force it into their own standardized set of data items. If the company reports something that doesn't seem to belong to one of these standardized line items, it will get forced into one of them. There are a few generic line items with 'other' in their description and line items without an obvious home are typically put into one of these catchalls. A related problem is that sometimes a company's financial statements won't list one of the standardized line items, so the service may dig through the notes to the financial statements to try and find an amount for this line item. In this case, ratios computed using the standardized financials can differ from those computed using the financial statements reported by the company. This can cause confusion when comparing ratios computed using the actual financial statements with those computed using the standardized data.

The simple solution to this problem is to use the company's 'as-reported' financials directly from its financial filings. This typically means that the data will have to be entered manually[1], but the advantage is that you will be speaking the same language as the company itself. Remember that the company customizes the financial statement line items to the nature of its underlying business. Moreover, most sell-side analysts use the as-reported financial format and so you will be speaking the same language as the professional investment community. The only qualification to this recommendation is that if you want to screen a large number of companies using a common set of ratios, you will basically be forced to use standardized financial data from one of the services. Even in this case, once you select a company for further analysis, we recommend reconciling the standardized data back to the as-reported financials to make sure you know what the standardized data represents.

In order to illustrate the significant differences that can exist between as-reported and standardized data, we will walk you through an example. The company that we use for the example is Salesforce.com, a provider of enterprise cloud computing solutions with a focus on customer relationship management. We provide Salesforce as-reported financial statements for the year ended January 31, 2017 in Figure 2.5. These financial statements are extracted directly from Salesforce's Form 10-K. Figure 2.6 provides the corresponding 'standardized' financial statements. The standardized data is obtained from the Compustat database, downloaded using the WRDS service and converted to the standardized data format used in our *eVal* workbook.[2]

---

[1] Some services are now making both the standardized and the 'as-reported' data available for download. FactSet is one such service.

[2] You can access the *eVal* workbook and the associated *Datamaker* workbook that is used to convert the data to the *eVal* standardized format on our website at http://www.lundholmandsloan.com/software.html . This webpage also provides a step-by-step user's guide for the *eVal* and *Datamaker* workbooks.

**salesforce.com, inc.**

**Consolidated Statements of Operations**
(in thousands, except per share data)

| | Fiscal Year Ended January 31, | | |
| --- | --- | --- | --- |
| | 2017 | 2016 | 2015 |
| Revenues: | | | |
| Subscription and support | $ 7,756,205 | $ 6,205,599 | $ 5,013,764 |
| Professional services and other | 635,779 | 461,617 | 359,822 |
| Total revenues | 8,391,984 | 6,667,216 | 5,373,586 |
| Cost of revenues (1)(2): | | | |
| Subscription and support | 1,556,353 | 1,188,967 | 924,638 |
| Professional services and other | 677,686 | 465,581 | 364,632 |
| Total cost of revenues | 2,234,039 | 1,654,548 | 1,289,270 |
| Gross profit | 6,157,945 | 5,012,668 | 4,084,316 |
| Operating expenses (1)(2): | | | |
| Research and development | 1,208,127 | 946,300 | 792,917 |
| Marketing and sales | 3,918,027 | 3,239,824 | 2,757,096 |
| General and administrative | 967,563 | 748,238 | 679,936 |
| Operating lease termination resulting from purchase of 50 Fremont | 0 | (36,617) | 0 |
| Total operating expenses | 6,093,717 | 4,897,745 | 4,229,949 |
| Income (loss) from operations | 64,228 | 114,923 | (145,633) |
| Investment income | 27,374 | 15,341 | 10,038 |
| Interest expense | (88,988) | (72,485) | (73,237) |
| Other income (expense) (1) | 9,072 | (15,292) | (19,878) |
| Gain on sales of land and building improvements | 0 | 21,792 | 15,625 |
| Gains from acquisitions of strategic investments | 13,697 | 0 | 0 |
| Income (loss) before benefit from (provision for) income taxes | 25,383 | 64,279 | (213,085) |
| Benefit from (provision for) income taxes (3) | 154,249 | (111,705) | (49,603) |
| Net income (loss) | $ 179,632 | $ (47,426) | $ (262,688) |

**FIGURE 2.5: Salesforce.com's 'As Reported' Income Statements and Balance Sheets for the Year Ended 1/31/2017. Extracted from Salesforce's Form 10-K for the Fiscal Year Ended January 31, 2017.**

**salesforce.com, inc.**
**Consolidated Balance Sheets**
(in thousands, except per share data)

| | January 31, 2017 | January 31, 2016 |
|---|---|---|
| **Assets** | | |
| Current assets: | | |
| Cash and cash equivalents | $ 1,606,549 | $ 1,158,363 |
| Marketable securities | 602,338 | 1,567,014 |
| Accounts receivable, net of allowance for doubtful accounts of $12,039 and $10,488 at January 31, 2017 and 2016, respectively | 3,196,643 | 2,496,165 |
| Deferred commissions | 311,770 | 259,187 |
| Prepaid expenses and other current assets | 279,527 | 250,594 |
| Total current assets | 5,996,827 | 5,731,323 |
| Property and equipment, net | 1,787,534 | 1,715,828 |
| Deferred commissions, noncurrent | 227,849 | 189,943 |
| Capitalized software, net | 141,671 | 123,065 |
| Strategic investments | 566,953 | 520,721 |
| Goodwill | 7,263,846 | 3,849,937 |
| Intangible assets acquired through business combinations, net | 1,113,374 | 490,006 |
| Other assets, net | 486,869 | 142,097 |
| Total assets | $ 17,584,923 | $ 12,762,920 |
| **Liabilities and stockholders' equity** | | |
| Current liabilities: | | |
| Accounts payable, accrued expenses and other liabilities | $ 1,752,664 | $ 1,349,338 |
| Deferred revenue | 5,505,689 | 4,267,667 |
| Total current liabilities | 7,258,353 | 5,617,005 |
| Deferred revenue, noncurrent | 37,113 | 23,886 |
| Convertible 0.25% senior notes, net | 1,116,360 | 1,088,097 |
| Term loan | 497,221 | 0 |
| Loan assumed on 50 Fremont | 198,268 | 197,998 |
| Revolving credit facility | 196,542 | 0 |
| Other noncurrent liabilities | 780,939 | 833,065 |
| Total liabilities | 10,084,796 | 7,760,051 |
| Commitments and contingencies (Notes 13 and 15) | | |
| Stockholders' equity: | | |
| Preferred stock, $0.001 par value; 5,000 shares authorized and none issued and outstanding | 0 | 0 |
| Common stock, $0.001 par value; 1,600,000 shares authorized, 707,460 and 670,929 issued and outstanding at January 31, 2017 and 2016, respectively | 708 | 671 |
| Additional paid-in capital | 8,040,170 | 5,705,386 |
| Accumulated other comprehensive loss | (75,841) | (49,917) |
| Accumulated deficit (Note 1) | (464,910) | (653,271) |
| Total stockholders' equity | 7,500,127 | 5,002,869 |
| Total liabilities and stockholders' equity | $ 17,584,923 | $ 12,762,920 |

**FIGURE 2.5: continued**

| Fiscal Year End (YYYY-MM-DD) | 2015/01/31 | 2016/01/31 | 2017/01/31 |
|---|---|---|---|
| **Income Statement** | | | |
| Sales (Net) | 5,373,586 | 6,667,216 | 8,391,984 |
| Cost of Goods Sold | (903,643) | (1,207,036) | (1,702,463) |
| Gross Profit | 4,469,943 | 5,460,180 | 6,689,521 |
| R&D Expense | (792,917) | (946,300) | (1,208,127) |
| SG&A Expense | (3,372,359) | (3,910,910) | (4,772,489) |
| EBITDA | 304,667 | 602,970 | 708,905 |
| Depreciation & Amortization | (450,300) | (528,300) | (631,668) |
| EBIT | (145,633) | 74,670 | 77,237 |
| Net Interest Expense | (73,237) | (72,485) | (88,988) |
| Non-Operating Income (Loss) | 5,785 | 62,094 | 37,134 |
| EBT | (213,085) | 64,279 | 25,383 |
| Income Taxes | (49,603) | (111,705) | 154,249 |
| Other Income (Loss) | 0 | 0 | 0 |
| Net Income Before Ext. Items | (262,688) | (47,426) | 179,632 |
| Ext. Items & Disc. Ops. | 0 | 0 | 0 |
| Minority Interest in Earnings | 0 | 0 | 0 |
| Preferred Dividends | 0 | 0 | 0 |
| Net Income (available to common) | (262,688) | (47,426) | 179,632 |

**FIGURE 2.6: Standardized Income Statements and Balance Sheets for Salesforce.com for the Year Ended 1/312017. Data is Obtained from Compustat via WRDS and Converted to *eVal's* Standardized Format.**

| Fiscal Year End (YYYY-MM-DD) | 2016/01/31 | 2017/01/31 |
|---|---|---|

**Balance Sheet**

| | 2016/01/31 | 2017/01/31 |
|---|---|---|
| Operating Cash and Market. Sec. | 1,341,381 | 2,208,887 |
| Receivables | 2,524,929 | 3,230,820 |
| Inventories | 0 | 0 |
| Other Current Assets | 481,017 | 557,120 |
| Total Current Assets | 4,347,327 | 5,996,827 |
| PP&E (Net) | 1,715,828 | 1,787,534 |
| Investments | 1,904,810 | 848,686 |
| Intangibles | 4,503,340 | 8,558,104 |
| Other Assets | 299,467 | 393,772 |
| Total Assets | 12,770,772 | 17,584,923 |
| | | |
| Current Debt | 15,402 | 19,594 |
| Accounts Payable | 71,481 | 115,257 |
| Income Taxes Payable | 205,781 | 239,699 |
| Other Current Liabilities | 5,324,341 | 6,883,803 |
| Total Current Liabilities | 5,617,005 | 7,258,353 |
| Long-Term Debt | 1,490,658 | 2,209,102 |
| Other Liabilities | 648,653 | 593,070 |
| Deferred Taxes | 11,587 | 24,271 |
| Total Liabilities | 7,767,903 | 10,084,796 |
| Minority Interest | 0 | 0 |
| Preferred Stock | 0 | 0 |
| Paid in Common Capital (Net) | 5,706,057 | 8,040,878 |
| Retained Earnings | (703,188) | (540,751) |
| Total Common Equity | 5,002,869 | 7,500,127 |
| Total Liabilities and Equity | 12,770,772 | 17,584,923 |

**FIGURE 2.6: Continued**

Let's start by reconciling the income statement for the year ended January 31, 2017 (also referred to as the 2016 fiscal year). The as-reported financials begin by listing revenues that total 8,391,984. This same amount is listed as 'Sales (Net)' on the standardized financial statements. All good so far, except that the as-reported financials also separately break out 'subscription and support' revenues versus 'professional services and other' revenues. These revenue streams likely have very different drivers and growth rates and so it is probably useful to analyze them individually.

Next, the as-reported financials list 'Total cost of revenues' of 2,234,039 while the standardized financials list 'Cost of Goods Sold' of only 1,702,463. It is not immediately clear what is going on here. For now, let's just keep track of the fact that the costs listed in the standardized financials are too low by 531,576. Both the as-reported financials and the standardized financials report R&D Expense of 1,208,127, so we are all good here. But the as-reported financial statements report 'Marketing and Sales' and 'General and Administrative' expenses summing to 4,885,590 while the standardized financials report 'SG&A Expense' of only 4,772,489. The standardized operating expenses are again too low, leading to a cumulative costs and expenses understatement of 644,677. Note, however, that the standardized financial statements next report a line item for 'Depreciation and Amortization' of 631,668 that does not appear on the as-reported financial statements. This expense makes up the bulk of the expenses that were missed previously and the standardized financials now only understate costs and expenses by 13,009. Can you see what happened here? The standardized financials have a line for depreciation and amortization expense, while the as-reported financial do not. Instead, depreciation and amortization is allocated to the underlying cost of goods sold and operating expenses. Nevertheless, the analyst preparing the standardized financial must have found an amount for depreciation elsewhere in the Form 10-K and put on this line, reducing some other expenses to balance things out. Next, note that both the as-reported and the standardized financial report interest expense of 88,988. The as-reported financials report other income summing to 50,143 while the standardized financials report Non-Operating Income of 37,134. The difference of 13,009 brings the cumulative expenses into balance and so both sets of statements report pre-tax income to 25,383. Both statements next report an income tax benefit of 154,249, leading to bottom line net income of 179,632.

Working through these reconciliations quickly gets pretty tedious, so we will stop here. But we encourage you to go through the same exercise with the as-reported versus the standardized balance sheets to see if you can reconcile them. You will find that the amounts for total assets, total liabilities and total stockholders' equity reconcile exactly, but that other intermediate line items often have very different names, and even when they have similar names, the amounts recorded in the standardized statements may differ. Our advice is to go with the as-reported financial statements whenever possible. The line items used here are those selected by management and they will also be the same numbers that management discusses in the MD&A and footnotes and that are used by most other analysts. The standardized financials can be useful if you want to do quantitative analysis on a large sample of companies. But even then, we suggest that after you identify a specific company for further analysis, you start working with the as-reported financials.

## 2.5 CONCLUDING COMMENTS

A forecast is only as good as the information on which it is based. The objective of this chapter has been to direct you to most relevant information for generating an efficient forecast. We also encouraged you to build your own objective forecasts rather than relying too heavily on the representations of management or sell-side analysts. Yet information alone is not enough. You need to know how to weave this information together in a meaningful way and how to combine hard information about past financial performance with soft information about management's ability to react to new industry developments and to sensibly invest free cash flow. We turn to these issues in the remaining chapters.

## 2.6 QUIZZES, CASES, LINKS AND REFERENCES

### Cases
• Analyzing Apple (Question 4)
• Building *eVal* (Part A)

### Links
• EDGAR website: https://www.sec.gov/edgar
• Listing of SEC Forms:  https://www.sec.gov/info/edgar/forms/edgform.pdf
• economy.com website: https://www.economy.com/
• economic indicators from Council of Economic Advisors:
   https://www.gpo.gov/fdsys/browse/collection.action?collectionCode=ECO NI
• Briefing.com website: https://www.briefing.com
• Briefing.com economic calendar:
   https://www.briefing.com/investor/calendars/economic/
• The complete GICS system:
   https://en.wikipedia.org/wiki/Global_Industry_Classification_Standard
• Fidelity.com website: https://www.fidelity.com/
• Hoovers.com industry analysis: http://www.hoovers.com/industry-analysis.html
• WRDS website: https://wrds-web.wharton.upenn.edu/wrds/
• *eVal* Valuation Workbook:
   http://www.lundholmandsloan.com/software.html
• Lundholm and Sloan website: www.lundholmandsloan.com

CHAPTER THREE

# Understanding the Business

## 3.1 INTRODUCTION

After collecting the wealth of data described in Chapter 2, your next task is to weave it together in a meaningful way. Your goal is to develop a thorough knowledge of the macroeconomic environment, the industry structure, and the operations and strategies of the particular business you are studying. We encourage you to adopt a top-down approach. First, you should consider general macroeconomic conditions. This will help you understand how the current economic climate affects the performance of each of the industries in which the business operates. Next, you should consider each industry in which the business operates. Most professional analysts concentrate on just one or two industries, and they know these industries like the back of their hand. So, if you are going to produce work of similar quality, you also will need to develop a thorough knowledge of each industry. The final stage is a detailed analysis of the operations and strategies of the business. What is the supposed source of competitive advantage in each of the industries in which the company operates, and what are the synergies between the different segments? We briefly review each of these steps below and refer you to the appropriate texts for a more detailed treatment.

Before devoting the next month to pouring over macroeconomic data and reading strategy textbooks, we also encourage you to use a healthy dose of economic intuition and common sense in your analysis. Macroeconomic and industry factors are only useful if you can draw a link between them and the particular firm you are studying.  Also, the strategy literature has seen many fads over time— remember the "new economy"? Don't just join the herd and assume that any firm that pours resources into implementing the latest fad will have stellar growth and staggering profitability for the foreseeable future. Your goal at this stage is to develop a working understanding of the business you are studying and how it fits into the larger economy.

## 3.2 MACROECONOMIC ANALYSIS

A top-down approach to understanding a business must start with the global economy. Most domestic businesses have direct exposure to the global economy through their product markets, input markets, or foreign operations. Even businesses without direct exposure to global markets are increasingly sensitive to the global factors as the world economy becomes more integrated. You need to understand the state of the global economy and the consensus among experts about where it is headed. You also should be aware of the state of the individual domestic economies that your business is exposed to and their individual sensitivities to the global economy. In particular, you should be aware of the expected economic growth rates, political risks, and currency risks in each of the domestic economies in which the firm operates. These factors can vary widely across countries. For example, expected growth is relatively low in large, mature economies such as North America and Europe, but can be much higher in emerging economies, such as those located in Asia and South America. But these economies also tend to have the greatest political risks and currency risks.

Armed with a basic understanding of the global economic environment, you should next focus on the domestic economy. Most businesses' operations and customers are concentrated in their home country and, consequently, the domestic economy is where you should begin your analysis. The overall state of the domestic economy and its future prospects are summarized by a few economic statistics.  We review these below for the United States, noting that most other countries report similar statistics.

## Gross Domestic Product

Gross domestic product (GDP) is the most widely used measure of macroeconomic performance. It measures the market value of final goods and services produced domestically. Figures for GDP are released quarterly by the Bureau of Economic Analysis of the U.S. Department of Commerce. These figures are typically expressed in real (i.e., inflation-adjusted) terms as an annualized quarter-to-quarter percentage change, which is referred to as the real GDP growth rate. The overall rate at which the economy is growing is an important determinant of the rate at which many businesses can grow, which is why the GDP growth rate is such a closely watched statistic. Over the last 40 years, the real GDP growth rate has averaged about 3 to 4 percent in the US, reaching highs of over 10 percent and lows of less than –5 percent. The most commonly used definition of an economic recession is two consecutive quarters of negative real GDP growth. Economists carefully monitor many leading indicators of GDP growth in an attempt to predict its future movements. Common leading indicators include unemployment insurance claims, consumer spending, consumer confidence, business orders, business productivity, and housing and construction activity. Projections of GDP growth and several of these leading indicators are made available by the Congressional Budget Office.

## Interest Rates

Interest rates reflect the cost of borrowing money and affect business performance in two important ways. First, interest rates determine the price that a firm must pay for its own capital. Other things equal, lower interest rates mean less interest expense and higher profits. Low interest rates also reduce the cost of capital, increasing the number of viable investment opportunities. For consumers, low interest rates reduce the cost of current consumption relative to future consumption. For example, you have a greater incentive to buy a new car today if the cost of borrowing declines. A decline in interest rates tends to spur consumer spending, thereby increasing sales growth for many businesses. It is important to note that it is *changes* in interest rates that cause changes in consumer spending. If interest rates are low today, but have been low for many years, then consumers are not going to suddenly rush out today to increase their current consumption. However, if interest rates have been running at high levels in recent years and suddenly drop to more moderate levels, we will see an increase in consumption as the relative cost of current versus future consumption has just dropped. Interest rates reflect not only the cost of current versus future consumption, but also expectations concerning inflation and credit risk. We can abstract from the credit risk portion of interest by examining the interest rate on low-credit-risk borrowings such as the federal funds rate or the yields on the bills, notes, and bonds issued by the U.S. Treasury. Over the past 40 years, nominal (i.e., not inflation-adjusted) interest rates on 10 Year Treasury Notes have ranged from less than 2 percent to over 15 percent, with an average of about 6 percent.

## Inflation

Inflation is defined as a general rise in price levels. Inflation creates the gap between real and nominal economic rates. In times of high inflation, businesses will generally find that they are better off in nominal terms because they are selling their goods for higher prices. But if those incoming dollars buy fewer goods and services, the businesses may actually be worse off in real terms. Armed with the inflation rate, it is possible to adjust nominal dollars into real dollars and get a clearer picture of economic performance. Inflation has other more pernicious effects. In times of high and uncertain inflation, the risk from investing in financial assets increases and the credibility of the domestic currency is undermined in global financial markets. Faced with such risk, investors will take their capital to countries without such uncertainty or invest directly in commodities such as gold that provide a hedge against inflation. The inflation rate is most commonly measured using the rate of change in the Consumer Price Index (CPI), published monthly by the <u>Bureau of Labor Statistics</u>. The CPI measures the price of a basket of goods bought by a typical U.S. consumer. Over the past 40 years, the annual rate of inflation, as measured by the CPI, has ranged from less than 0 percent to over 12 percent, and has averaged around 4 percent.

## Foreign Exchange Rates

Foreign exchange rates describe how many units of one currency can be bought with a unit of another currency. Many of the inputs bought and outputs sold by domestic businesses are in transactions with foreign entities. As the relative value of the U.S. dollar rises, the cost of foreign inputs decreases and the revenue from foreign sales decreases. Thus, the impact of foreign exchange rate fluctuations on a business depends not only on whether exchange rates go up or down, but also on whether the firm is a net buyer or seller of goods and services denominated in a particular currency. Foreign exchange rates are driven by a complex variety of factors, including the relative productivity of capital and labor, relative inflation rates, and relative real interest rates.

## Oil Prices and Other Key Commodity Prices

Commodity prices affect the costs of all businesses. The most important commodity price at the macro level is the price of oil. Oil is critical to the successful functioning of an industrialized economy. Oil prices tend to be volatile, due to the concentration of a large proportion of the world's oil reserves in a small number of countries and the high fixed costs involved in extracting oil. Increases in oil prices lead to increases in transportation and energy costs that affect nearly all businesses. Increases in oil prices also reduce the amount of income that consumers have to spend on other products. Other important commodity prices include natural gas and various metals. Obviously, different industries have different key commodity inputs: the price of steel is important for the auto industry and the price of palladium is important for the semiconductor industry. Make sure you identify the commodities that are important to the industry that you are studying.

Aside from the economic indicators above, other important factors to consider in your macroeconomic analysis are corporate hedging activities and the business cycle.

## Hedging

A firm can effectively hedge its exposure to interest rates, foreign exchange rates, and most commodity prices. Consequently, two firms in the exact same business may have completely different exposures to these factors. For instance, one gold-mining firm may sell its entire production forward, so that its economic profits are unaffected by changes in gold prices, while another firm may not, so that its profits are tied closely to the price of gold. Similarly, financial institutions can alter their interest rate exposure by entering into various interest rate derivative contracts. Firms can also create natural hedges by the way they structure their business. For instance, a firm anticipating a large increase in receivables denominated in a foreign currency can arrange its operations in such a way that it also has a large increase in payables denominated in the same currency. The currency gains or losses on receivables will offset the gains or losses on the payables. The point is that, even if a firm's underlying business is exposed to changes in interest rates, foreign exchange rates, or commodity prices, you won't know its net exposure until you understand its real and financial hedging activities. Recall from Chapter 2 that Item 7A of Form 10-K requires disclosure of exposures to macroeconomic risks. This is the best place to learn about a company's net exposure to interest rate, currency, and commodity risks.

## The Business Cycle

The *business cycle* is an important concept for understanding the current state and future prospects of the domestic economy. Historically, domestic economies have exhibited systematic periods of expansion (characterized by high GDP growth, low unemployment, and high consumer confidence) and contraction (characterized by low GDP growth, high unemployment, and low consumer confidence). While there is no guarantee that these cycles will continue, many macroeconomists believe that these cycles are a permanent feature of the economy. Hence, you should have a good sense of the current state of the business cycle as well as when and how it is most likely to change. The profitability of some sectors is much more sensitive to movements in the business cycle than others, as we will discuss below.

## A Realistic Goal for Macroeconomic Analysis

If you set out to become an expert in all the factors that influence the global and domestic economies, you may never get to the point of analyzing your particular firm. Your goal should be to understand the general consensus about major macroeconomic factors. You don't need to develop your own independent forecasts of future GDP or interest rate movements, but you should understand what the experts are saying about these factors and how they might influence your firm's performance in the future.

## 3.3 INDUSTRY ANALYSIS

Before studying the detailed operations and strategies of an individual firm, it is first important to think about the industry that the firm operates in. Professional analysts tend to specialize in particular economic sectors and industries to achieve efficiencies in business analysis. Industry analysis has three primary objectives:
• To understand the sensitivity of the industry to key macroeconomic factors.
• To understand how the industry operates and the key performance metrics for evaluating these operations.
• To understand the competitive structure of the industry.

We discuss each of these objectives in more detail below.

## Sensitivity to Macroeconomic Factors

Recall from Chapter 2 that economic sectors represent groups of industries that have similar exposures to key macroeconomic factors. Figure 3.1 provides an overview of the sensitivities of each economic sector to three key macroeconomic factors: the GDP growth rate, interest rates, and oil prices.

| | Macroeconomic Factor | | |
|---|---|---|---|
| Sector | GDP | Interest Rate | Oil Price |
| Energy | ++ | − | ++ |
| Materials | ++ | − − | − − |
| Industrials | ++ | − − | − − |
| Consumer | ++ | − − | − |
| Consumer Staples | + | − | − |
| Healthcare | + | − | − |
| Financials | + | − − | − |
| Information | ++ | − − | − |
| Telecommunication | + | − − | − |
| Utilities | + | − | − − |
| Real Estate | ++ | -- | - |

**FIGURE 3.1:  Sensitivity of Sector Profitability to Macroeconomic Factors**

Key: ++ = strong positive relation; + = positive relation; − = negative relation; − − = strong negative relation.

The GDP growth rate is a key driver of profitability for all sectors of the economy. However, some sectors are much more sensitive to The GDP growth rate than others. For example, the materials, consumer goods, industrials, and information technology sectors all have high sensitivity to the GDP growth rate. Many of the industries in these sectors have high operating leverage (i.e., relatively high fixed costs), so small movements in economic activity have big impacts on profitability.

Increases in interest rates tend to have a negative effect on the profitability of all sectors, but some sectors are affected more than others. The industrials and information technology sectors are particularly sensitive to the reductions in corporate capital expenditures that accompany increased interest rates. The financial sector can also suffer from the reduced borrowing activity associated with higher interest rates.

Increases in oil prices also tend to have a negative effect on the profitability of nearly all sectors. The one obvious exception is the energy sector, which consists largely of companies involved in the exploration, extraction, transportation, refining, and marketing of oil.

## Industry Operation and Key Industry Ratios and Statistics

Firms in the same industry generally produce similar goods and services using similar production technologies. You should begin your industry analysis by figuring out how the industry operates. This involves finding the answers to questions such as: What is the nature of the production process that takes place in the industry? What are the key inputs in the production process? What is the nature of the marketing and distribution process? Is after sales service a significant factor?

Once you understand how the industry operates, you should identify the key ratios and statistics that capture the financial health of the industry and firms within the industry. The particular metrics vary widely based on the nature of the industry's operations. In the oil production industry, for example, key statistics include oil prices, the current demand for oil, crude oil and petroleum inventories, oil refinery capacity utilization rates, and oil services equipment utilization rates. In contrast, in the semiconductor industry, key ratios and statistics include the semiconductor industry monthly global sales report, the semiconductor equipment book-to-bill ratio, wafer fabrication plant utilization rates, the purchasing managers' index, and business capital spending. Sell-side analyst reports are a good sources of information about the most popular ratios and statistics.

## Competitive Structure of the Industry

Your study of the industry should include an assessment of the intensity of industry competition. As a benchmark, recall the old microeconomic concept of perfect competition. In a perfectly competitive market, there are many firms using the same production technology and facing the same input and output prices. In equilibrium, just enough firms enter the market to ensure that the equilibrium price provides a "normal" return on the invested capital to all firms in the market. In such a market, valuation is easy. In expectation, each firm simply generates a normal return on its invested capital. Thus, if we know the magnitude of the invested capital and the normal rate of return, we simply multiply the two together to forecast the expected profit. Indeed, this is exactly the logic that is applied to securities markets by efficient market theorists: in an efficient market, each investor is simply expected to earn a normal return on his or her investment. However, it is generally accepted that there are inefficiencies in the market for real assets. Firms in certain industries have been known to generate abnormally high returns for extended periods of time. For example, Coke and Pepsi have both sustained high profitability over prolonged periods, and they do so selling sugared water (with a touch of addictive caffeine)! When studying the industry, you should look for characteristics that might allow firms to generate abnormal profits over a prolonged period of time.

Famed strategist Michael Porter highlights five forces that determine the degree of competition in an industry:

1. Rivalry among existing firms
2. Threat of new entrants
3. Availability of substitute products
4. Bargaining power with suppliers
5. Bargaining power with customers

The first three forces relate to sources of direct competition. Let's apply these three forces to the restaurant industry, focusing particularly on chains of fast-food restaurants. Clearly there is intense rivalry among existing firms—next to every McDonald's is a Burger King, with Wendy's, Taco Bell, and Subway just around the corner. Similarly, new entrants face relatively low barriers to entry; patents are not available for food items, capital expenditures are relatively minor, and franchisees can help fund investment. The competitive pressure from substitute products depends entirely on how narrowly you define the industry. Customers of fast-food restaurants could switch to full-service restaurants at reasonably low cost. However, if the industry is more broadly defined as "restaurants," then the substitute product is cooking food at home. The switching costs here are somewhat higher, insofar as this requires a significant lifestyle change on the part of customers. Putting the three forces together, one would have to conclude that the fast-food restaurant industry is highly competitive, possibly even approaching the textbook definition of perfect competition.

The final two forces in Porter's framework relate to a company's relative bargaining position with its suppliers and customers. Both suppliers and customers can alter input and output prices in order to extract a firm's profits if they have a bargaining advantage. Consider the desperate situation of a small firm in the automotive parts industry, one that manufactures plastic parts. A few large corporations control the market for the raw plastic pellets that are used as inputs, leaving little room to negotiate a better price on the input side. And on the output side, the situation is even worse. The automotive firms have many alternative sources for plastic parts. They enjoy so much power over their suppliers that they occasionally give themselves price concessions on existing contracts. Without even consulting the supplier, they simply pay less than the full amount on their accounts payable, expecting that the supplier will either acquiesce or lose all business in the future.

As you analyze the industry, remember that less competition means that abnormal levels of industry profitability are easier to sustain. Of course, we also should remember that various regulatory bodies are charged with preventing business practices that restrain competition. In the United States, the Federal Trade Commission's Bureau of Competition and the U.S. Department of Justice's Antitrust Division are the pertinent regulatory bodies.

## 3.4 THE FIRM'S STRATEGY

Firm profitability is not solely a function of industry profitability. For example, McDonald's has been able to generate consistently high profits while operating in the highly competitive restaurant industry. What explains this anomaly? Strategists would say that McDonald's has developed a strategy for creating and sustaining competitive advantage. Strategy textbooks attempt to identify and categorize such winning strategies. Three common categories are cost leadership, product differentiation, and focus. A cost leadership strategy aims for low production costs and thin margins, with profits coming from a high volume as customers are attracted by the low price. Wal-Mart successfully implemented such a strategy in the variety retail industry. Product differentiation is achieved by producing a product with unique attributes that are valued by buyers who will pay a premium price, resulting in higher profits. Revlon pioneered this strategy in the cosmetics industry and Apple has finessed it in the smart phone industry. Finally, the idea behind focus is to develop a niche strategy that supplies one segment of the market with exactly what they want, be it low cost or a differentiated product. Carhartt, the U.S-based maker of heavy-duty work clothing, has successfully implemented such a strategy in the apparel industry.

In evaluating a company's strategy, the most important point to keep in mind is that it is extremely difficult to sustain a competitive advantage. Each of the generic strategies described above will be difficult to sustain in the long run. A cost leadership strategy is vulnerable to imitation and to shifts in technology that lead to lower-cost production methods. A differentiation strategy also is subject to imitation. Moreover, differentiation strategies are often short-lived fads. For example, the specialty retail and apparel industries are characterized by many differentiated brands that go in and out of style over time—in the market for denim jeans, Mudd Jeans are out and Diesel is in, at least as of this writing. Finally, a focus strategy also is subject to imitation and to the risk that changes in market conditions render the targeted segment nonviable.

The best source for information concerning a firm's strategy for achieving competitive advantage is the first section of a firm's Form 10-K filing with the Securities and Exchange Commission. This section must provide a description of the registrant's business. The applicable securities laws require the description of business to include:

"Competitive conditions in the business involved including, where material, the identity of the particular markets in which the registrant competes, an estimate of the number of competitors and the registrant's competitive position, if known or reasonably available to the registrant. Separate consideration shall be given to the principal products or services or classes of products or services of the segment, if any. Generally, the names of competitors need not be disclosed. The registrant may include such names, unless in the particular case the effect of including the names would be misleading. Where, however, the registrant knows or has reason to know that one or a small number of competitors is dominant in the industry it shall be identified. The principal methods of competition (e.g., price, service, warranty or product performance) shall be identified, and positive and negative factors pertaining to the competitive position of the registrant, to the extent that they exist, shall be explained if known or reasonably available to the registrant." [Extracted from SEC Regulation S-K, Item 101(c)(1)(x)]

Thus, management is required to give its best shot at describing both the degree of industry competition and the firm's own perceived source of competitive advantage in Item 1 of Form 10-K. However, you should always take management's ravings about their sources of competitive advantage with a grain of salt. Simply admitting that the firm doesn't really have any competitive advantage would probably not sit well with investors, so management will typically spin some sort of yarn. Your job is to check that the alleged source of competitive advantage is plausible and delivers superior financial performance.

Finally, you should remember that there are two elements of a successful strategy – long-term profitability and growth.   Long-term profitability is essential.   Unless a business is profitable enough to provide a competitive return on invested capital, it cannot justify its existence.   Assuming that a business is profitable, growth becomes the multiplier that allows a strong return on capital to be converted into lots of dollars of profit.  So your analysis of a business strategy should include both the profitability of the business and the growth potential of the business.  You should also remember that while most managers would like to grow their businesses, growth generally results in declining profitability.  Basic economics tells us that demand curves usually slope down, so an increase in supply shifts us down the demand curve and leads to a reduction in price.  Also, a strategy that is successful in one market may be difficult to replicate in another market.  A classic example is the Home Depot's attempt to replicate its do-it-yourself home improvement superstores in Mexico.  The market for do-it-yourself home improvement was more limited in Mexico due to the smaller middle class segment of the population, making the business less profitable.

## Synergy Analysis

Not all firms operate a single business in a single industry. Corporate synergy analysis focuses on how firms can generate abnormal profits by bringing two or more businesses under the same corporate umbrella. Theories abound in this area. Synergies are created by leveraging proprietary assets, eliminating transaction costs, eliminating redundant overhead, increasing market power, or any number of other activities. The important point to remember here is that the free market is a very good disciplining mechanism, but it is eliminated when activities are brought inside a single firm. For instance, it could be that synergy is created when a sawmill company acquires a timber company, or it could be that the timber segment no longer harvests trees efficiently, because it no longer has to sell logs on the open market—the sawmill segment simply takes their timber as an input. Without the discipline of competing in an open market, the timber segment may respond to inefficient transfer prices or simply get lazy. Empire-building managers are often quick to identify the benefits of mergers but fail to appreciate the costs that can result from coordination and control issues that surface once market discipline is removed.

## 3.5 UNDERSTANDING SALESFORCE'S BUSINESS

We will wrap up this chapter by applying what we have learned to review Salesforce's business. Our goal is not to do a comprehensive analysis, as that would take up too much time and space. Instead, we aim to highlight the key facts that you should uncover and the areas on which you should focus your comprehensive analysis. We will focus on the early months of 2017, around the time that Salesforce issued its Form 10-K for the 2016 fiscal year. Salesforce provides enterprise software with a focus on customer relations' management, primarily via the 'cloud'. You can think of Salesforce as a very specialized version of Facebook that is customized for a company's sales representatives. It allows sales representatives to interact with customers and each other in real time and provides a wide array of related analytics. Prior to the advent of Salesforce, most large companies tracked customer relationship management using customized onsite enterprise management software, while smaller companies used ad hoc approaches based on emails, spreadsheets and the like. Thus, Salesforce provides a cheaper and more convenient solution for large companies and a much more powerful and efficient solution for smaller companies. Salesforce generates revenue through annual subscription fees that are typically paid in advance. At the time of writing, Salesforce was expanding its cloud-based subscription offerings beyond customer relations to areas such as service, marketing and analytics.

Before digging into Salesforce's strategy in more detail, we will begin by studying the macroeconomic environment facing Salesforce in early 2017. Next, we will understand the key characteristics of the industry in which Salesforce operates. Finally, we will analyze Salesforce's strategy within that industry.

The first quarter of 2017 marked the continuation of a long and slow economic recovery in the U.S.[1] The annualized GDP growth rate had rebounded from a low of -6.8% in the fourth quarter of 2008 to stabilize at around 2% by the first quarter of 2017. Unemployment had stabilized around its 'natural' rate of 5%, interest rates were slowly climbing from their historically low levels and inflation was running right around the Federal Reserves long-run target rate of 2%. This environment was accompanied by a modest resurgence in consumer spending, though business investment remained soft. The Congressional Budget

---

[1] The macroeconomic data discussed here is extracted from the *Congressional Budget Office's* publication "The Budget and Economic Outlook: 2017 to 2027" dated January 2017.

Office summarized its outlook for the next three years as follows:

> "The CBO expects real GDP to grow by 2.3% this year and by around 1.9% next year on a fourth-quarter-to-fourth-quarter basis. The agency anticipates that most of that growth will come from consumer spending, business investment and residential investment" [2]

The global macroeconomic picture was similar to that in the U.S. China had been the engine of the global economy for the last decade, but growth in China was stabilizing. Brexit and related political events had caused a hiccup in UK and European growth. Currencies in the UK and Europe were also weaker, causing a drop in US denominated revenues from these markets.

As far as Salesforce is concerned, there are two major takeaways from our macroeconomic analysis. First, since economic growth and business spending are both fairly muted, we can't expect Salesforce to generate a lot of growth from general growth in the underlying macroeconomy. Second, weaknesses in U.K. and European currencies will put pressure on any revenues that Salesforce derives from these markets.

We next turn to our industry analysis. Salesforce is assigned a GICS code of 45103010. We can break this down using the complete GICS system. The first two digits '45' refer to the economic sector 'Information Technology'. The next two digits '10' refer to the industry group 'Software and Services'. The next set of digits '30' refer to the industry 'Software'. The final two digits '10' refer to the sub-industry 'Application Software'. Other large players in this GIC code include Adobe Systems and Citrix Systems. As we sill see later, however, Salesforce's major competitors are not in this sub-industry group and so it is better to analyze Salesforce within the context of the entire software industry. The software industry in early 2017 was characterized by healthy revenue growth driven primarily by innovations in 'cloud' computing. S&P summarized the situation as follows:

> "The emergence of accessible, faster, and more reliable Internet, coupled with secure and robust software platforms and applications, has helped cloud computing become not just a notable trend, but arguably the single most important theme impacting the business of software." [3]

Thus, revenue and earnings prospects in this industry depend critically on the provision of competitive cloud computing services.

We begin our industry analysis by applying Porter's 5 forces to understand the competitive structure of the industry. In terms of rivalry among existing firms, Microsoft and Oracle, had traditionally dominated the software industry. This high industry concentration had led to concerns with lack of competition. Cloud computing, however, was shaking up the old order and younger companies such as

---

[2] *Ibid.* p. 42.
[3] Extracted from "Industry Surveys: Software", *Standard & Poor's*, April, 2017.

Salesforce that specialized in cloud computing applications were stealing market share and increasing competition. In terms of new entrants, there is a significant first-mover advantage as the switching costs in migrating to a new software system can be high. Threat of substitutes at the industry level are low, though as we have already mentioned, a massive substitution from traditional in-house software to cloud-based services was currently underway. New entrants such as Salesforce dominated the cloud business, while traditional players such as Microsoft and Cisco were playing catch-up. Finally, the power of suppliers and customers is fairly low, as both tend to be relatively large and fragmented groups.

Turning now to a more specific analysis of Salesforce, we start by reading Item 1 of Form 10-k. Salesforce begins by summarizing its business as follows:

> "Salesforce is a leading provider of enterprise software, delivered through the cloud, with a focus on customer relationship management, or CRM."

Salesforce goes on to summarize its key cloud-based services. Its first and most popular offering is called Sales Cloud. This is a cloud-based service for businesses to manage their relations with current and potential customers. Salesforce has also branched out into other cloud-based services including offerings to help businesses manage their customer service, marketing and e-commerce activities.

On page 5, Salesforce lays out what it sees as the key competitive advantages of its services. These include (i) secure, private, scalable and reliable, (ii) rapid deployment and lower total cost of ownership, (iii) ease of integration and configuration, (iv) high levels of user adoption, (v) rapid development of apps and increased innovation, and (vi) continuous innovation. You should evaluate these sources of competitive advantage. Do they make sense? Are they sustainable in the face of competition? These are the mechanisms through which Salesforce hopes to create 'moats' around its business and achieve above normal rates of return on investment. Overall, it appears that Salesforce is offering an innovative and differentiated product, but the competition has noticed and is trying hard to play catch up.

Next, Salesforce describes they key elements of its ongoing strategy. This includes various plans to improve its existing services and provide new services. One factor that you should consider here is the past track record of management in executing the key elements of its strategy. Much of Salesforce's success is attributed to the vision and business acumen of its prominent CEO, Mark Benioff. Mr. Benioff represents a key asset to Salesforce and his leadership provides Salesforce with a potential advantage over competitors that operate with less visionary management teams.

Salesforce goes on to describe another of other features of its business. You should read all of these. One area that you should focus on is the required discussion of the competitive environment. You will see this on page 9 of Form 10-K. Here, Salesforce emphasizes that:

> "We believe that as traditional enterprise software application and platform vendors

shift more of their focus to cloud computing, they may become a greater competitive threat."

You can see that Salesforce is very much aware that traditional enterprise software vendors such as Microsoft and Oracle have realized that Salesforce is stealing their lunch in the cloud and are trying to play catch up. You should evaluate the effectiveness of their strategies and the strength of Salesforce's first mover advantage in the cloud.

Next, Item 1A of Form 10-K provides a very legalistic list of many risk factors potentially affecting the business. You should read through this with an eye to identifying the key risk factors. Important risk factors include concerns about the security of client data in the cloud, competition from traditional enterprise software vendors and key person risk with the CEO.

The information discussed above provides the foundation for your analysis and should provide a basis for where you need to dig deeper. In the case of Salesforce, you should understand what the big traditional competitors are doing to develop competing cloud-based services. You should also study Salesforce's recent SEC filings and press releases. Finally, it would be a good idea to check out what the sell-side analysts are saying to make sure that you haven't missed anything important.

## 3.6 CONCLUSION

There is no substitute for a thorough understanding of the business underlying an equity security. Anyone who tries to convince you that you can accurately value most businesses by extrapolating past trends or applying fixed multiples to key historical financial statement variables is wrong.

But there is still plenty of work to do before you are ready to value a firm's equity. We still need to talk about how to use the financial statements to evaluate the effectiveness of the firm's strategy and how to develop good forecasts of the future financial statements. These forecasts are the ultimate drivers of your valuation. We turn to these tasks in the remaining chapters.

## 3.7 QUIZZES, CASES, LINKS AND REFERENCES

### Quizzes
• Chipotle Mexican Grill (Problem 1)
• Pandora (Problem 1)
• LinkedIn (Problem 1)
• Salesforce (Problem 1)

### Cases
• Analyzing Apple (Questions 1-3)
• Apple and the iFad (Questions 1-3)

- Boston Chicken, Inc. (Questions 1 through 3)
- Netflix, Inc. (Questions 1 and 2)
- Overstock.com (Questions 1 and 2)
- Sirius Satellite Radio (Questions 1-3)
- High Yields at Annaly Capital (Questions 1-2)
- Has Zynga Lost Its Zing? (Questions 1-2)
- Is Tesla's Stock Price in Ludicrous Mode? (Questions 1-2)

## Links
- Bureau of Economic Analysis: https://www.bea.gov
- Congressional Budget Office Economic Projections:
    https://www.cbo.gov/about/products/budget-economic-data
- Bureau of Labor Statistics: https://www.bls.gov
- Salesforce website: https://www.salesforce.com/
- The complete GICS system:
    https://en.wikipedia.org/wiki/Global_Industry_Classification_Standard

## References
### *Further Readings in Macroeconomics*
- *Principles of Macroeconomics,* by N. Gregory Mankiw (2014) is a good standard text on macroeconomics.

### *Further Readings in Strategy*
- *Competitive Strategy,* by Michael Porter (1998), is a landmark book in the strategy literature. It lays out Porter's five forces for industry analysis and his three generic strategies for achieving competitive advantage.
- *Gaining and Sustaining Competitive Advantage,* by Jay Barney (2011) covers the basics of business strategy.

CHAPTER FOUR

# Accounting Analysis

## 4.1 INTRODUCTION

Traditional valuation texts are usually very good at telling you how to value a business assuming that you already know the future cash flows. But, in practice, forecasting these cash flows is the most important and difficult task in conducting a valuation. Moreover, past cash flows are rarely a good indicator of either past performance or future cash flows. For example, successful growth firms often generate negative cash flows as they invest in growing their business activities. The problem with cash flows is that they measure the distribution of value rather than the creation of value. For this reason, financial statements, prepared in accordance with 'generally accepted accounting principles' (GAAP), have evolved to provide more useful information about value creation in a business. These statements provide a "language" for evaluating a firm's past performance and forecasting its future performance. It is the language that is spoken by the financial community, and it is the language that we will use throughout the valuation exercise.

At this point, you may ask yourself, "If accountants already measure value creation, what is left for the rest of us to do?" It turns out that financial statements are not designed to provide a direct valuation of a company. Instead, the financial statements are intended to provide information that is useful in helping others to conduct their own valuation. For the most part, this information is based on past transactions, while firm value depends on forecasts of future transactions. Since we are the "others" who actually get to do the valuation, we must convert the information about past transactions to forecasts of future transactions. To do this, we need to understand the answers to three questions:

1.   What information do financial statements provide?
2.   What are the key limitations of this information?
3.   How do we overcome these limitations?

The purpose of this chapter is to address these questions.

We begin by reviewing some basic investment concepts that will help you understand what accountants are trying to measure. Foremost among these is the concept of 'return on investment'. We next review some basic accounting concepts and the key financial statements. Our objective is not to teach you accounting. In fact, we assume that you already have a working knowledge of basic accounting. Instead, our objective is to discuss the nature of the information provided in the financial statements and how this information relates to firm value. We close by describing the limitations of financial statement information and providing guidelines for addressing these limitations.

## 4.2 BASIC INVESTMENT CONCEPTS

The primary purpose of investing cash and other financial resources is to generate a periodic return on that investment. Other relevant factors include minimizing risk, maintaining liquidity and seeking to make the world a cleaner, healthier and happier place. We will come back to these other factors later, but for now, we will focus on the return.

We will start by illustrating the concept of return on investment with a simple example. Assume that you put $100 in a savings account at the beginning of the year. You leave it there all year and let it earn interest. At the end of the year, your bank statement shows that your balance plus earned interest totals $105. What is your return on investment for the year? You should automatically know that it is 5%, but let's go through the computation and spell out the terminology:

Initial Investment at Beginning of Year = $100
Earned Interest for the Year = $5
Annual Return on Investment = $5/$100 = 5%.

This all seems very straightforward and you should immediately recognize the 5% return on investment as the interest rate on the bank account. There are several special features of this example that make it so straightforward. First, we know exactly when and how much we invested to generate the earnings. Second, we know exactly how much we earned. We could go along to the bank at the end of the year and take out the $105, liquidating the bank account and realizing the $5 of earnings. Third, you are the sole beneficiary of the bank account, and so you can be sure that all of the earnings belong to you. Unfortunately, most businesses have much more complex financial situations and accountants face the challenge of figuring out the amount of investment and earnings in these more complex situations.

The use of return on investment is pervasive in the financial world and the acronym 'ROI' is frequently used as shorthand for this important investment concept. We also see many specialized measures of ROI that are assigned their own special names. Here are three common specialized measures that you may be familiar with:

1.   The internal rate of return (IRR) on an investment project.
2.   The yield to maturity (YTM) on a fixed income security.
3.   The return on equity (ROE) for the common equity holders in a company.

The IRR should be a familiar concept from your introductory finance coursework. The IRR is essentially a generalized measure of ROI that can be applied to cases where the investment is made and/or the return is received over multiple periods. Because of the multi-period nature of the investment flows, we can't simply compute the ROI by dividing the earnings by the beginning investment, but functions in computer programs can easily do so. If you used the IRR function in any such program to evaluate our savings account example above, it would dutifully return an IRR of 5%.

The YTM is essentially the IRR on a fixed income security, where the current price and the promised future cash flows (coupons and principal repayments) are used to compute the IRR. For example, we could say that the YTM on our savings account at the time of investment is 5%. The YTM terminology is most commonly applied to bonds. One of the most common uses of the YTM is in the construction of 'yield curves'. A yield curve plots the YTM on a class of securities against the time to maturity. The U.S. Treasury yield curve is a particularly useful benchmark for evaluating the ROI of any investment. U.S. Treasuries have low credit risk and high liquidity. It therefore stands to reason that any relatively risky and/or illiquid investment should be expected to generate an ROI at least as high as the corresponding U.S. Treasury with similar maturity. For equity investments, the convention is to use the yield on the 10 Year Treasury Note as the benchmark. You can take a look at the current U.S. Treasury yield curve on the U.S. Department of the Treasury website.

Finally, the ROE is a measure of ROI for the owners of the 'common equity' in a company. It is computed by dividing the earnings belonging to the common equity holders by the beginning book value of the common equity, as determined by our faithful accountants. Why do we need to distinguish between the ROI and the ROE of a business? It is because, as mentioned earlier, businesses can have other investors who contribute capital and share in the earnings of the business, such as debtholders and preferred stockholders. To understand the difference between ROI and ROE, we can make some modifications to our earlier savings account example. Let's assume that you only have $25 to invest, but that you can also borrow an additional $75 at an interest rate of 4%. By doing so, you can again invest $100 and earn interest of $5. The ROI on the $100 total investment is still clearly 5%. But the ROE on your $25 equity investment is:

Equity Investment = $25
Equity Earnings = $5-(4% of $75) = $5-$3=$2
Return on Equity = $2/$25 = 8%.

Thus, while your equity investment and equity earnings are lower, your ROE is higher. How did this happen? Intuitively, by borrowing at an interest rate that is lower than the ROI on your investment, you get to keep a disproportionate share of the earnings for yourself.

It turns out that the following simple and intuitive formula links the ROI with the ROE:

ROE = ROI + (ROI – Borrowing Rate)×(Borrowings/Equity).

If we further define:

Spread = ROI - Borrowing Rate; and
Leverage = Borrowings/Equity, then we get

ROE = ROI + (Spread × Leverage).

Applying the formula to our example, we have

ROE = 5% + (1% × 3) = 8%.

Thus, for a given ROI, two financial metrics contribute to the excess of ROE over ROI. The first is the spread between the ROI and the borrowing rate. The second is the leverage ratio. Higher spreads and higher leverage generate higher ROEs.

At this stage, you are probably wondering whether it can be this easy to generate a high ROE. In practice, it is difficult to find positive spreads. They typically exist only when the ROI involves significant risks. And this is exactly the case where it can be dangerous to take on too much leverage. Note that our formula also indicates that if the spread turns out to be negative, then ROE will be less than ROI and higher leverage will drive the ROE even lower! So leverage is a double-edged sword that should be used with caution.

Nevertheless, this simple formula forms the underpinnings for many successful business models, the prime example being the banking industry. The basic banking model involves sourcing capital at low interest rates from demand deposit accounts and CDs, and then lending the proceeds to borrowers via residential, consumer and commercial loans. Banks typically run very high leverage ratios, often in the order of 8-10, and keep a very careful eye on their spreads. As the financial crisis illustrated, poor loan quality can result in negative spreads that can combine with high leverage to yield disastrous results.

Our simple example reveals four key metrics that are needed to compute the ROE for a business. First, we need to know the amount of the **investment** in the business. Second, we need to know how much of the investment has been funded by **equity** versus other sources of capital. Third, we need to know the periodic **earnings** of the business. Fourth, we need to know how much of the earnings must be paid to the borrowers in the form of **interest**. These amounts were all obvious in our simple example. But they are far from obvious for many real businesses. This is where we must turn to our trusty accountants.

## 4.3 BASIC ACCOUNTING CONCEPTS

If all businesses were as simple as the one described in the last section, then we could fire all the accountants. But in practice, each of the four key metrics described above are much more difficult to measure in practice. Let's consider each in turn:

## Investment

In our simple example, we had only one investment: cash in a bank account. Most real businesses have a multitude of investments such as inventory, receivables, equipment, land, marketable securities and so forth. These investments all have one thing in common. They are economic resources of the business that are expected to provide future benefits. Accountants attempt to identify and measure these different investments. From your introductory accounting class, you should remember that the term used by accountants to refer to these investments is **assets**. Here is the formal definition of an asset, direct from the Financial Accounting Standards Board (FASB):

> "Assets are probable future economic benefits obtained or controlled by a particular entity as a result of past transactions or events."

This definition may sound straightforward, but as we will see later in the chapter, accounting standard setters and corporate accountants go through a lot of sleepless nights trying to decide whether certain investments qualify as assets, and if so, how to value of these assets.

## Equity

In our modified simple example, the equity was the $25 of cash that we invested ourselves, as distinct from the other $75 of the investment that was funded by borrowings. The most common way to measure equity is to start with the total assets and then deduct the value of all the other obligations of the business. Equity represents the resulting residual interest in the assets. This is exactly how the FASB defines equity:

> "Equity or net assets is the residual interest in the assets of an entity that remains after deducting its liabilities."

The astute reader may have noticed that while we have defined equity, we have only done so by introducing a new undefined term: **liabilities**. These liabilities represent all the other obligations of the business. In our simple example, the only liability was the borrowings. In practice, there are many other claims. Examples include accounts payable, taxes payable, preferred stock, minority interest and so forth. Accountants try to identify and measure all such obligations and refer to them collectively as liabilities. Here is the formal definition of a liability from the FASB:

> "Liabilities are probable future sacrifices of economic benefits arising from present obligations of a particular entity to transfer assets or provide services to other entities in the future as a result of past transactions or events."

Our accountants again spend many sleepless nights debating the grey areas in this definition. Armed with definitions of assets and liabilities, we can now measure equity via the following relation:

Equity = Assets – Liabilities.

This is often referred to as "the accounting equation" or the "balance sheet equation". One of the four major financial statements is the *Balance Sheet* (also known as the *Statement of Financial Position*). The balance sheet simply lists the assets, liabilities and equity of the business, grouping each into broad categories referred to as 'line items'. And as our equation suggests, the balance sheet must always balance. To make sure that this happens, the accountant measures the assets and the liabilities of the business and then uses equity as the 'plug'. As we will see later, the key line item in the equity section of the balance sheet that is used as the plug is called 'retained earnings'.

## Earnings

Earnings represent the net increase in the economic resources generated by a business over a period of time (typically a quarter of a year). Earnings are the key measure of financial performance of a business. Since the equity of a business represents the net economic resources of a business at a point in time, we can measure the earnings to the equity holders of a business for a period by taking the change in the equity from the beginning to the end of the period. This is exactly how we computed the earnings in our simple bank account example. Since the bank balance increased from $100 to $105, our earnings must have been $105-$100=$5. There is, however, one very important exception to this rule. In this simple example, we did not contribute or withdraw any capital from the business during the period. What if we had instead withdrawn the $5 of interest at the very end of the period, so that we closed with an investment balance of $100? The change in investment would have been $100-$100=$0, but intuitively, we know that our earnings is still $5 regardless of whether or not we withdraw it at the end of the period.

To deal with this issue, we must measure earnings by adding the amount of the withdrawal to the change in the investment. Alternatively, lets assume that instead of withdrawing the $5 on the last day of the period, we had instead invested another $10 on the last day. In this case, our investment would grow to $115 at the end of the period, but intuitively, our earnings are still $5. To deal with this issue, we need to subtract the new investment (also know as a capital contribution) that we made during the period.

Putting all this together, you should see that we define the periodic earnings to the equity holders of a business as:

Periodic Earnings to Equity Owners  =  End of Period Equity
                                     –  Beginning of Period Equity
                                     +  Withdrawals by Equity Owners
                                        during the Period
                                     –  Contributions from Equity Owners
                                        during the Period.

Note that the measurement of earnings flows directly from the measurement of assets and liabilities. Our definitions of assets and liabilities determine the beginning and ending values of equity. To compute earnings, we also need to keep track of the withdrawals and contributions made by equity holders during the year. For corporations, withdrawals typically take the form of cash dividends or stock repurchases and contributions typically take the form of stock issuances. To simplify things moving forward we will refer to the excess of withdrawals over contributions as the 'net equity distributions' of the business. We can then define earnings as:

Earnings to Equity Owners     =     Ending Equity
    −     Beginning Equity
    +     Net Equity Distributions.

The primary reason that most businesses exist is to generate earning. Earnings are also referred to as net income and are the most common measure of financial performance. Not surprisingly, investors therefore want to know not only the amount of earnings, but also how they were produced. This is where our second financial statement, the *Income Statement* (or *Statement of Earnings*) comes into play.

Net income sits at the bottom of the *Income Statement*. The line items above net income provide additional information about the drivers of net income. Businesses generate income by providing goods and services to customers in return for cash and other consideration. The income statement starts by listing revenues. Remember that income represents an increase in equity, which is in turn generated by increasing assets or reducing liabilities. Thus, revenues represent increases in assets or reductions in liabilities that arise from providing goods and services to customers. In many cases, the asset that goes up is cash, but it could also be an increase in the accounts receivable asset or a reduction in the deferred revenue liability.

Next, the income statement lists the various costs and expenses that were incurred in providing the goods and services to customers. These costs and expenses represent reductions in assets or increases in liabilities. In many cases, the asset that goes down is cash, but it could also be a reduction in an asset such as inventory or an increase in a liability such as wages payable.

Finally, we must subtract any earnings that do not belong to the owners. This includes amounts owing to other capital providers, such as interest owed to debtholders, and any income taxes owing to government authorities. This leaves us with the net income of the owners.

The *Balance Sheet* and the *Income Statement* are the two primary financial statements. The other two most common financial statements are the *Statement of Owner's Equity* and the *Statement of Cash Flows*. We will analyze the *Statement of Cash Flows* in Chapter 6. The *Statement of Owners Equity* helps to round out the first two financial statements by reconciling the beginning and ending balances of equity. Rearranging the definition of earnings provided earlier gives:

Ending Equity     =     Beginning Equity
    +     Earnings to Equity Owners
    −     Net Equity Distributions.

The *Statement of Owners' Equity* provides us with this reconciliation, showing us exactly which line items in the equity section of the balance sheet changed and why. The relation between the *Balance Sheet*, the *Income Statement* and the *Statement of Owner's Equity* is illustrated in Figure 4.1.

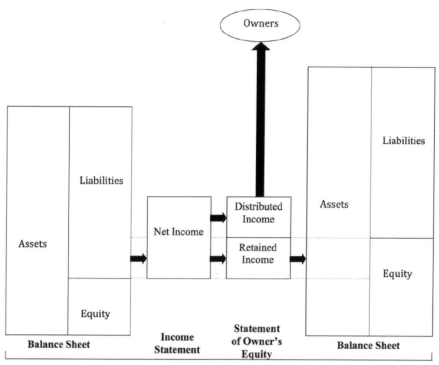

**FIGURE 4.1: Overview of Basic Building Blocks of Accounting.**

We will close this section by examining the annual financial statement of Salesforce.com for the year ending January 31, 2017. Recall that you can access these financial statements in the Salesforce.com 2016 Form 10-K on EDGAR. The balance sheet is located on p. 58. Total assets on January 31, 2017 are $17.6B, up from $12.8B in the previous year. The biggest assets are goodwill ($7.3B), accounts receivable ($3.2B) and property and equipment ($1.8B). Total liabilities are $10.1B, up from $7.8B in the previous year. The biggest liabilities are deferred revenue ($5.5B) and accounts payable ($1.8B). Salesforce also has some debt financing, the most notable being the convertible 0.25% senior notes at $1.1B. Subtracting the total assets from the total liabilities leaves stockholders equity of $7.5B, up from $5.0B in the previous year. The biggest stockholders equity account is additional paid-in capital of $8.0B, up from $5.7B in the previous year. The big increase in this account suggests that Salesforce must have raised some new equity during the past year. Unlike most companies, Salesforce does not have a 'retained earnings' account as part of equity. Instead, it has an 'accumulated deficit' account. This is because it has a history of accumulated losses rather than earnings. Note, however, that the accumulated deficit became less negative in the most recent year, suggesting that Salesforce has finally started generating earnings.

Salesforce's income statement is provided on page 59 and Salesforce has chosen to call it the *Statement of Operations*. As we guessed from the balance sheet, net income was positive for the most recent year and amounted to $.2B. Net income comprised of revenues of $8.4B, less cost of revenues of $2.2B, less operating expenses of $6.1B. There are also a number of other small items included in income, including interest expense of $0.1B and a tax benefit of $.2B. At the very bottom of the income statement, net income is expressed on a per-share basis. This is because the ownership in a public corporation is through a large number of shares, and so each shareholder is interested in how much earnings they generate per-share.

Salesforce's *Statement of Stockholders' Equity* is provided on page 62 and provides reconciliations for each of the shareholders' equity accounts over the past 3 years. We will focus on the reconciliation for the most recent year at the bottom of the statement. The final column provides the reconciliation for total shareholders' equity, reconciling the beginning balance of 5.0B to the ending balance of $7.5B, amounts we already saw in the balance sheet. The reconciliation identifies two major causes of the increase. First, there was a $1.2B increase for 'Shares issued related to business combination'. Second, there was a $0.8B increase for 'Stock-based expenses'. Thus, as we guessed from the balance sheet, Salesforce has been issuing new shares. But note that it has been using the shares to acquire other businesses and pay employees rather than the more traditional approach of issuing shares to raise cash. Note that these share issuances are mostly credited to the 'Additional Paid-in Capital' account within stockholders' equity. Finally, right at the bottom of the statement, we see the Net Income of $0.2B being added back to the 'Accumulated Deficit' account. This lowers the amount of the accumulated deficit, and hopefully one glorious day in the not to distant future, the accumulated deficit will turn positive and the account will be renamed 'Retained Earnings'.

# 4.4 LIMITATIONS OF ACCOUNTING INFORMATION

Unfortunately, our love fest with accounting is officially over. It's time to look at accounting's dark side. If accountants were to recognize all economic assets and liabilities and record each item on the balance sheet at fair market value, then the value of equity on the balance sheet would equal the fair value of the equity and the amount recorded for net income in the income statement would represent the economic earnings. But accountants are adamant about the fact that they are not trying to measure the fair value of the business. For this reason, the numbers in the financial statements are often referred to as 'book values' and do not even pretend to represent fair values. The good news here is that because accountants wash their hands of the valuation exercise, they provide the opportunity for the rest of us to do the interesting stuff!

The key limitation of accounting information from a valuation perspective is that accounting rules rely primarily on past transactions. This is great from the perspective that it makes the information reliable and verifiable. It is of enormous help to have our trusty accountants providing information about past sales and costs. However, because accountants are reluctant to try and forecast future transactions, the accounting system misses a lot of information about fair value. For a good example, let's go back to Salesforce's balance sheet.

Recall that Salesforce's biggest asset is 'Goodwill', which was most recently valued at $7.3B. It turns out that this is the sum of all the amounts that Salesforce has paid over and above the fair value of the recognized assets and liabilities in past acquisitions. In other words, this account captures everything that the accountants missed out on recognizing in these acquired businesses.[1] The good news is that the book value of the acquisition will therefore reflect the amount paid for the acquisition, at least at the time of the acquisition. The bad news is that after the acquisition has taken place, the goodwill is not consistently marked to fair value. If the fair value of the goodwill goes up, the book value is not touched. If, on the other hand, the fair value of the goodwill goes down, the accounting rules specify that, under certain conditions, the book value should be marked down to fair value. The problem is that this process involves subjectivity, so as a practical matter, most goodwill impairments take place with a delay.[2] The bad news doesn't stop here. So far, we have only considered goodwill related to acquisitions, but most companies generate their own goodwill internally. Without an acquisition, this goodwill will not show up on the balance sheet until it generates sales and hence earnings. To put this problem in perspective, Salesforce stock price in early 2017 was over seven times its book value. The difference represents the stock market's valuation of internally generated goodwill and other assets that have been missed by the accountants.

Given the limitations inherent in accounting, the primary role of accounting analysis is to determine which benefits and obligations have been ignored in the financial statements and which have been recognized but incorrectly valued. We start with the accounting rules governing the recognition and measurement of assets and liabilities. But before we start, we need to acknowledge that different countries have different accounting rules. For instance, the U.S. has its own 'Generally Accepted Accounting Principles,' or U.S. GAAP, while Canada and most of Europe use 'International Financial Reporting Standards,' or IFRS. Fortunately, U.S. GAAP and IFRS are slowly converging. But because our examples and cases focus on U.S. companies, we will use U.S. GAAP unless we specify otherwise.

---

[1] Note that this statement assumes that Salesforce acquired the businesses at fair value. It is also possible that Salesforce overpaid for the businesses, in which case goodwill was overstated. Alternatively, Salesforce could also have underpaid, in which case the economic value of the goodwill was understated.

[2] See "Has Goodwill Accounting Gone Bad?" by Kevin Li and Richard Sloan, forthcoming, *Review of Accounting Studies*.

## Assets

As mentioned earlier, accountants define assets as probable future economic benefits obtained or controlled by a particular entity as a result of past transactions or events. This rather dry definition imposes two important hurdles for a future economic benefit to be recognized as an asset. First, the future benefit must be *expected*. Accountants have developed a long list of attributes to help determine whether a benefit is sufficiently probable to make it into the financial statements. Important examples of future benefits that are *not* deemed to be probable include those associated with most research and development and marketing activities. Second, the future benefits must have resulted from past transactions or events. The most important manifestation of this hurdle is that future benefits associated with selling goods and services cannot be recognized until the sale has actually been consummated (the realization principle). So future benefits associated with anticipated future sales revenues are not recognized. It is virtually certain that Apple will sell some iPhones at a fat margin during the next few years, but the accounting system does not recognize the value of these future transactions. And many start-up pharmaceutical companies have zero current sales (because they have not yet marketed their first drug) but are valued by the stock market as being worth millions of dollars. The market is valuing cash flows from anticipated future sales. Accountants ignore such future benefits unless they are purchased as part of a business acquisition, in which case they are included in goodwill.

So what future benefits are the accountants willing to recognize? There are three broad types of assets. First, there is cash and cash equivalents, which are valued quite simply at their face value. Second, there are amounts of cash owed to the firm as a result of past transactions or events (e.g., trade receivables). These monetary receivables are generally valued using the net present value of the expected future payments. Third, there are future benefits acquired by the firm as part of a past transaction or event (e.g., marketable securities, inventory, property, acquired intangibles). If the acquired future benefits are financial assets, such as marketable securities, they are sometimes valued using their observed market value. If the acquired future benefits are nonfinancial assets, such as a truck or a building, they are generally valued at historical cost, adjusted downward to the extent that the anticipated future benefits have either been used up or impaired.

Overall, accountants do a good job at recognizing and valuing future benefits associated with financial resources but do a poor job at recognizing and valuing future benefits associated with nonfinancial resources. Accountants only recognize a subset of the future benefits associated with nonfinancial resources and they usually value these benefits based on what they cost rather than on the value of the cash flow streams they are expected to generate.

## Liabilities

Liabilities are essentially the opposite of assets. Liabilities are probable future sacrifices of economic benefits arising from present obligations as a result of past transactions or events. The recognition hurdles imposed on liabilities correspond closely to those imposed on assets. The future sacrifices must be *probable*. Important examples of future sacrifices that are usually *not* deemed probable include the expected costs associated with unsettled litigation and third-party loan guarantees. The future sacrifices must also arise from present obligations as a result of past transactions or events. For example, we may have contracted with suppliers to purchase inventory in the future. But we are not obliged to recognize a liability for the promised future payments until such time as we assume ownership of the inventory. Most liabilities are monetary in nature and are valued based on the present value of the promised payments. Obligations to provide future goods and services to customers represent an important exception and are valued based on the price paid by the customer to receive the future goods/services. While this sounds like a simple valuation rule, things can get tricky. For example, assume that a software company sells a software program bundled with a contract to update the software. The accountant must decide how to divide the selling price between the software program and the future update obligation. The latter is recognized as a liability on the balance sheet until the update envisioned by the contract has been provided.

## Accounting Earnings

Recall that accounting earnings are the change in the book value of equity arising from business activities other than transactions with the equity holders. Formally:

Earnings to Equity Owners  = Change in Equity  + Net Equity Distributions

The good news here is that we don't need any new recognition and measurement rules to determine earnings. That's because the change in the book value of equity equals the change in assets less the change in liabilities. But the bad news is that earnings inherit all the shortcomings of assets and liabilities. The *Income Statement* provides insights into how the firm's business activities have generated the bottom line earnings. The key components of the income statement are illustrated in Figure 4.2. Each of these components has a different definition that facilitates the interpretation of past performance and the forecasting of future performance. The most important components are revenues and expenses and so we will explore them in a bit more detail.

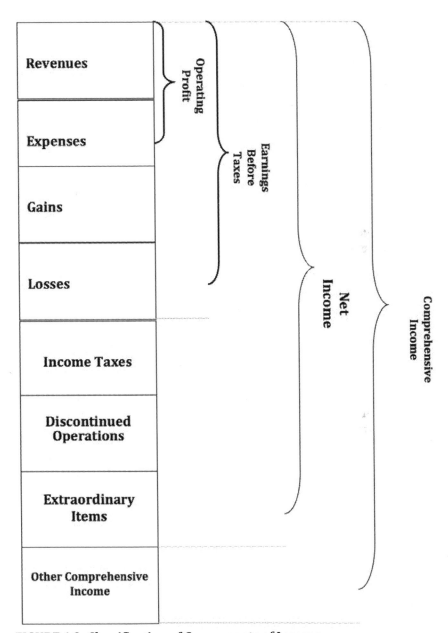

**FIGURE 4.2: Classification of Components of Income**

## Revenues

Revenues are defined as increases in assets or reductions in liabilities that arise from the provision of the goods and services in the course of a firm's operating activities. For the most part, revenues are simply the proceeds received by the firm in return for providing goods and services. Note that the goods and services sold must be part of the firm's intended operating activities. If a firm that is in the business of operating restaurants sells an entire restaurant, the proceeds from the sale will not be recorded as part of revenue, because the firm's intended operating activity is operating rather than selling restaurants. Instead, they will be reported as part of the gain or loss on the sale of the restaurant (more on this below).

A central question in accounting for revenues is establishing exactly when the revenues are earned. In what period do the associated assets increase in value? The general revenue recognition rule is called the *realization principle* and states that revenue is recognized when an exchange transaction has taken place, the earnings process is substantially complete, and collection of the proceeds is reasonably assured. While this sounds very reasonable, it clearly leaves room for interpretation. Consider a company that purchases land, does some minor improvements, subdivides it, and then sells plots to customers who pay 10 percent of the selling price and sign a 10-year mortgage for the balance. Is the selling price recognized as revenue when the firm purchases the land, when it finishes the minor improvements, when a customer pays the initial 10 percent, or when the customer pays off the mortgage? In most situations, the accounting rule is easy: revenue is recognized when a sale is made and the customer takes possession of the goods. But even this seemingly simple rule has received its share of abuse, as we discuss later.

Sales transactions are a key driver of certain expenses on the income statement. Once a sale transaction occurs and revenues are recognized, the accounting rules attempt to measure the assets that are consumed in generating these revenues. Revenue recognition is the kick-off event for the measurement of earnings and, because of this, plays a central role in ratio analysis and forecasting.

## Operating Expenses

Operating expenses are defined as the mirror image of revenues: they are decreases in assets or increases in liabilities that arise from the provision of goods and services in the course of a firm's operating activities. As with revenues, the expenses must be associated with the firm's intended operating activities. For example, the carrying value of a restaurant that is sold by a restaurant operating company would not be an expense (see discussion on gains and losses below).

Wherever possible, expense recognition rules attempt to match the consumption of specific assets to the production of specific revenues, but these rules frequently have to resort to ad hoc allocations of costs. For example, we might all agree that the cost of the raw materials used to produce finished goods should be matched against the revenue generated by the sale of the goods. But exactly how much property, plant, and equipment was consumed to convert the raw materials into finished goods? How much of the corporate Lear jet was consumed in the production of the goods? What about the cost of deferred compensation to the sales force? There are a myriad of principles to provide guidance in this respect, but they can lead to poor matching and are also prone to manipulation, so you need to do your homework.

## Operating Profit

The difference between a firm's revenues and expenses represents the profit associated with the firm's ongoing operating activities. This amount is also referred to as the *operating income* and is the primary driver of firm value. If a firm can't generate a respectable operating profit, then it probably won't be around for very long.

An important role for the income statement is in distinguishing operating profit from the myriad of other, largely nonrecurring transactions and events that cause assets and liabilities to change. Revenues and expenses are intended to capture the financial consequences of a firm's ongoing operating activities. The remaining bits and pieces of income are discussed below. But just because an item is classified as revenue or expense does not rule out the possibility that it may be nonrecurring. Even the ongoing operations of a company are subject to special charges and nonrecurring demand and supply shocks. Recall from Chapter 2 that the management discussion and analysis provided in Forms 10-K and 10-Q is required to identify any potentially nonrecurring components of revenue and expense. As you study a firm's income statement, think carefully about the extent to which each item is likely to be recurring.

## Gains, Losses and Other Items

The remaining items in the income statement are typically more transitory in nature. Gains are increases in the net assets of a firm that occur in the normal course of business and contribute to the earnings of a firm but are incidental or peripheral to the firm's main operating activities. Returning to our previous example of the restaurant-operating firm that sells an entire restaurant, if the proceeds from the sale exceed the carrying value of the restaurant sold, then we would report a gain. Since we are not in the business of selling restaurants, the proceeds and costs associated with the sale are not classified as revenues and expenses. Common examples of gains include proceeds from the sale of assets, awards from winning a lawsuit, and certain increases in the value of marketable securities. Losses are the mirror image of gains.  As shown in Figure 4.2, revenues, expenses, gains, and losses combine to produce a firm's *earnings before taxes.*  All of the categories discussed thus far are presented on a pretax basis.  Thus, the next step shown in Figure 4.2 is to deduct the applicable income taxes.

There are a few other oddities on the income statement that are zero for most firms most of the time. These items are mostly unusual and nonrecurring. They include discontinued operations, extraordinary items, preferred stock dividends, minority interest in earnings and other comprehensive income. Refer to an intermediate accounting text if you want to learn more.

## Accounting Distortions

Remember that we started out this chapter by introducing the important investment concept of return on equity (ROE). What we ultimately want to know is the economic rate of return that is being generated on our investment. However, the accounting ROE will only measure the economic rate of return if the accounting rules correctly measure the economic resources and obligations of the business. While such measurements are easy with a savings account, they are highly subjective for most real businesses. Recall that the book value of equity isn't represented by a cash deposit, but by the net value of all the assets and liabilities recognized and measured under GAAP. For example, if a firm has invested substantial amounts in R&D, its book value will likely be understated because accountants don't allow most past R&D investments to be recognized as assets.

To illustrate how ROE is affected by imperfections in accounting measurements, we will introduce some new notation. Suppose that, due to divine intervention, we could create the perfect accounting system. Let *Beginning Investment* denote the amount of the equity investment at the beginning of the period and let *Economic Earnings* denote amount of earnings to equity holders under this perfect accounting system. The underlying economic rate of return (ERR) is given by:

ERR = Economic Earnings/ Beginning Investment.

Now define $\varepsilon$ as the *measurement error* in equity. It is the difference between the book value of equity, as computed by the real imperfect accounting system, and the true value of the Investment, computed with our hypothetical perfect accounting system:

Beginning $\varepsilon$ = Accounting Equity − Beginning Investment.

Note that if equity is measured with error, then that error will also enter the computation of accounting earnings. Because accounting earnings is derived from the change in equity, the error in accounting earnings will be equal to the change in $\varepsilon$:

Error in Accounting Earnings  =  Accounting Earnings
                                                  –  Economic Earnings
                                             =  Change in ε.

So the accounting ROE can be expressed as:

$$ROE = \frac{\text{Economic Income} + \text{Change in } \epsilon}{\text{Beginning Investment} + \text{Beginning } \epsilon}.$$

In practice, we refer to these measurement errors as 'accounting distortions.' An important job of the financial analyst is to identify and quantify these distortions. Accounting distortions have a two-pronged effect on ROE. First, changes in the measurement error during the period are reflected in the numerator. Second, the level of error at the beginning of the period is reflected in the denominator. The overall distortion in ROE relative to the economic rate of return (ERR) depends on the relative size of the numerator and denominator effects.

The effects of accounting distortions on investment are pretty easy to understand. Overstating (understating) an asset leads to overstating (understating) investment. Conversely, overstating (understating) a liability leads to understating (overstating) investment. But the effects of accounting distortions on the earnings are more complicated. The distortion depends critically on three characteristics of the error:

1.  Does the error relate to an asset or a liability?
2.  Does the error result in an overstatement or an understatement of the asset or liability?
3.  Is the error originating (i.e., getting bigger) or reversing (i.e., getting smaller) during the period?

Figure 4.3 summarizes the impact of all the possible combinations of the above characteristics. Let's start with the first one, which is the origination of an overstatement related to an asset. This is the classic accounting distortion and at the heart of many well-known accounting debacles. It is illustrated in the top left cell in Panel A of Figure 4.3. The origination of an asset overstatement causes us to overstate earnings in the current period, because earnings include an increase in assets that does not correspond to an increase in economic resources. A very common case in point here would be the failure of a company to write-down the carrying value of inventory that has become obsolete. From an economic perspective, the value of the inventory falls. But the accounting system fails to pick up the decline, leading to the origination of a positive error in the book value of the inventory. Earnings, in turn, are overstated by the amount of the inventory write-down that should have been recorded during the period. Other examples include booking a receivable that doesn't exist, failing to write down loans that have turned bad and inappropriately capitalizing expenditures that yield no future benefits. The infamous accounting fraud at WorldCom is a classic case of the latter.[3]

**Panel A: Asset Distortions**

|  | Asset Overstatement | Asset Understatement |
|---|---|---|
| Originating | **Earnings Overstated** Example: Failing to write down obsolete inventory | **Earnings Understated** Example: Failing to capitalize R&D expenditure |
| Reversing | **Earnings Understated** Example: Subsequent write down of obsolete inventory | **Earnings Overstated** Example: Realization of benefits from R&D expenditure |

**Panel B: Liability Distortions**

|  | Liability Overstatement | Liability Understatement |
|---|---|---|
| Originating | **Earnings Understated** Example: Excessive revenue deferral | **Earnings Overstated** Example: Failure to accrue future retirement benefits |
| Reversing | **Earnings Overstated** Example: Subsequent recognition of deferred revenue | **Earnings Understated** Example: Subsequent recognition of retirement benefits |

**FIGURE 4.3: The Impact of Accounting Distortions on Earnings**

---

[3] See https://www.sec.gov/litigation/complaints/comp17829.htm. We are interested in the part where "WorldCom improperly reduced its operating expenses by recharacterizing certain expenses as capital assets".

Asset overstatements cause earnings to be overstated and so are often referred to as *aggressive accounting*. But just as whatever goes up must eventually come down, asset overstatements must eventually be corrected. These corrections cause an offsetting effect in a subsequent period's earnings. This is illustrated in the bottom-left cell of Panel A of Figure 4.3, which extends our previous example of obsolete inventory that is not impaired in a timely manner. At some point in the future, our hapless auditor will hopefully figure out that the inventory is overstated. Or perhaps a new manager will take charge and start by reversing the outgoing manager's chicanery. Either way, the inventory will be written down in this subsequent period. Note that because the inventory was already overvalued at the beginning of the period and is being written down to the correct value during the period, there is a negative change in the error that causes earnings to be understated. So aggressive accounting causes earnings to be overstated in an early period and understated in a later period. We are essentially delaying the bad news. An astute investor may have been able to identify early warning signs that inventory was overstated, such as an unexplained build-up of finished goods inventory or write-downs at competitor firms holding similar inventory.

The right hand side of Panel A of Figure 4.3 illustrates the effect of asset understatements on earnings. The origination of an asset understatement causes earnings to be understated, as no error existed at the beginning of the period and a negative error exists at the end of the period. A classic example here is the failure to capitalize expenditures on R&D. U.S. GAAP does not allow most expenditures of R&D to be capitalized, but such expenditures are typically expected to generate future benefits. Thus, in a period during which a firm invests in R&D, a negative error originates, causing earnings to be understated. For this reason, asset understatements are often referred to as *conservative accounting*. In some future period, we will hopefully receive benefits from the R&D, in which case the error will reverse, and earnings will be overstated. In other words, the reversal of conservative accounting leads to overstated earnings. Many firms are continuously investing in R&D. For these firms, the distortion in current earnings is the net effect of benefits received from prior period R&D (reversal effect) less expenses recognized for current period R&D (origination). We will work through an example shortly. Note that regardless of earnings distortion in any given period, the immediate expensing of R&D will always lead to understated assets and book equity, imparting an upward bias in ROE.

Panel B of Figure 4.3 illustrates the accounting distortions created by the misstatement of liabilities. These are the mirror image of those reported in Panel A, because liabilities relate to future obligations rather than future benefits. So the origination of an overstated liability causes earnings to be understated. A classic example here would be deferring the recognition of revenue when a sales transaction has occurred, cash has been received and the good or service has been largely provided. The origination of a liability overstatement is another case of conservative accounting. But again, what goes up must come down, so earnings will be overstated in the future period during which the deferred revenue is finally recognized. All this is shown on the left-hand side of Panel B, Figure 4.3.

The right-hand side of Panel B shows the distortions created by liability understatements. The origination of a liability understatement causes earnings to be overstated, while the subsequent reversal of the understatement causes earnings to be understated. In case you haven't recognized, this is another case of aggressive accounting. A good example would be the failure to record a liability for retirement obligations earned by employees in the current period. This will come back to bite earnings when the workers retire and receive their benefits. Fortunately, U.S. GAAP now do a much better job than they used to in requiring firms to recognize their economic obligations under pension plans as liabilities.

We've now covered all the possible combinations of asset and liability misstatements. Let's try and drive this home by applying what we have leaned to Salesforce's financial statements. We will start with an understated asset. Salesforce reports significant research and development expenses on its income statement. Recall that most research and development must be expensed as incurred under U.S. GAAP. Since these expenditures are expected to create future benefits, there is a missing asset on Salesforce's balance sheet. In order to determine the value of the missing asset, we need to determine the amount and timing of the future benefits. To make things easy let's assume that the future benefits from Salesforce's R&D start at the beginning of the fiscal year immediately following the one in which they are incurred and are realized evenly over the subsequent two-year period. Using these assumptions, the missing R&D asset for the 2015 and 2016 fiscal years (i.e., the fiscal years ending in January 31 2016 and 2017 respectively) are (in $ thousands):

$$
\begin{aligned}
\text{2015 Missing R\&D Asset} &= \text{2015 R\&D Expenditure} \\
&+ \tfrac{1}{2}\,\text{2014 R\&D Expenditure} \\
&= 946,300 + \tfrac{1}{2}\,792,917 \\
&= 1,342,759.
\end{aligned}
$$

$$
\begin{aligned}
\text{2016 Missing R\&D Asset} &= \text{2016 R\&D Expenditure} \\
&+ \tfrac{1}{2}\,\text{2015 R\&D Expenditure} \\
&= 1,208,127 + \tfrac{1}{2}\,946,300 \\
&= 1,681,277.
\end{aligned}
$$

So assets are understated by over $1B in each of the last two years. Next, remember that earnings will be understated by the amount of the increase in the error (i.e., the amount by which the missing asset increased):

$$
\text{2016 Earnings Understatement} = 1,681,277 - 1,342,759 = 338,519
$$

Another way of looking at this adjustment is to net the new error that originated in 2016 from the old error that reversed in 2016. The originating error is the 1,208,127 of R&D that was not capitalized in 2016. The reversing error is the half of the 2014 and 2015 expenditures that produced assets expiring in 2016 and hence should have been amortized against earnings in 2016:

$$
\begin{aligned}
\text{2016 Earnings Understatement} &= \text{Originating Error} - \text{Reversing Error} \\
&= 1,208,127 - \tfrac{1}{2}\,(946,300 + 792,917) = 338,519.
\end{aligned}
$$

In this case, because R&D expenditures have been growing, the originating error exceeds the reversing error and so there is a net origination that causes earnings to be understated.

Note that the amount of the understatement is a very large number compared to Salesforce's reported earnings of only 179,632. Since this understatement is computed on a before-tax basis, it can be directly compared to Salesforce's income before taxes of only $25,383. Salesforce is using conservative accounting for R&D and removing this distortion increases Salesforce's before-tax earnings by tenfold!

To round things out, let's also look at the case of a liability that is potentially overstated on Salesforce's financial statements. Salesforce's biggest liability is deferred revenue. If you look carefully at Salesforce's balance sheet for the 2016 fiscal year, you will see both a deferred revenue account under current liabilities of 5,505,689 and a noncurrent deferred revenue of 37,113. These amounts, for the most part, represent subscription revenues for annual contracts to use Salesforce's cloud-based services. Customers have signed contracts and paid for services, but U.S. GAAP says that none of the revenue can be recognized until the customer exercises the right to use the cloud-based service, which happens ratably over the course of the contracts. This seems very conservative, and most of the economic value is probably realized when the customer signs up and pays the cash. What if we adopt this alternative approach and recognize no liability for deferred revenue? In this case liabilities are overstated by the following amounts:

2016 Overstated Deferred Revenue Liability = 5,505,689 + 37,113 = 5,542,802

2015 Overstated Deferred Revenue Liability = 4,267,667 + 23,886 = 4,291,553

So liabilities are considerably overstated in both years. Remember that earnings are understated by an originating liability overstatement, so we have:

2016 Earnings Understatement = 5,542,802 − 4,291,553 = 1,251,249

In this case, new originating deferred revenues exceeded old reversing deferred revenues, causing deferred revenues to increase for the year. This increase translates into an earnings understatement.

It turns out that we are not done yet. Along with deferring revenue, Salesforce also defers the commissions that it pays to employees in generating this revenue. You can see these amounts as assets on the balance sheet. These commissions are paid in cash shortly after the contract is signed. Because Salesforce defers revenues on the grounds that it still has an obligation to provide the service, it also defers the commissions paid to employees in generating these revenues. It stands to reason that if we adjust for revenue deferrals, we should also adjust for associated commission deferrals. Going through the same process for commissions, we have:

2016 Overstated Deferred Commissions Asset = 311,770 + 227,849 = 539,619

2015 Overstated Deferred Commissions Asset = 259,187 + 189,943 = 449,130

Remembering that earnings will be overstated by an originating asset overstatement. So for 2016:

2016 Earnings Overstatement= 539,619 – 449,130 = 90,489

So in this case, new originating deferred commissions exceeded old reversing deferred commissions resulting in an increase in deferred commissions and an earnings overstatement.

So far, we have conservative accounting for deferred revenues leading to an earnings understatement and aggressive accounting for deferred commissions leading to an earnings overstatement. Since these two accounting distortions go hand-in-hand, the net effect of these distortions on earnings is:

Net 2016 Earnings Understatement = 1,251,149 – 90,489 = 1,160,760.

You should immediately see that this is a whopping understatement of earnings. Reported before-tax earnings are only 25,383.[4] If we agree that the deferred contract revenue represents an economic asset, earnings are understated by over 1,000,000! The astute reader may wonder whether we should recognize all of this deferred revenue, since we still have to provide the customer with access to cloud-based services. But it turns out that we might not have gone far enough. Salesforce also has very significant unbilled deferred revenues that don't even show up as a liability. The reason that they are not recorded as a liability is that while customers have signed multi-year contracts, they are only billed in annual installments. Deferred revenue is only recognized when a billing is made, at which point an account receivable is also recorded as an asset. You can read about this on p. 36 of Form 10-K, where you see that unbilled deferred revenue grew from 7,100,000 in 2015 to 9,000,000 in 2016. The bottom line is that customers have committed to pay Salesforce a bundle to use its services for many years, yet a lot of it isn't recognized in the income statement or even deferred on the balance sheet! We will leave you to ponder these awe-inspiring accounting distortions.

We will wrap up this section by pulling together all of the distortions that we have quantified above and seeing how they impact before-tax ROE. Reported before-tax ROE for Salesforce in 2016 is:

Salesforce 2016 Reported Before-Tax ROE
        = 2016 Before-Tax Income/2015 Shareholders Equity
        = 25,383/5,002,869 = 0.5%.

---

[4] You may have noticed that Salesforce's before tax earnings is actually lower than it's after tax earnings. This unusual situation arose in fiscal 2016 because Salesforce recorded an income tax benefit instead of an income tax expense. This benefit results from the reversal of a valuation allowance on Salesforce's deferred tax assets. Now that Salesforce looks like it will be profitable, it can use its past losses to reduce the taxes on future income.

This is clearly a pretty lousy rate of return, given that we could have got a 2.5% return on a 10-Year U.S. Treasury Note. But adjusted for the distortions documented above, we have:

Salesforce Adjusted 2016 Before-Tax ROE
    = 2016 Adjusted Before-Tax Income/2015 Adjusted Equity
    = (25,383+338,519+1,160,760)/(5,002,869+1,342,759 +4,291,553 – 449,130)
    = 15.0%

This is a healthy rate of return and suggests that Salesforce is growing a lucrative business. It helps to explain why investors have priced Salesforce at a significant premium to accounting book value.

# 4.5 COMMON SOURCES OF ACCOUNTING DISTORTIONS

You should now realize that accounting assets and liabilities can represent economic resources and obligations with considerable error. The only way to identify these errors is to understand the underlying economics of the business, understand how much of this is reflected in the accounting system, and do your best to quantify the resulting distortions. To help you think about potential accounting distortions, we can divide the distortions into three broad categories:

1.   Distortions caused by GAAP,
2.   Distortions caused by lack of perfect foresight in the use of accounting estimates, and
3.   Distortions caused by management's intentional manipulation of accounting estimates.

We discuss each of these sources of error in more detail below.

## Measurement Error Caused by GAAP

The major source of measurement error introduced by GAAP is in the recognition and valuation of nonfinancial assets. Measurement error arises because investments made in nonfinancial assets are typically expected to generate uncertain benefits over multiple future periods. Because the timing and amount of these benefits are not known early in the life of the asset, measurement error is unavoidable. But worse still, the accounting rules for many types of investments often result in systematic and predictable measurement errors. Recall that GAAP accounting rules trade off relevance and reliability, with reliability often winning the day. Consequently, GAAP often require simple and objective procedures because they can be reliably computed and easily verified. Examples include the immediate expensing of certain investment expenditures and the use of mechanical depreciation and amortization schedules for others. We discuss the biases created by these simple procedures next.

## Immediate Expensing of Internally Generated Intangibles

This is an example of a hugely important class of assets that GAAP largely ignores. Under GAAP, expenditures made on internally developed intangible assets are generally required to be expensed immediately. It is as if these expenditures produce no benefits beyond the accounting period in which they are incurred. Examples include most research and development expenditures, expenditures to develop patents, most advertising expenditures, and most administrative expenditures. Many of these expenditures clearly generate benefits that extend well beyond the period in which they are incurred, but, rather than attempt to estimate the unused amount of these investments, GAAP use the safe and reliable value of zero. So a firm gets to capitalize the cost of constructing a new building, but not the cost of developing a valuable patent. Immediate expensing of internally developed intangibles is a classic example of conservative accounting. This accounting results in the systematic understatement of equity (because assets are understated) in all periods during which there has been a past expenditure that is expected to generate future benefits.

As with any asset understatement, the impact of this accounting distortion on net income relative to economic income depends on whether the understatement is originating or reversing. If the firm is increasing investment in intangibles, the understatement is originating, and lowers net income relative to economic income. If investment is constant, there is no effect on net income. Finally, if investment is decreasing, net income is overstated relative to economic income.

## Depreciation and Amortization of Capitalized Nonfinancial Assets

Unlike internally developed intangible assets, GAAP generally allow for the capitalization of expenditures on tangible assets (e.g., property, plant, and equipment) and purchased intangibles (e.g., patents). The accounting for such expenditures at their inception is straightforward. Since these expenditures are investments that are expected to generate future benefits, the full amount of the expenditures is initially *capitalized* on the balance sheet as an asset. The difficult part is deciding how to subsequently reduce the value of the asset over the future periods in which it generates benefits. This process is known as *depreciation* for tangible assets and *amortization* for purchased intangible assets. Ideally, the depreciation/amortization method should reflect the flow of expected future benefits generated by the initial investment expenditure. However, implementing such a method would entail subjective forecasts of the future benefits. So GAAP generally sacrifice relevance for reliability, requiring firms to follow a predetermined depreciation schedule, with the most common method being straight-line, whereby the initial value of the asset is reduced in equal increments over the expected life of the asset.

The most common effect of these rules is to understate asset values by depreciating them too quickly. This represents conservative accounting, resulting in the same biases as for the immediate expensing of expenditures on internally developed intangibles. However, the degree of bias is not as great, because we simply depreciate the asset too quickly rather than expensing the entire asset immediately. One consequence is the so-called *old plant trap*. Firms with old plant that has been almost completely depreciated will have low book values that result in high accounting rates of return. But once the old plant is replaced, book values will increase, causing accounting rates of return to fall. The old plant trap is sprung when investors mistake the high accounting rates of return for firms with old plants for high economic rates of return.

An important exception to the above rules applies to the case of purchased intangibles that are judged to have 'indefinite' lives, with goodwill being the most common example. In such cases, current GAAP requires no amortization, but instead applies a periodic impairment test. We will talk more about asset impairments below. But for now we note that determining the value of such assets is an incredibly subjective process. Consequently, management typically defers impairments until there is overwhelming evidence of a substantial decline in the value of the asset. This results in asset overstatements and aggressive accounting. Thus, we get something of a mismatch, with conservative accounting for many tangible assets and aggressive accounting for many purchased intangible assets.

## Asset Impairments

As discussed above, GAAP generally require that nonfinancial assets be carried at their amortized historical cost. This means that the carrying value of the asset represents a fraction of the amount that was originally invested in order to generate future benefits rather than a forecast of the value of the expected future benefits. However, GAAP also contain an important exception to this rule. If it is determined that the value of an asset has been sufficiently impaired, GAAP require that the asset be written down to fair value. The nature of the impairment tests depends on whether the asset is subject to amortization or falls into the special class of indefinitely lived intangibles that are not subject to amortization. In the former case, an impairment charge must be taken when the sum of the expected <u>undiscounted</u> cash flows from the asset is less than its carrying value. In the latter case, an impairment charge must be taken when the <u>discounted</u> sum of the expected future cash flows is less than the carrying value of the asset. The stricter test for indefinitely lived intangibles is an attempt to counter the aggressive accounting that can result from not requiring such assets to be amortized.

Asset impairments are a manifestation of the aforementioned conservatism convention, and introduce a nasty asymmetry into asset valuations. If an asset's value falls significantly below its carrying value, it gets revalued downward based on its estimated fair value, but if the asset's value significantly exceeds its current carrying value, no upward revaluation is allowed. Hence, we cannot interpret book value as either an estimate of past investment or an estimate of fair value. Rather, it is something of a mongrel, representing a mixture of these two amounts.

From a practical perspective, we need to remember that firms with asset impairments have potentially flawed business models. Corporate managers often encourage investors to focus on net income before asset impairment charges, reasoning that these charges are nonrecurring and are not indicative of future performance. Moreover, while asset impairments often represent the reversal of past aggressive accounting, management often use the opportunity to take 'big baths', booking a much larger impairment than is really justified. This is a form of conservative accounting. By writing down the value of an asset today, equity goes down and future expenses go down, so future income and ROE will be overstated . You should also remember that asset impairments are basically an admission by management that they have invested in unprofitable businesses. If a asset impairment is recorded every time management makes a bad investment, it stands to reason that income and ROE before impairments should look good, since they exclude the effects of all the bad investments. However, we should not draw the conclusion that management is doing a good job. We need to look at the aggregate performance of both the good and bad investments to draw overall conclusions about management performance.

### *Omission of Contingent Liabilities*

We have already discussed the fact that the accounting rules do not allow for the recognition of investments in internally generated intangibles as assets. The reason for this is that the future benefits are deemed to be so uncertain that they cannot be reliably measured. For the same reason, contingent liabilities also are not recognized on the balance sheet. A contingent liability is an expected future obligation that is not sufficiently probable or not reasonably estimable. Two common examples of contingent liabilities are ongoing litigation against a firm and potential environmental cleanup costs. Because liabilities are not recognized, net assets and equity are overstated. This results in aggressive accounting. In the period that a contingent liability arises, a liability understatement originates, so net income is overstated (i.e., we are in the top-right cell of Figure 4.3 Panel B). Manufacturers of tobacco products represent good examples of companies with unrecognized liabilities. These companies have reported high past accounting profits, but these profits most likely overstate the companies' true economic profitability, because they ignore the cost of future litigation stemming from tobacco-related illnesses.

## Measurement Error Caused by Lack of Perfect Foresight

The measurement of many assets and liabilities requires the estimation of future benefits and costs. GAAP require that future amounts be measured with some minimum level of reliability before qualifying for recognition in the financial statements. However, this certainly doesn't mean that, just because accountants found the nerve to recognize and measure them, they have little estimation error. In fact, quite the opposite is often true. For example, employee postretirement benefit liabilities require forecasts of health care costs decades into the future. Even if management has made a good-faith estimate, we should recognize that the amount recorded on the balance sheet might differ greatly from the actual future obligations it represents.

If management has done a thorough job at estimating inherently subjective future amounts, then there is probably little that you can do to improve upon their estimates. However, it is very important that you understand the amount of potential estimation error involved in the various assets and liabilities presented on a company's balance sheets. Understanding estimation error is important for at least two reasons. First, the precision of forecasts based on financial statement data is directly related to the precision of the financial statement data themselves. Second, the inherent risk of a business is a direct function of the risk of its underlying assets and liabilities.

Unfortunately, there are only a few broad-brush rules we can give you for establishing the amount of potential measurement error associated with particular classes of assets and liabilities. For example, we can safely tell you that cash and short-term investments have little measurement error. For accounts receivable, however, the amount of potential measurement error can be very small or incredibly large. A bank that lends only to highly creditworthy customers will generally be able to measure its receivables with much less potential error than a firm that makes subprime loans. A detailed understanding of the nature of the assets and liabilities being measured and the techniques used to measure them is required to make a good assessment of the amount of potential measurement error. This can only be accomplished through a thorough understanding of the business and careful analysis of the financial statements and their notes.

## Measurement Error Caused by Managerial Manipulation

The final source of error in the financial statements is introduced through intentional managerial manipulation (shock and horror!). Given the many estimates that GAAP entail, it is an inevitable fact that some managers will use this discretion to achieve their own short-term objectives. The most common type of managerial manipulation is aggressive accounting. This allows management to temporarily boost earnings and ROE. Possible motivations include hitting key bonus thresholds, meeting analysts' earnings forecasts, and creating the illusion of a profitable business for the purpose of raising new capital. Recall that aggressive accounting involves overstating assets or understating liabilities. This results in either the overstatement of revenue (e.g., overstating receivables or understating deferred revenues) or understatement of expenses (e.g., overstating inventory or understating pension liabilities). But aggressive accounting must ultimately reverse, so this type of *earnings management* is really about shifting income from one period to another.

The key to detecting aggressive accounting is to pin down the assets and liabilities over which management exercises the most discretion. This typically rules out things like cash, short-term investments, debt, and most payables. GAAP for these items are fairly rigid and there isn't much room for managerial manipulation.[5] As we advised in the previous section, you should devote extra attention to assets and liabilities that require the most estimation. This is where managers are most likely to perpetrate their dastardly deeds. Recall that Item 7 of Form 10-K requires management to describe their firm's critical accounting policies. This represents a good starting point for the identification of likely areas for earnings management. But you should not stop here, since management is usually sneaky enough not to tell you where the earnings management is taking place.

Another technique is to analyze situations where high earnings are not matched by correspondingly high cash flows. We will talk more about this method of analysis in Chapter 6. Unfortunately, a big difference between earnings and cash flows does not always signal aggressive accounting. It may instead reflect legitimate growth in real investment. Without a detailed analysis, it is difficult to discriminate between these two potential explanations.

Below, we categorize common earnings management techniques based on where they impact the income statement. We briefly discuss each category, identifying the assets and liabilities that are most likely to be involved.

## *Revenue Manipulation*

Revenue manipulation is the most common type of earnings management. The sales transaction is a key trigger for the recognition of future benefits under GAAP, so there is no better place to start looking for earnings management. The asset most commonly involved in revenue manipulation is accounts receivable. A cash payment from a customer is a pretty good indication that the customer is committed to the transaction (although the revenue may still not have been earned—more on this below). However, when the customer has not yet paid, the balance lives in the accounts receivable, and there is greater uncertainty about whether the payment will be made. The customer may not be committed to the transaction, may not have the ability to make the contracted payment, or may not even know that the company recorded a transaction.

A common form of revenue manipulation is *trade loading* or *channel*

---

[5] There have nevertheless been cases where cash and short-term investments have been manipulated. The accounting scandals at Parmalat and Satyam are two such examples.

*stuffing*, whereby product is shipped to a customer before the customer really needs it. This type of activity is most prevalent at the end of a reporting period. Management is effectively stealing from next period's sales in order to inflate this period's sales. Another form of revenue manipulation overstates the value of the net receivables by understating the allowance for uncollectible accounts. It is easy to increase the volume of sales transactions by granting more generous credit terms or by selling on credit to customers with lower credit quality. However, the cost of increasing sales in this way is the increased amount of expected uncollectible accounts. If accounts receivable is not adjusted downwards to reflect the increased expected uncollectibles, then accounts receivable, revenue, and earnings will all be overstated.

A variety of ratio analysis techniques can be used to identify firms that are potentially overstating revenue and accounts receivable, and we discuss them in Chapters 5 and 6. However, it is important to analyze these ratios in the context of the firm's business strategy and accounting policies. There have been examples of firms that have made strategic choices to loosen their credit terms that have paid off nicely. While unusually high receivables are an important red flag, they are not a definitive indicator of revenue manipulation.

Accounts receivable is not the only account that can be used for revenue manipulation. Suppose a customer pays in advance for a product or service, such as a subscription or a product that includes a servicing agreement. In such cases, GAAP require that revenue recognition should be delayed until the good or service is delivered to the customer. This creates a liability representing the future obligation of the firm to provide the promised goods/services. Common titles for such a liability are Deferred Revenue, Unearned Revenue and Advances from Customers. In this case the total sales price is allocated to different periods based on subjective proration schedules. Unlike receivables, the collection of cash is already assured. It is simply the timing of the revenue recognition that is at issue. Nevertheless, understatement of the liability to provide future goods/services can be a powerful tool for revenue manipulation. For example, a firm can boost current period revenues by promising to provide enhanced future service or additional future products at discounted prices. If the cost of these future obligations is not recorded as a liability, then current period equity and earnings will be overstated.

## Expense Manipulation

Whenever an asset is used up or a liability is created in the process of providing goods and services to customers, GAAP require an expense to be recognized. The theory is straightforward. However, like revenue recognition, there are many gray areas that open the door for earnings management.

Perhaps the biggest gray area is the 'capitalize versus expense' decision. Whenever an asset is used up in a firm's operating activities, an expense must be recognized *unless* a new asset is created. In other words, there must be a future benefit that satisfies the criteria for recognition as an asset. Therefore, earnings can be manipulated by capitalizing costs that should really be expensed. This is the means by which WorldCom perpetrated its well-known earnings management scheme. WorldCom capitalized approximately $10 billion of its regular operating costs as part of Property and Equipment.

Another common real-world example is the aggressive capitalization of costs incurred to develop and produce software. GAAP require that only costs incurred beyond the point of technological feasibility can be capitalized. But the determination of technological feasibility is subjective and lends itself to manipulation. In order to lower expenses, management can simply claim technological feasibility has been achieved. The auditor, not being an expert in software development, is in a poor position to question such a judgment. In an interesting twist on earnings management, Microsoft has been accused of understating income by expensing too much of its software development costs, regardless of technological feasibility. A good check for expense manipulation of this kind is to compare the total proportion of costs that are capitalized by a firm with its industry counterparts. If a firm is capitalizing a very different proportion of its costs from other firms in the industry, it is more likely to be manipulating earnings. But it is always possible that the firm really is different from its industry counterparts and its capitalization policies are appropriate.

Inventory accounting also lends itself to expense manipulation. In times of changing prices, the cost flow assumption used to account for inventory (FIFO, LIFO, etc.) can be important in determining the cost of inventory that has been used up and therefore recognized as cost of goods sold. Management can also manipulate the allocation of joint costs. In a slaughterhouse that produces pork products, how should we allocate the cost of the pig between bacon and sausage? If we sell bacon more quickly than we sell sausage, we can temporarily boost earnings by assigning more costs to sausage, hence leaving these costs in inventory longer.

Yet another technique for manipulating earnings using inventory accounting is to purchase a diverse range of inventory and offer it for sale at a high markup. The firm makes big profits on the product that sells and leaves the product that doesn't sell in inventory. The problem here, of course, is inventory obsolescence. This type of earnings management is particularly prevalent in the specialty retail industry, where seasonal fashions are difficult to predict. By failing to write down the obsolete inventory on a timely basis, management can understate expenses and overstate income.

Another avenue for expense manipulation involves noncurrent assets that are used up gradually over many periods, such as property, plant, and equipment. GAAP call for these assets to be depreciated, amortized, or impaired over time using a variety of rules. However, all of these rules provide management with considerable latitude in determining the periodic expenses recorded. An interesting example here is Blockbuster, a video rental chain. In the early years of video, Blockbuster depreciated its rental videos over a longer time period than its competitors. At the time, there was considerable uncertainty concerning the useful lives of rental videos, particularly because the demographics of video renters were changing rapidly as video players became more affordable. As a result, Blockbuster looked more profitable than its competitors, and so attracted more capital and became the leading player in this industry - until Netflix came along and put them out of business.

Expense manipulation is not restricted to assets. Understating liabilities is another technique for understating expenses. Consider the accounting for warranty liabilities. When a firm sells a product with a warranty, the expected future costs of the warranty should be recognized as an obligation of the company at the same time that the sales transaction is recognized. This will result in an increase in liabilities and a decrease in equity and earnings. By understating or ignoring the warranty liability, management can overstate earnings. One spectacular example of expense manipulation in this vein involved Regina Company. Regina manufactured vacuum cleaners that were reputably so durable that they would last a lifetime. In fact, Regina offered a lifetime warranty on its products, but the high quality of its products meant that few warranty costs were ever incurred. Then, a new CEO boosted Regina's earnings and stock price by using cheaper components in the vacuum cleaners. The lower costs meant higher profits in the short run. But, as you would expect, costs associated with the lifetime warranty started to skyrocket, and Regina subsequently went broke. The higher expected warranty costs should have been recorded as a liability, and an associated expense recognized in the income statement. If this had been done, Regina would never have shown higher profits in the first place.

A final important area for expense manipulation is employee pensions and other retirement benefits. GAAP require these amounts be estimated, recognized as a liability, and charged off as an expense in the period that employees earn the right to these future benefits. There is huge subjectivity involved in estimating these amounts. What will be the ultimate amount of the benefits? What discount rate should be used to calculate the present value of the future benefits? Small changes in these assumptions can have huge impacts on the financial statements, so management has considerable leeway to manipulate earnings. Again, you should conduct an industry comparison of the accounting assumptions to determine whether a particular firm appears to be managing earnings.

In summary, most earnings management involves misstated assets or liabilities on the balance sheet. Consequently, the key to detecting earnings management is a careful examination of the balance sheet. So far, we have focused exclusively on traditional revenue and expense manipulation. However, there are other more subtle forms of financial statement manipulation. We provide a brief discussion of four of the most common forms below.

## *Related-Party Transactions*
A key prerequisite for the recognition of many assets and liabilities on the

balance sheet is a transaction with another party. The maintained assumption under GAAP is that these transactions represent arms'-length business dealings. For example, if inventory is purchased, the underlying assumption is that the purchase price represents the fair market value at the date of purchase. Also, if a sale is made, the assumption is that the sale will not be reversed at a later date.

Given GAAP's heavy reliance on transactions with other parties, one possible technique for manipulating the financial statements is to engage in "sham" transactions with related parties. For example, a firm with an earnings shortfall could sell product to a customer with a verbal agreement that the sale will be reversed or the customer reimbursed in some other manner (e.g., future price discounts). Such practices are technical violations of GAAP, but they can be difficult to prove. Further, related-party transactions extend from earnings management to balance sheet management. A director may make a "long-term loan" to a company just before the end of a reporting period in order to create the impression of improved short-term liquidity on the balance sheet, and then reverse the loan shortly thereafter.

Fortunately, U.S. reporting requirements require that all material related-party transactions must be disclosed in the financial statements of the reporting entity. The nature of the relationship and the amount and nature of the transactions must be reported in the notes to the financial statements. Unfortunately, if management really wants to deceive you with related-party transactions, it is unlikely that they will say so in plain English in the financial statement footnotes.

## *Off-Balance-Sheet Entities*

Off-balance-sheet entities have many similarities with related-party transactions. With off-balance-sheet entities, management creates a separate legal entity that is not required to be consolidated in the firm's financial statements. Management nevertheless exercises influence over this new entity and uses the entity to manipulate the firm's financial statements. Management usually exercises influence over the off-balance-sheet entity by appointing related parties to the management of the entity or by being a key financier, supplier, customer, or guarantor of the entity. Once established, there are several ways in which the off-balance-sheet entity can then be used to manipulate the financial statements of the firm. For example, the off-balance-sheet entity may purchase goods and services from the firm at inflated prices, directly boosting equity and earnings. In many past cases, these purchases have been funded by loans from the firm itself and simply represent sham transactions designed with the sole intent of boosting earnings. Alternatively, a firm could boost revenue by using an off-balance-sheet entity to provide customers with loans for making purchases from the firm. If the firm itself guarantees these loans, then the risk associated with the loans is ultimately borne by the firm but is hidden from investors because the loans themselves are in the off-balance-sheet entity. Off-balance-sheet entities also can be used to hide financial leverage and other sources of risk from investors.

The analysis of off-balance-sheet entities can be extremely difficult. Firms that create such structures in order to manage the financial statements will go to great lengths to make it as difficult as possible for investors to figure out what is going on. Moreover, because we typically don't have financial information for these off-balance-sheet entities, we really don't have much to work with. The well-known rise and sudden fall of Enron was primarily attributable to the aggressive use of off-balance-sheet entities to boost earnings and hide risks from investors. The best advice we can give you here is that if you see any sign that off-balance-sheet entities are being used, you should make sure that you understand how they are being used. If you don't feel that you have enough information to make a meaningful assessment, you may want to assume the worst.

How do you know if any off-balance-sheet entities are out there? There are three potential disclosures in the notes to the financial statements that you should look for. First, there is the related-party note. This note must report any unconsolidated transactions with entities in which the firm has ownership, control, or significant influence. Second, there is the note relating to equity investments and other unconsolidated investments. You should ascertain whether any of these investments give the firm influence over the operating policies of the investee. Finally, there is the contingent liabilities note. If the firm has guaranteed the debt of any unconsolidated entities, then these guarantees should be identified in the contingent liabilities note.

## *Off-Balance-Sheet Financing*

Off-balance-sheet financing is used to finance the acquisition of resources without showing the associated assets and liabilities on the balance sheet. By doing so, the firm usually hopes to create the impression that it has less financial risk than it really does. The most common type of off-balance-sheet financing is an operating lease. A firm enters into a contract in which it acquires the right to use an asset in return for periodic payments to the owner of the asset. If the contract covers a substantial portion of the useful life of the asset, then the economic substance of the transaction is identical to one in which the firm borrows money and then buys the asset. But because the legal form of the transaction is a lease contract, no assets and liabilities are recognized.

GAAP have developed a complex set of rules to determine whether leases can be kept off the books as operating leases or must be put on the books as capital leases (the future benefits and obligations associated with capital leases must be estimated and placed on the balance sheet). While we won't drag you through all the rules, suffice it to say that creative accountants have found ways to help management get whatever accounting treatment they want, regardless of the economic substance of the lease transaction. As a result, most leases remain off balance sheet.[6]

Fortunately, figuring out the impact of operating leases is straightforward. Firms are required to disclose future minimum lease payments on most operating leases in the notes to the financial statements. By taking the present value of these payments, you can immediately get a good idea of how much off-balance-sheet financing is attributable to operating leases.

Operating leases are not the only way off-balance-sheet financing can be achieved. Any contract in which a firm acquires the right to use a resource and incurs future obligations in return represents off-balance-sheet financing. Other common forms of off-balance-sheet financing include purchase commitments, take-or-pay contracts, sale of receivables with recourse, unconsolidated finance subsidiaries, joint ventures, and equity investments. You should be able to discover the existence of these and other off-balance-sheet financing techniques by studying the MD&A and notes to the financial statements, particularly the contractual obligations section of MD&A and the contingent liabilities note.

### Nonrecurring Charges and Pro Forma Earnings

A final form of financial statement manipulation that has become popular of late is the strategic use of nonrecurring charges, such as asset impairments, losses on the sale of long-lived assets, and restructuring charges. Because these charges are nonrecurring, it has become usual for management, analysts, and investors to focus on the recurring component of earnings that excludes such charges. This non-GAAP definition of earnings is often referred to as *pro forma* earnings in analyst reports and firms' press releases.

In recent years, the magnitude and frequency of nonrecurring charges has exploded. Moreover, firms have started to exclude recurring charges from pro forma earnings with the lamest of excuses. The idea is to reclassify as many recurring expenses as possible into a nonrecurring charge and, hence, report higher recurring or pro forma earnings. For example, if a firm writes down its fixed assets today in a nonrecurring impairment charge, recurring earnings will be higher moving forward, because the carrying value of these assets is lower and hence future depreciation expense will be lower. As a result, many firms consistently report large nonrecurring charges year after year. Management wins twice with this manipulation. First, they convince you to ignore the nonrecurring charge in the period that they take it, arguing that it is old news and irrelevant to the future. Second, expenses in the future are lower because of the writedown of assets in the current period. Ignoring expenses that management labels as nonrecurring is like evaluating a fund manager's performance after excluding the bottom 10 percent performers in her portfolio. You should determine what is really included in these charges and make a

---

[6] New leasing standards that make it more difficult to keep leases off balance sheet will take effect for fiscal years ending after December 15, 2018. For details, see
http://www.fasb.org/jsp/FASB/FASBContent_C/NewsPage&cid=1176167901466 .

careful assessment of their implications for the soundness of the firm's financial health. A bad management team will blunder from one bad business decision to the next. Are the losses associated with each of these bad decisions nonrecurring simply because they relate to different business decisions? The answer is no.

## 4.6 CONCLUSION

You should take away three lessons from this chapter. First, the GAAP-based financial statements provide the universal language for evaluating the past performance and forecasting the future performance of a business. Second, the financial statements only provide timely information on a subset of value-relevant events. The financial statements are not the accountants' attempt to value the firm. Rather, the goal of the financial statements is to provide people like us with transaction-based information that is useful in conducting our own valuations. Third, while the financial statements are restricted to reasonably reliable information, lots of subjectivity is still involved in the estimation of assets and liabilities. This opens the financial statements to potential errors and managerial manipulation. A careful examination of a firm's assets and liabilities is the best starting point for identifying potential errors and manipulation.

To build a good valuation model, you must become intimately familiar with a firm's financial statements and the accounting policies underlying those financial statements. Are the accounting policies consistent with the underlying economics of the business operations and strategies? What important events are captured in the financial statements on a timely basis and what events are missing? Which assets, liabilities, revenues, and expenses are likely measured with the most error? Is there any evidence suggesting management is manipulating the financial statements? You need to answer all of these questions before you attempt to forecast the firm's future financial statements and produce a valuation.

## 4.7 QUIZZES, CASES, LINKS AND REFERENCES

### Quizzes
• Chipotle Mexican Grill (Problem 2)
• Pandora (Problem 2)
• LinkedIn (Problem 2)
• Salesforce (Problem 2)

### Cases
• Analyzing Apple (Questions 4-7)

• Apple and the iFad (Questions 4-6)
• Boston Chicken, Inc.
• EnCom Corporation (Stages 1 and 2)
• Netflix, Inc. (Questions 3-5)
• Overstock.com (Questions 3-6)
• Pre-Paid Legal Services
• Sirius Satellite Radio (Questions 4-9)
• High Yields at Annaly Capital (Questions 3-4)
• Has Zynga Lost Its Zing? (Questions 3-7)
• Is Tesla's Stock Price in Ludicrous Mode? (Questions 3-6)

## Links

• U.S. Treasury Yield Curve: https://www.treasury.gov/resource-center/data-chart-center/interest-rates/Pages/Historic-Yield-Data-Visualization.aspx
• Salesforce.com 2016 Form 10-K on EDGAR: https://www.sec.gov/Archives/edgar/data/1108524/000110852417000006/crm-2017131x10k.htm

CHAPTER FIVE

# Financial Ratio Analysis

## 5.1 INTRODUCTION

Valuing an equity security requires you to interpret and forecast a huge quantity of financial data. Ratio analysis provides a framework for doing this in an organized and systematic manner. By converting the financial statement data into ratios, we are converting data into information. For instance, margin analysis reveals how much profit a firm makes from each dollar of revenue it generates and turnover analysis reveals the amount of assets needed to generate each dollar of revenue. It is extremely important that you learn to identify a firm's performance in terms of the financial ratios presented here. This is the language that analysts and management use to discuss a company's performance, and we will use this language to construct forecasts of the future. Ratio analysis is traditionally applied to historical data to evaluate past performance, but we will also use it to evaluate the plausibility of our forecasted future financial statements.

## 5.2 TIME-SERIES AND CROSS-SECTIONS

Ratio analysis involves comparing individual ratios with their levels in prior years and their levels in other firms. Comparing a firm's ratios with their levels in prior years is called *time-series analysis*. Time-series analysis identifies changes in financial performance and helps to detect the underlying cause. It also helps you to see whether the firm's most recent performance is unusual, in which case it may be less likely to recur in the future, or whether it is just one in a series of normal outcomes. If you have a flair for quantitative analysis, you might be tempted to estimate a complicated time-series model of a firm's past ratios in order to predict their future values. We don't recommend such an approach. As a general rule, financial ratios don't follow mechanical time-series models. Instead, it is more important that you evaluate changes in ratios in the context of changes in the underlying business operations and strategy of the firm.

Comparing a firm's ratios with the corresponding ratios in competitor firms is called *cross-sectional analysis*. This type of ratio analysis is also called *comparative analysis* (often shortened to *comps*). If management has done a consistently good job, then this will not be readily apparent in a time-series analysis. But it will be revealed by a cross-sectional ratio analysis with competitors. Does the company command a higher margin on its products? Is it the most efficient producer in its industry? Is it gaining market share from competitors? These are the types of questions that you can only answer by comparing a firm's financial ratios with competitor firms or the industry average. It isn't always easy, but you should try to triangulate a firm's ratios with its business strategy. If the firm is attempting to differentiate its product, it should enjoy higher margins than its competitors. If a firm is attempting to be a cost leader, it should have a higher asset turnover than its competitors. We'll discuss how different strategies influence particular ratios later in the chapter.

You conduct cross-sectional analysis by computing the same set of ratios for a comparable firm and then comparing ratios across the two firms. If you don't have any idea how to choose a comparable firm, you can get some help from the www.hoovers.com website. Find your company by entering its name in the box at the top right and then click on the company to load its profile, where its top competitors will be listed. Note that some of these competitors may be private companies, in which case it will be difficult to obtain financial data for a cross-sectional analysis. You can also use ratio analysis to gain insights into industry structure and bargaining power with customers and suppliers. For example, Priceline.com generates commissions by selling airline tickets. By studying margins in the airline industry, you can get a sense for the maximum commission rate that Priceline.com could plausibly charge the airlines.

## Ratios Tend to Mean-Revert

From a valuation perspective, the main reason we want to study the historical performance of a firm's financial ratios is to guide us in forecasting the future values of these ratios. To this end, you should remember a common theme in the evolution of financial ratios over time – they tend to mean-revert. This means that if they are unusually high they tend to fall and if they are unusually low they tend to rise. For example, firms that experience an extremely high or extremely low return on equity (net income over common equity) in a given year probably had something unusual happen – a windfall gain on the sale of an asset, a write-off of inventory, a surprisingly successful advertising campaign, or an embarrassing product recall, to list just a few possibilities. In these cases it is unlikely that the extreme return on equity will persist into the future, because the unusual event that happened once is unlikely to happen again. Later we will graph some common ratios to illustrate their rates of mean reversion.

We don't want to over-sell the power of mean-reversion. It is an observable tendency for many different ratios in a large sample of firms, but there are many exceptions. And, as we discuss below, how quickly and how completely a ratio mean reverts varies greatly by both ratio and firm.

## 5.3 SOME CAVEATS

Despite their usefulness, ratios are also frequently misunderstood and abused. So before launching into a discussion of specific ratios, we offer some important caveats regarding ratio analysis.

## There is no 'correct' way to compute many ratios

Many people assign the same name to ratios that are computed quite differently. Consider the Return on Assets (ROA) ratio. The numerator (income) is sometimes measured on a before-tax basis and sometimes measured on an after-tax basis. It is sometimes measured on a before interest basis and sometimes on an after interest basis. It may or may not include any non-recurring and/or non-operating items for the period. The denominator (assets) usually represents total assets, but it is sometimes measured as net operating assets (in which case the ratio is sometimes referred to as the Return on Net Operating Assets). The key point here is that there are no standards like 'GAAP' governing the computation of ratios. Basically, anything goes, and both management and sell-side analysts can be creative in coming up with ratios that put firms in the best possible light. Thus, when interpreting a ratio, you should first make sure you understand how it was computed.

## Ratios do not provide answers, they just tell you where to look for answers

It is common to hear rules of thumb that attach certain interpretations to ratios falling in certain ranges. For example, a firm with an Interest Coverage ratio less than 2 is often deemed to be financially distressed, or a firm with an ROA less than the yield on the 10-year US Treasury is deemed to be a candidate for liquidation. Unfortunately, financial analysis is not that simple. There are many reasons why ratios can have unusual values; from accounting distortions to subtle differences in firms' strategies. Ratio analysis guides you in your search for answers, but ratios themselves rarely provide the answers.

## Managers know that investors use ratios

Managers are well aware that investors rely on ratios to summarize their firm's financial performance. Hence, they can and do use their discretion over accounting, operating, investing and financing decisions to make their key ratios look more appealing. This practice is often referred to as 'window dressing'. A common example is the use of operating leases and other off-balance sheet financing techniques to reduce leverage ratios. It is therefore important to anticipate and undo the effects of any managerial window dressing of a firm's financial ratios.

# 5.4 A FRAMEWORK FOR RATIO ANALYSIS

We suggest that as you read through the section you conduct your own ratio analysis on a real company (see the cases at the end of the chapter for some suggestions). If you are using a spreadsheet program like *eVal* you will find it helpful to display Excel's formula bar so that you can see how the ratios in each cell have been computed. The formula bar can be displayed by selecting the Formula Bar menu item from the View menu in Excel.

Ratio analysis begins with the two pillars of firm value: *growth* and *profitability*. Growth measures changes in the scale of the business on which the firm is able to generate profitability. Profitability measures the return on investment generated by the business, which we already encountered in chapter 4. The key to value creation is to simultaneously achieve high growth and high profitability. Our ratio analysis starts with summary measures of each of these pillars. We then examine the underlying drivers of profitability to learn more about its sources and sustainability.

# 5.5 GROWTH

The analysis of growth is relatively straightforward. Growth rates are commonly reported for a variety of financial statement line items such as sales, assets, common equity, earnings and free cash flows. But *growth in sales* is the most commonly discussed growth statistic. Growth rates in assets, common equity, earnings and free cash flows are closely related to the sales growth rate. In fact, when sales growth and profitability reach 'steady state' (which we will define in detail later), the growth rates in all financial statement line items converge to the steady-state sales growth rate. However, during years when sales growth and profitability are fluctuating, the growth rates in the other line items will generally differ from the growth rate in sales. The intuition behind these differences is usually straightforward. For example, asset growth will differ from sales growth when there is a change in the level of assets that is required to generate a given level of sales.

The final growth rate that we will define is the *sustainable growth rate*. This ratio is computed as:

### Sustainable Growth Rate
$$= Return\ on\ Equity\ \times\ (1 - Dividend\ Payout\ Ratio).$$

Given its current level of profitability and dividend policy, the sustainable growth rate is the maximum rate that a firm can grow without resorting to additional external financing. If a firm's forecasted sales growth rate exceeds its sustainable growth rate, be sure you understand how the additional growth will be financed. One possibility is through increased future profitability. However, if the increased profitability is not achieved, then the growth plans may have to be curtailed. Alternatively, the additional growth may be financed externally through the issuance of debt and/or equity. This introduces uncertainty, because capital markets must be receptive to the firm's growth plans if they are going to provide financing. A final option is for the firm to cut its dividend payout ratio. However, given that the dividend payout ratio is usually zero for growth firms, this option is often not available.

Sales growth rates have very little memory; an unusually high growth rate this year rarely translates into a similarly high growth rate next year. To illustrate, Figure 5.1 takes all the firms in the US economy between 1962 and 2016, computes their percentage sales growth each year, sorts them into five portfolios from low growth to high growth (labeled as year 0 on the figure), and then plots the median sales growth for each portfolio over the next five years. The fact that all the lines snap back to the middle very quickly is something you should never forget. Consider the top line. Firms in the highest portfolio have median sales growth of 55% in year 0. But in the very next year the median growth for these high flyers falls to 22% and after five years, their growth rate is barely distinguishable from all the other firms. If all you know about a firm is that they had huge sales growth last year, don't be too impressed. Remind yourself that sales growth mean reverts very quickly.

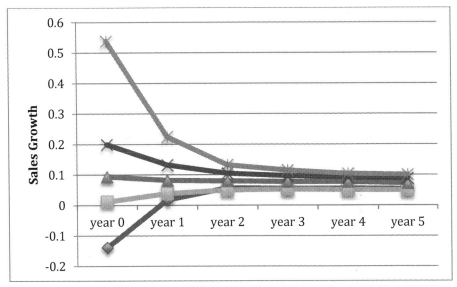

**Figure 5.1 Mean-Reversion in Sales Growth. US Firms from 1962 to 2016**

## 5.6 PROFITABILITY

While the analysis of growth is relatively straightforward, the analysis of profitability has endless nuance. The starting point for the analysis of profitability is our old friend from chapter 4, the return on investment. For the owners of the common equity of a business, this means the *return on equity*, computed as net income divided by common equity:[1]

$$Return\ on\ Equity\ (ROE) = \frac{Net\ Income}{Common\ Equity}.$$

ROE is the ultimate accounting measure of a firm's profitability and will be the focus of our financial analysis of the past and our forecasts of the future. We therefore devote most of the remainder of this chapter to the analysis of ROE.

Before proceeding, we need to discuss a nuance regarding timing conventions in computing the return on equity. The numerator represents the net income for the period over which we want to measure the profitability of the business, typically a year. The denominator represents the amount of common equity invested in the

---

[1] Note that we use net income in the numerator and not comprehensive income. While comprehensive income is the final bottom line, the convention is to use net income because, as a practical matter, the items included in comprehensive income are generally non-recurring fair value adjustments.

business. But at what point in time should we measure the amount of common equity? Back in chapter 4, we measured common equity at the beginning of the year. We motivated this choice using the example of a bank savings account. If we invested $100 in a bank account at the beginning of the year, left it there all year, and received interest income of $5 for the year, then our rate of return would be 5%. So this example suggests that we divide the earnings for the year by the amount of common equity at the beginning of the year. But what if we invested another $100 in the bank account on the <u>second</u> day of the year and received interest of $10 for the year? Since we had $200 invested in the bank account for essentially the whole year, our rate of return would be approximately $10/$200=5%. Alternatively, what if we had invested another $100 in the bank account on the very <u>last</u> day of the year and received interest of $5? Since we had only $100 invested in the bank account for essentially the whole year, our rate of return would be approximately $5/$100=5%.

The previous two examples should make it clear that we don't necessarily use the amount invested at the beginning of the year or at the end of the year. Instead, we want to use the time-weighted average investment outstanding during the year. If no new investment is made during the year, we just use the beginning balance. But if new investment is made during the year, we need to multiply the amount of the new investment by the fraction of the year it is outstanding and add that to the beginning investment. For example, if $100 is invested at the beginning of the year and another $100 is invested 9 months into the year, the time-weighed average capital invested during the year is $100+$100*(3/12)=$125, since the additional capital is outstanding for 3 months. In practice, it can be cumbersome to determine exactly when new capital is issued. Therefore, a common convention is to use the simple average of the beginning and ending investment balances:

$$\textbf{\textit{Return on Equity (ROE)}} = \frac{Net\ Income}{Average\ Common\ Equity}.$$

This convention is reasonable when the amount of new investment is a relatively small fraction of the beginning balance, and we will use this convention throughout the remainder of the text. You should remember, however, that this is a simple approximation, and if a large amount of new investment takes place during the year, it may be worth pinpointing the timing of the new investment and using the time-weighted average. This timing issue arises any time we compute a ratio that compares a flow variable (an amount generated over the course of the year – such as one on the income statement) with a stock variable (an amount existing at a point in time – such as one found on the balance sheet).

## Benchmarking the Return on Equity
ROE is one of the few ratios that can be compared to a well-defined benchmark. If you were considering investing in a fixed income investment, you would compare its interest rate to the interest rates offered by like investments. Similarly, to evaluate firm profitability, you can compare the firm's ROE with its competitors' ROEs. Other things equal, the higher a firm's ROE, the greater the return generated per

dollar of book equity invested in the firm. Moreover, to value a firm, you must estimate the firm's cost of equity capital. We will discuss the cost of capital in more detail in chapter 9, but loosely speaking, the cost of equity capital represents the expected return that an equity investment must generate to make it competitive with similar investment opportunities. So, accounting distortions aside, a firm with an ROE at least as high as its cost of equity capital is generating a competitive return for its equity holders. Thus, the cost of equity capital is a natural benchmark for a firm's ROE. Historically, the cost of equity capital has been estimated at about 10% for the average firm in the US economy, so this is a crude benchmark you can use to assess a firm's ROE. Unfortunately, there are two key drawbacks with such comparisons. First, as we will see in Chapter 9, it is difficult to estimate a firm's cost of equity capital with any certainty. Second, as we have mentioned before, the vagaries of GAAP accounting rarely result in measures of net income and common equity that correspond with their economic counterparts. So, to make these constructs more meaningful, we need to do more work.

## Mean Reversion in ROE

We stated earlier that many measures of financial performance tend to mean revert, and ROE is no exception. Figure 5.2 shows the mean reversion in return on equity for the entire sample of publicly traded firms between 1962 and 2016. Each year, we sort the firms into five groups from lowest to highest ROE and then we plot the median ROE for each of these groups over the next five years. As the plot shows, the highest groups move down over time and the lowest groups move up over time, consistent with the notion of mean reversion. And note that the lines are reverting toward the middle group with an ROE of about 10%, the historical long-term average ROE in the US economy.

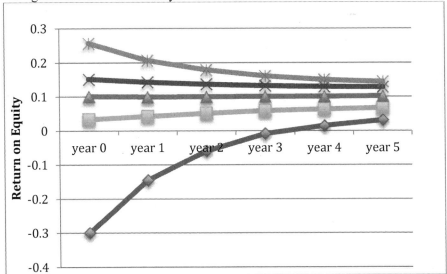

**Figure 5.2 Mean-Reversion in ROE. US Firms from 1962 to 2016**

There are a few other observations to take away from Figure 5.2. First, the drastic improvement in the lowest ROE group in year 1 is a bit misleading. If the firm goes bankrupt, it drops out of the sample, leaving only those firms who improved their performance enough to stay alive five more years and hence remain on the graph. Even with this selection bias, it takes this bottom group three years to get back to zero ROE. So they mean-revert, but slowly. Second, while the top two ROE groups decline and the bottom two groups improve, at no time do the lines completely converge. Even after five years the highest group has an ROE of about 15% and the lowest group has an ROE of about 2%. While mean reversion over 5 years has definitely brought the two groups closer together, it has not eliminated the disparity in ROE.

Why does ROE tend to mean-revert? The short answer is competition. If a firm enjoys a high return on equity, this catches the attention of other firms. Existing rivals undercut the firm's prices and new firms enter the market. As the firm responds to these competitive threats with a price cut of its own, its profitability suffers, driving down the ROE. Why is the mean-reversion in ROE less than complete? For reasons we discussed in Chapter 3, many firms enjoy imperfect competition and are therefore partially shielded from competitive forces. In addition, accounting distortions can generate long-term disparity in ROE across firms. Firms in the pharmaceutical industry report among the economy's highest ROEs, but this is partly due to the fact that their most prominent economic asset – their past R&D expenditures – are expensed immediately. Because an asset is not recorded, assets and common equity are understated, causing ROE to be overstated.

It is reasonable to expect some components of income to be more persistent than others. For this reason we also compute *return on equity before non-recurring items*. The idea is to exclude from the numerator items that are likely to completely disappear in subsequent years, thus providing a better indication of a firm's long-run sustainable ROE. We expect that ROE before non-recurring items will mean-revert more slowly than regular ROE. Non-recurring items are most commonly found in the extraordinary items and discontinued operations (Ext. Items & Disc. Ops.), other income and non-operating income line items on the income statement. You can exclude these line items from the definition of net income used to compute ROE before non-recurring items. Non-operating income is a pre-tax item on the income statement, so it must be tax-adjusted before adding it back to net income. The resulting measure is as follows:

**Return on Equity Before NonRecurring Items**
$$= \frac{\text{Net Income} - \text{After Tax NonRecurring Items}}{\text{Average Common Equity}},$$

where

After-Tax Non-Recurring Items = Ext. Items & Disc. Ops. + Other Income (Loss) + (1-effective tax rate)*(Non-Operating Income (Loss)), and
effective tax rate = Income Taxes/Pre-Tax Income.

You should remember that while canned ratio analyses using standardized data may produce a ratio called 'ROE Before Non-Recurring Items', it is only a first approximation and you should engage in more detailed analysis in order to classify items as recurring or non-recurring. For example, the 'Other Income' line item sometimes includes earnings from equity affiliates, which may well be recurring. Also, non-recurring items may be buried in other line items on the income statement, such as the effects of an inventory write-down, which will usually be hidden in the cost of goods sold (but can be recovered from the financial statement footnotes).

## Decomposing ROE – the Basic DuPont Model

It is very useful to decompose ROE into a few fundamental drivers of profitability. The Basic DuPont Model, pioneered by management at a predecessor of the DuPont Chemical Company, factors ROE into three components, as shown below.

$$\frac{Net\ Income}{Common\ Equity} = \frac{Net\ Income}{Sales} \times \frac{Sales}{Total\ Assets} \times \frac{Total\ Assets}{Common\ Equity}, or$$

$$ROE = Net\ Profit\ Margin \times Total\ Asset\ Turnover \times Total\ Leverage.$$

The basic DuPont model does a good job at highlighting the three key drivers of the accounting rate of return on equity. First, the *Net Profit Margin* measures the amount of net income generated per dollar of sales. Second, the *Asset Turnover Ratio* measures the amount of sales generated per dollar of assets. Third, the *Total Leverage Ratio* measures the amount of assets that are supported by a dollar of common equity. The product of the three gives the net income generated per dollar of common equity, which is just ROE.

The DuPont breakdown provides a variety of insights. First, if a firm can't earn a positive net profit margin, then it will generate a negative return regardless of how efficiently it utilizes its assets or how much leverage it applies. The first order of business at any hotdog stand is to sell the hotdogs for more than the cost of the meat and buns. The net profit margin extends this intuition all the way to the bottom line of the income statement – how much of each sales dollar remains after all expenses are deducted. Second, assuming the firm is making a net profit, the trick is to do so with the minimum investment in assets. If selling hotdogs requires an elaborate kiosk, or a fleet of home-delivery trucks, then the profit made might not be sufficient to justify the investment. Fortunately for the hotdog business, most stands run a large volume past a relatively inexpensive investment in assets; hence, the asset turnover is high.

Figure 5.2 illustrated the mean reversion in ROE. Figure 5.3 plots the evolution of the three components of ROE. As the panel A shows, most of the mean reversion in ROE is due to mean reversion in the profit margin, which makes sense if price competition is the driving force behind the mean reversion. In contrast, the total asset turnover ratio and the total leverage ratios are remarkably stable, as seen in the second and third panels of the figure. These ratios are largely determined by the structure of the industry. It takes lots of equipment and a long time to construct buildings, for example, and so the construction industry necessarily has a slow asset turnover ratio. And, as we illustrate later in the chapter, financial institutions necessarily have lots of leverage. In fact, financial institutions dominate the top group of total leverage, which stands out from the rest, with a median value of about eight.

**Panel A**

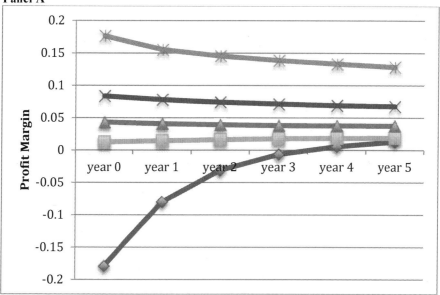

**Panel B**

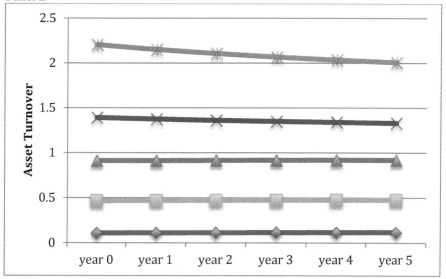

**FIGURE 5.3: Mean Reversion in Net Profit Margin, Total Asset Turnover and Total Leverage, US Firms from 1962 to 2016**

**Panel C**

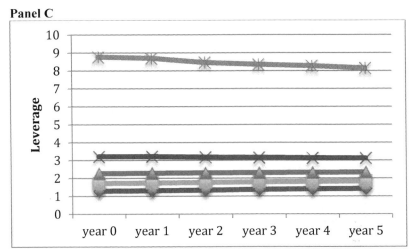

**Figure 5.3 Continued**

The first two components of the Basic DuPont model capture the operations of the business. How does the firm use its assets to make sales, and how profitably can it convert the sales into net income? These two components tend to trade off against one another; if you multiply them together, you get Net Income/Average Total Assets, labeled the *return on assets*. We can characterize different firms and industries by the different trade-offs that are required between margin and turnover. Capital-intensive industries, such as construction and heavy equipment manufacturing, have low turnovers and must therefore charge higher margins to get a competitive return on assets. On the other end of the spectrum, high turnover discount retailers and fast food chains generally have razor thin profit margins and generate a decent return through high asset turnover. Within industries, we can also characterize firms based on the different margin and turnover trade-offs that they make. Firms that choose a cost leadership strategy, producing at the lowest possible cost and selling in large quantities, tend to have low margins and high turnover. On the other hand, firms that choose a product differentiation strategy, producing a premium product and selling in smaller quantities, tend to have higher margins and lower turnover.

As an example, contrast the net profit margin and total asset turnover of Nordstrom, a luxury retailer, and Ross Stores, a close-out discount retailer, back in fiscal 2006 (well before the 2008 recession completely altered the retail landscape), as shown in Figure 5.4. For fiscal 2006, Nordstrom had a return on assets of about 13.8% and Ross Stores had a return on assets of about 11.1% - not exactly the same but reasonably close. How the two firms got to this similar return on assets was completely different. Nordstrom, the luxury retailer, had a net profit margin of 7.7% and an asset turnover of 1.8 while Ross Stores, the discount retailer, had a profit margin of 4.3% and an asset turnover of 2.6. These numbers reveal the very different strategies the two firms have. Nordstrom makes a significantly larger investment in assets – deeper inventory and fancier stores – and charges a premium for this. While

Ross Stores keeps significantly less net income per dollar of sales, they make up for it by economizing on the stores and inventory; consequently, they generate significantly more sales per dollar of asset invested. While both firms would like to have a high margin *and* a high turnover, in practice this is very hard to achieve. If Ross Stores were to raise its prices in order to improve its margin, its sales volume would probably suffer, driving down its asset turnover. And if Nordstrom were to carry lower quantities of less expensive inventory in an effort in improve its asset turnover, its customers would probably be unwilling to pay its higher margins. The very nature of each firm's strategy dictates where they will be on the margin versus turnover trade-off.

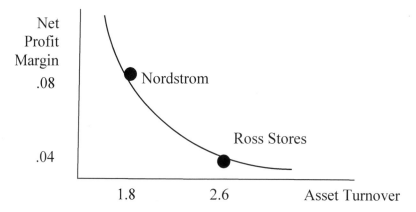

**FIGURE 5.4: Trade-Off Between Margin and Turnover for Nordstrom and Ross Stores in fiscal 2006.**

The trade-off between margins and turnover plays out in a number of different business decisions. Putting inventory on sale lowers the profit margin but improves the asset turnover (assuming, of course, that the sale causes a buying frenzy among customers). Outsourcing production improves turnover, but lowers margins. Aging vinegar longer improves the quality and allows the vinegar-maker to charge a greater margin, but necessarily lowers the asset turnover.

The first two terms in the Basic DuPont Model determine the firm's return on total assets. The return on equity can be made larger than the return on assets by leveraging the assets. This effect is captured by the third factor in the Basic DuPont Model, Total Leverage. Imagine a firm whose assets are financed by a small amount of equity and a large amount of liabilities. The small equity base claims the entire return on assets and will therefore enjoy a very high return on equity.

Management has lots of control over the firm's leverage, so why don't all firms increase their ROE simply by borrowing more money? Ignoring for a moment the added risk that additional leverage brings, the more basic answer is that the additional debt comes with additional interest expense, and interest expense lowers net income and therefore lowers the Net Profit Margin. Thus, as Total Leverage increases, the Net Profit Margin decreases. Which effect dominates depends on whether the interest rate on the borrowed money is less than the pre-interest return that the firm earns with the borrowed money. This last effect is a weakness of the Basic DuPont Model; it doesn't cleanly separate operating decisions from financing decisions. For this, we must turn to the Advanced DuPont Model.

## Decomposing ROE – The Advanced DuPont Model

The Advanced DuPont Model isolates operating performance more cleanly than the basic DuPont Model by introducing a new measure of profitability: the *return on net operating assets* (RNOA). This core measure of operating performance is then adjusted for the effect of Leverage to arrive at the ROE. While this decomposition more cleanly separates operating and financing effects, it is also more complicated. Before we can present detailed definitions and computations, we need to associate each line item on the income statement and balance sheet with either operating or financing activities. What is operating and what is financing? The answer will not always be clear but as a guiding principle, financing activities relate to sources of capital, and typically come with some type of financing cost (e.g., interest expense), while operating activities relate to the provision of goods and services to customers.

The income statement items are divided into Net Operating Income (NOI) and Net Financing Expense (NFE). Both amounts are net of tax, so that Net Income = NOI – NFE. The tax rate used is not arbitrary; it is the effective tax rate for the period, defined as Income Taxes/EBT (where EBT denotes earnings before taxes). The balance sheet assets and liabilities are divided into Net Operating Assets (NOA) and Net Financial Obligations (NFO), so that Common Equity = NOA – NFO. There will be some ambiguous items, but the general goal is to isolate the effects of operating activities from financing activities. The most important thing is to be consistent across classifications on the income statement and balance sheet. It would be wrong, for instance, to classify the interest on capital leases as part of Net Financing Expense but then classify the capital lease obligation as part of Net Operating Assets. Figure 5.5 illustrates how we have made these classifications using the standardized financial statement data items in our spreadsheet program, *eVal*. Remember, spreadsheet programs like *eVal* can't read and interpret the detailed financial statements, so some of the classifications are crude. You need to read the actual financial statements and adjust the data inputs accordingly.

Having allocated the line items in the income statement and balance sheet into operating and financing components, we can now conduct our ratio analysis on each activity separately, and then examine how they come together to determine ROE. The two key ratios are shown at the bottom of Figure 5.5. They are

**Income Statement**
Sales (Net)
- Cost of Goods Sold
= Gross Profit
- R&D Expense
- SG&A Expense
= EBITDA
- Depreciation & Amortization
= EBIT
- Interest Expense
+ Non-Operating Income (Loss)
= EBT
- Income Taxes
+ Other Income (Loss)
= Net Income Before Ext. Items
- Ext. Items & Disc. Ops.
- Minority Interest in Earnings
- Preferred Dividends
= Net Income (available to common)

**Net Operating Income (NOI) =**
   (EBIT + Non-Operating Income)*(1-tax)
   + Other Income (Loss)
   - Ext. Items and Disc. Ops.

**Net Financing Expense (NFE) =**
   Interest Expense*(1-tax)
   + Minority Interest in Earnings
   + Preferred Dividends
where the effective tax rate (tax)
   = Income Taxes/EBT.

**Balance Sheet**
Operating Cash and Market. Sec.
+ Receivables
+ Inventories
+ Other Current Assets
= Total Current Assets
+ PP&E (Net)
+ Investments
+ Intangibles
+ Other Assets
= Total Assets

Current Debt
+ Accounts Payable
+ Income Taxes Payable
+ Other Current Liabilities
= Total Current Liabilities
+ Long-Term Debt
+ Other Liabilities
+ Deferred Taxes
= Total Liabilities
+ Minority Interest
+ Preferred Stock
+ Paid in Common Capital (Net)
+ Retained Earnings
= Total Common Equity

**Net Operating Assets (NOA) =**
   Total Assets
   - Accounts Payable
   - Income Taxes Payable
   - Other Current Liabilities
   - Other Liabilities
   - Deferred Taxes

**Net Financial Obligations (NFO) =**
   Current Debt
   + Long-Term Debt
   + Minority Interest
   + Preferred Stock

**Return on Net Operating Assets**
$$(\textbf{RNOA}) = \frac{\text{NOI}}{\text{NOA}}$$

$$\textbf{Net Borrowing Cost (NBC)} = \frac{\text{NFE}}{\text{NFO}}$$

**FIGURE 5.5: How *eVal* decomposes the Financial Statements into Operating and Financing Components**

**Return on Net Operating Assets (RNOA)** $= \dfrac{Net\ Operating\ Income\ (NOI)}{Net\ Operating\ Assets\ (NOA)}$

and

**Net Borrowing Cost (NBC)** $= \dfrac{Net\ Financing\ Expense\ (NFE)}{Net\ Financial\ Obligation\ (NFO)},$

where

Net Financing Expense (NFE) = Interest Expense*(1-tax) + Preferred Dividends + Minority Interest in Earnings,
Net Operating Income (NOI) = Net Income + Net Financing Expense,
Net Financial Obligations (NFO) = Current Debt + Long-Term Debt + Minority Interest + Preferred Stock,
Net Operating Assets (NOA) = Common Equity + Net Financial Obligation, and
Effective Tax Rate (tax) = Income Taxes/Earnings Before Taxes.

Each ratio associates the income statement flows with the balance sheet items that caused them. Consider the RNOA. In the numerator, NOI represents the after-tax income earned by the operating assets; equivalently, it is net income with the after-tax financing charges added back. In the denominator, NOA represents the operating assets used to generate the NOI. Equivalently, it is common equity with the net financial obligations added back. Common equity and net financial obligations represent the sources of capital that are used to finance the net operating assets. The result is a measure of the firm's operating performance that abstracts from the manner in which these operations are financed. For instance, RNOA is not affected by the firm's level of debt, the interest rate it borrows at, or the tax shield that the interest creates. All these effects are isolated in the net borrowing cost (NBC), which associates the after-tax income statement flows that go to debt, minority interests, and preferred stock providers with the amount of capital they provided.

The absolute interpretation of the RNOA as a profitability measure is similar to the interpretation of ROE. The key difference is that the long-term 'hurdle rate' for RNOA is the after-tax weighted average cost of capital – a blend of the cost of equity capital and debt capital that we will discuss in Chapter 9.

We offer a final word of warning about RNOA. In practice, there are many different definitions and terminologies used for RNOA. For example, it is not uncommon to use total assets in the denominator, in which case the measure is usually referred to simply as return on assets (ROA). Another common variant measures the numerator before taxes, in which case the measure is usually referred to as the pre-tax RNOA. Finally, the term return on invested capital (ROIC) is frequently used in place of the term RNOA. Recall that net operating assets are equal to invested capital (the sum of debt, minority interests, preferred stock and common stock). So the terms net operating assets and invested capital are often used interchangeably. The bottom line is that when you see a return on "something" you should make sure that you understand how it is computed before attempting to interpret it.

Putting all the pieces together, the Advanced DuPont Model decomposes ROE as shown below.

$$
\begin{aligned}
\text{ROE} &= \text{RNOA} & + & \quad \text{Leverage} & * & \quad \text{Spread} \\
&= \text{NOI/NOA} & + & \quad (\text{NFO/Common Equity}) * & & \quad (\text{RNOA} - \text{NBC}) \\
&= \text{NOI/NOA} & + & \quad (\text{NFO/Common Equity}) * (\text{NOI/NOA} - \text{NFE/NFO}).
\end{aligned}
$$

Note that Leverage in this decomposition differs from the Total Leverage definition in the Basic DuPont Model. This measure of leverage only includes financial obligations in the numerator, whereas the Basic DuPont Model uses total assets. The Advanced DuPont Model describes ROE as RNOA plus an adjustment for the amount of Leverage the firm employs times the 'Spread' between RNOA and NBC. To interpret this relation, first recall that RNOA measures a firm's operating performance. ROE, on the other hand, measures the return to the common equity holders after satisfying the claims of all the other capital providers that are funding the firm's operations. The common equity holders are the residual claimants on any operating earnings that remain after satisfying these other capital providers. Thus, if a firm's RNOA exceeds its net borrowing costs (NBC), then the ROE will exceed the RNOA, because the common equity holders get more than a proportionate share in the net operating income. The extent to which ROE exceeds RNOA depends on the 'Spread' between RNOA and the NBC, and the amount of Leverage the firm applies.

You may remember that we previously introduced the relation between ROE and ROI in chapter 4. The Advanced DuPont model basically tells us how to compute the RNOA, which is just the ROI for the operations of a business. As simple illustration, consider a bank that borrows funds at one rate and lends at another (hopefully higher) rate. The bank's RNOA is given by its lending rate adjusted for the other costs of operating the bank (i.e., the rate it earns on its operating assets, which consist of its loan portfolio). The ROE generated for the bank's owners depends on its borrowing rate relative to its adjusted lending rate (i.e. its spread) and the proportion of its lending that is funded by debt. For example, if a bank generates an RNOA of 6%, uses nine dollars of debt for each dollar of equity and pays 5% interest on the debt, then the bank's ROE is given by

$$\text{ROE} = 6\% + (9/1) \times (6\% - 5\%) = 15\%.$$

In this case the Leverage is 9 and the Spread is 1%, adding 9% to the RNOA of 6% to yield an ROE of 15%. Note that leverage does not always increase ROE relative to RNOA. If a firm has a negative spread, then additional leverage reduces ROE relative to RNOA. For example, assume that the bank in our example only generates an RNOA of 4%. In this case we have:

$$\text{ROE} = 4\% + (9/1) \times (4\% - 5\%) = -5\%.$$

Thus, higher leverage increases ROE when RNOA is greater than the cost of non-equity financing and reduces ROE when RNOA is less than the cost of non-equity financing. In other words, additional leverage makes the good times better and the bad times worse. This is just another way of saying that additional leverage increases the risk of the returns to common equity holders.

The next stage of the Advanced DuPont Model is to decompose RNOA into net operating margin and the net operating asset turnover, much like we did in the Basic DuPont model, as shown below.

NOI/NOA        = NOI/Sales              *  Sales/NOA, or
RNOA           = Net Operating Margin   *  Net Operating Asset Turnover.

Thus, RNOA is increasing in both the margin that a firm generates on its sales and the amount of sales that can be generated per unit of assets, just as in the Basic DuPont Model. The difference between the two models is that the margin and turnover measures are based on 'cleaner' measures of operating activities in the advanced model, and this has some important consequences. First, the net operating margin isn't polluted by interest expense, minority interest in earnings, or preferred dividends, as it was in the Basic DuPont Model. Second, the treatment of operating liabilities is very different between the two models. Imagine using operating cash to pay off an extra dollar of accounts payable on the last day of the year. Clearly this has no effect on the ROE. And no terms in the Advanced DuPont Model would change because the definition of NOA nets the operating liabilities against the operating assets. However, in the Basic DuPont Model, the Asset Turnover Ratio would increase because there is a dollar less of total assets (the dollar of cash is gone) and the Total Leverage would decrease because there is a dollar less total liabilities (because the dollar of accounts payable is gone). Again, because the Basic DuPont Model doesn't make a clean distinction between operating and financing, seemingly minor transactions can influence the ratios. The Advanced DuPont model is relatively immune to these distortions.

## Financial Assets in the Advanced DuPont Model

By default, most spreadsheet programs (including our spreadsheet program, *eVal*) classify all cash and marketable securities as part of net operating assets. Yet in many cases, these are really financial assets that are not directly tied to the operations. The firm needs to maintain some balance of cash to fund its ongoing operating activities, but this is rarely more than a few percent of sales. To pick an extreme example, at the end of September 2016 Apple had over $67 billion in cash and marketable securities. This is more than 20% of their total assets, and 2.5 times more than their balance of property and equipment. Apple doesn't need to maintain this much cash for normal operations; rather, much of this cash is "trapped" overseas; if Apple were to send it back to the USA they would have to pay tax on it. How should we deal with these financial assets in our Advanced DuPont Model? Ideally, we would net them against the Net Financial Obligations and we would net the investment income they produce against Net Financing Expense. They aren't really part of operations, so we should reclassify them into financing. *eVal* doesn't do this for a few reasons. First, we would be hard-pressed to specify for all firms at all times what the right amount of operating cash is, making it almost impossible to isolate the true financial assets. Second, without examining the 'as reported' financial statements and footnotes, it is impossible to know where the investment income has been included on the income statement, and hence impossible to know the income statement line item where the data standardization process has allocated this income. It could be netted against Interest Expense and therefore included in that line item, it could be included in Non-Operating Income (Loss), or it could be netted against SG&A Expense. As we discussed in chapter 2, you need to look at the 'as reported' financial statements and make sure your standardized income statement and balance sheet are in good order. Part of that exercise is making sure that the line item "Interest Expense" is only the interest outflow on the Current and Long Term Debt; any interest income should ideally be included in "Non-Operating Income (Loss). An early indicator that your financial statements might have a problem in this regard is an extremely low (or even negative) Net Borrowing Cost.

## The Advanced DuPont Model in Three Retail Stores

Let's apply the Advanced DuPont Model to three large department store chains; Kohl's (KSS), Ross Stores (ROST), and Nordstrom (JWN). Kohl's targets middle-income families with moderately priced apparel, Nordstrom provides a more upscale retail experience, and Ross Stores is a discount closeout retailer. If you want to investigate the computation of these ratios in more detail, the standardized financial statements for each are available on the Case Data sheet in *eVal*.

Figure 5.6 gives the Advanced DuPont Model for the three companies in fiscal 2009. Notice the close similarity in net operating margins and yet the enormous differences in ROE. Kohl's reports 13.6%, a respectable amount in absolute terms, but it pales in comparison to Nordstrom's healthy 31.7% and Ross Store's very impressive 41.1%! Nordstrom's RNOA is only a bit larger than Kohl's, but with a leverage ratio of almost 2 and a spread of almost 10%, they get a huge boost from their leverage. Ross Stores, with almost no financial leverage, gets to their impressive ROE a completely different way. They earn a net operating margin as large as Kohl's and Nordstrom, yet they have a net operating asset turnover that is about three times larger than the other two companies, resulting in a RNOA of 36.6%. Ross Stores' high margins are surprising. Following a discount retail strategy, it is supposed to have lower margins and make up for it with higher net operating asset turnover. And Nordstrom, following a luxury retail strategy, is supposed to have higher margins but pay for it with a slower asset turnover. And yet Kohl's, Nordstrom and Ross Stores have almost identical operating margins. Consequently, Ross Stores cleans up in 2009 by enjoying a high margin *and* a high asset turnover. We will explore the margins and turnover ratios of these three companies in more detail in the next section.

| | Kohls | Nordstrom | Ross |
|---|---|---|---|
| **Advanced Dupont Model** | fiscal 2009 | fiscal 2009 | fiscal 2009 |
| Net Operating Margin | 0.063 | 0.062 | 0.062 |
| x Net Operating Asset Turnover | 1.834 | 2.182 | 5.856 |
| = Return on Net Operating Assets | 0.115 | 0.135 | 0.366 |
| Net Borrowing Cost (NBC) | 0.040 | 0.037 | 0.039 |
| Spread (RNOA - NBC) | 0.074 | 0.099 | 0.327 |
| Financial Leverage (LEV) | 0.284 | 1.843 | 0.139 |
| ROE = RNOA + LEV*Spread | 0.136 | 0.317 | 0.411 |
| | Kohls | Nordstrom | Ross |
| **Margin Analysis** | fiscal 2009 | fiscal 2009 | fiscal 2009 |
| Gross Margin | 0.378 | 0.419 | 0.258 |
| EBITDA Margin | 0.100 | 0.133 | 0.101 |
| EBIT Margin | 0.100 | 0.097 | 0.101 |
| Net Operating Margin (b4 non-rec. | 0.062 | 0.061 | 0.062 |
| Net Operating Margin | 0.063 | 0.062 | 0.062 |
| | | | |
| **Turnover Analysis** | | | |
| Net Operating Asset Turnover | 1.834 | 2.182 | 5.856 |
| Net Working Capital Turnover | 6.853 | 4.002 | 15.731 |
| Avge Days to Collect Receivables | 0.000 | 84.132 | 5.062 |
| Avge Inventory Holding Period | 97.778 | 65.431 | 60.073 |
| Avge Days to Pay Payables | 34.949 | 46.926 | 41.005 |
| PP&E Turnover | 2.454 | 3.866 | 7.584 |

**FIGURE 5.6: Advanced DuPont Model for Kohl's, Nordstrom and Ross Stores in fiscal 2009.**

## 5.7 PROFIT MARGINS

The net operating margin used in the Advanced DuPont Model represents after-tax operating income divided by sales. In order to understand the drivers of net operating margin, we must look at each of the components of after-tax operating income as a proportion of sales. If the bottom line net operating margin is unusual, then work your way down this list of intermediate margins to identify the underlying line items that are driving this behavior.

The starting point is the *Gross Margin*, which measures the difference between sales and cost of goods sold as a proportion of sales:

$$Gross\ Margin = \frac{Gross\ Profit}{Sales} = \frac{(Sales - Cost\ of\ Goods\ Sold)}{Sales}.$$

This is the first level of profitability -- the mark-up on the product. For each dollar of sales, how much more can the firm charge over the cost of making or buying the product. It is generally all down hill from here, so if a firm can't generate a decent gross margin, there is not much point in looking any further. This is also the ratio to watch if you are worried about increased competition. If the firm is lowering its prices to retain market share, you will see it here.

The next key margin we report is the *EBITDA margin*, which gives 'earnings before interest, taxes depreciation and amortization' as a proportion of Sales. Another way to define the numerator is Sales less Cost of Goods Sold, R&D Expense, and SG&A Expense. The ratio is shown below:

$$EBITDA\ Margin = \frac{EBITDA}{Sales}.$$

The firm may enjoy a large mark-up on its product, but it could be that the key costs aren't due to the actual production of the goods. For instance, the drug company Pfizer (ticker = PFE) has a gross margin of approximately 80% for the past few years. But the real costs at a pharmaceutical company are R&D and SG&A; the actual manufacturing of the drug is a relatively minor cost. Consequently, Pfizer's EBITDA margin is about 25%. If you discover that the EBITDA margin is unusual, then you should go back to the detailed income statement to identify the specific line items that are responsible. Note that this ratio excludes depreciation and amortization, so it can be quite high for capital-intensive firms. Analysts often tout the EBITDA ratio, reasoning that depreciation and amortization represent non-cash charges and are therefore irrelevant. But don't be tricked into relying too heavily on this ratio (as many Telecom investors did in the late 1990s). While depreciation and amortization are accounting adjustments, they nevertheless represent the allocation of real past capital expenditures. A capital-intensive firm may look great on an EBITDA basis, but sooner or later, it will have to reinvest real cash in its capital base in order to stay in business.

The *EBIT margin* is the EBITDA margin with the 'DA' taken out. As such, it provides a useful summary measure of operating performance. The numerator is sales less all operating expenses except interest and taxes; hence the name 'Earnings Before Interest and Taxes':

$$EBIT\ Margin = \frac{EBIT}{Sales}.$$

The after-tax operating margin can fluctuate due to changes in leverage or tax rates. The EBIT margin abstracts from these effects, providing a clean measure of underlying operating performance

As we move down the page from Gross margin to EBIT margin, the relation between sales and profits gets weaker. As sales increase, cost of goods sold will necessarily have to increase – the firm needs to pay for the goods that it is selling – so the gross margin is relatively stable over time. But an increase in sales does not necessarily mean that R&D expense will increase, as this is a much more discretionary expenditure. Similarly, administrative expenses bear no direct relation to sales. In the long run a firm needs these expenses to generate its sales, but in a given year there is no reason why they should vary in proportion to sales.

The final margin that we report is the *Net Operating Margin Before Non-Recurring Items*. This margin starts with net operating income but then adds back any non-recurring expenses, adjusted for their tax consequences (specifically, it adds back tax-adjusted Non-Operating Income, Other Income, and Extraordinary Items and Discontinued Operations). Unusual behavior in this margin that does not show up in the EBIT margin is attributable to taxes or costs of non-equity capital (specifically, tax-adjusted Interest Expense, Minority Interest in Earnings and Preferred Dividends).

$$Net\ Operating\ Margin\ before\ Non - Recurring\ Items$$
$$= \frac{Net\ Operating\ Income + AfterTax\ NonRecurring\ Items}{Sales}.$$

Finally, any unusual behavior in the bottom line net operating margin that does not show up in the above margin should be due to non-recurring items. You should identify the nature of these items from the as-reported financial statements and ascertain that they are indeed unlikely to recur.

## Economies of Scale and Operating Risk

Many young and growing firms have negative net operating margins. They all claim that this is a temporary situation and that once they grow past some critical size, they will be hugely profitable. Of course, many of them never achieve this dream and fail, but the ones that succeed do so because they experience economies of scale. A typical situation might be a firm with a positive gross margin but a negative EBITDA margin, due mainly to its SG&A expense. If the SG&A expense is composed of mostly fixed costs, then as sales grow, the SG&A expense does not increase proportionately, and eventually the EBITDA margin becomes positive. Moreover, expenditures on R&D and marketing have to be expensed immediately, but usually benefit future sales. Be on the lookout for such effects as you study a company's margins. If sales are growing and the margins are steadily improving, this is a sign that the firm is exploiting economies of scale. Alternatively, if a firm claims that it will not be profitable until it grows to some larger size, but its past sales growth has not generated any significant improvement in its margins, then you should be suspicious. The company's claims of great margins in the future may be nothing more than wishful thinking.

While a cost structure with a large fixed cost component helps achieve economies of scale, it also imposes *operating risk* (also referred to as *operating leverage*) on the company. If the sales volume is highly variable then in periods of low volume the firm will be stuck with its fixed costs and insufficient revenue to cover them; in periods of high volume it will easily cover its fixed costs and enjoy huge margins. In other words, the good times are really good and the bad times are really bad. As an example, consider a firm's decision to buy equipment or enter short-term rental contacts for the same equipment. Short-term rentals can be varied with sales, resulting in lower operating risk. For this reason managers often attempt to lower their operating risk by outsourcing many aspects of production. Frequently, however, they find that there is little profit left over when they do this. No risk often means no return. For example, most oil exploration companies rent exploration equipment from dedicated oil services companies. This lowers their operating risk. But when the price of oil is high, the oil services firms jack up their rental rates, cutting into the potential profits of the oil exploration companies.

Earlier we compared Kohl's, Nordstrom and Ross Stores to illustrate the trade-off between margins and turnovers in the DuPont model. The middle of Figure 5.6 we show the detailed margin analysis. First, the basic value-luxury pricing structure remains the same: the gross margin is 41.9% at Nordstrom, compared to 37.8% at Kohl's and 25.8% at Ross Stores. But, as we noted earlier, in fiscal 2009 the net operating margin at the three companies is almost identical at around 0.063. What happened between the gross margin and the net operating margin for these three companies? Why is Ross Stores "too high" and why is Nordstrom "too low?" If we compare the EBITDA margins, we get the answer. The only relevant expense between the gross margin and the EBITDA margin for these companies is SG&A. Ross keeps this expense at 15.7% of sales, while Nordstrom reports 28.6%. Besides turning over their assets much faster than Kohl's and Nordstrom, Ross Stores spends much less on advertising and general administration. Further, through the recessionary period of 2006 and 2009, as consumers shifted toward value and away from luxury, Ross Stores steadily increased their sales while sales at Nordstrom fell precipitously. This caused the fixed component of SG&A to be spread over a larger base of sales at Ross Stores but a smaller base of sales at Nordstrom, with the net result of a better EBITDA margin at Ross Stores and worse EBITDA ratio at Nordstrom.

# 5.8 TURNOVER RATIOS

We now turn our attention to ratios measuring the amount of assets that the firm requires to generate its sales, known as turnover ratios. These ratios are also referred to as efficiency ratios, because they tell us how efficiently management is employing the firm's assets. A net operating asset turnover ratio of 2 indicates that $.50 of net operating assets are required to generate $1.00 of sales. We use turnover analysis to examine how the underlying operating asset and liability line items on the balance sheet contribute to the overall net operating asset turnover ratio. The basic approach is to compute a turnover ratio for specific groups of operating assets and operating liabilities. A common turnover ratio is the *Net Working Capital Turnover Ratio*, computed as

**Net Working Capital Turnover Ratio**

$$= \frac{Sales}{Current\ Operating\ Assets - Current\ Operating\ Liabilities}$$

Typically, all the current assets are classified as operating and all the current liabilities except current debt are classified as operating. The net working capital turnover ratio measures how efficiently a firm is managing its working capital accounts. Ideally, a firm would like to generate sales with a minimum investment in working capital. Obviously this presents the firm with trade-offs. It is difficult to minimize the investment in inventory while still presenting the customers with a wide variety of choices and fast delivery. And all firms would like to collect on their sales immediately and pay their accounts payable very slowly, but customers often prefer to delay payments and suppliers often give incentives to pay early.

It is common to compute individual turnover ratios for the three most important components of working capital – receivables, inventories and payables – and there are a number of common modifications that are made in the computation of these ratios. First, they are often stated in the form of the average number of days that a dollar sits in the account. The relation between an annual turnover ratio and the average days outstanding metric is simply:

$$Average\ Days\ Outstanding\ = \frac{365}{Annual\ Turnover\ Ratio}.$$

For example, if we turn over our receivables 12 times per year, then the average receivable must have a life of approximately 365/12 = 30 days. Using this approach, the average days to collect receivables is given by:

$$Average\ Days\ to\ Collect\ Receivables\ = \frac{365}{(Sales/Average\ Receivables)}.$$

Similarly, the average inventory holding period is given by:

$$Average\ Days\ to\ Sell\ Inventory = \frac{365}{Cost\ of\ Goods\ Sold/Average\ Inventory}.$$

Note that we made an additional modification in computing the average inventory holding period; we replaced sales with cost of goods sold. This is because inventories are carried at cost, and so we want a flow variable that measures the cost of inventories consumed during the period. Lastly, the average days to pay payables is computed as:

$$Average\ Days\ to\ Pay\ Payables = \frac{365}{Purchases/Average\ Accounts\ Payable},$$

where

Purchases = Cost of Goods Sold + Ending Inventory – Beginning Inventory.

Note here that the denominator is measured using purchases. This represents the dollars of payables that were added during the period, and so is directly comparable with the average balance in the payables account in the numerator.

The final turnover ratio that we report is property, plant and equipment (PP&E) turnover, computed as:

$$PP\&E\ Turnover\ =\ \frac{Sales}{Average\ Net\ PP\&E}.$$

PP&E isn't literally consumed in the sale the same way that inventory is. Nonetheless, it is an asset that is necessary in the production of sales, albeit indirectly at times. In the very short run, a company's corporate headquarters and distribution centers could probably blow up and sales in the department stores wouldn't be affected, but in the long run, headquarters and distribution centers are necessary. We want to know if the firm is using its PP&E efficiently. Does it have idle capacity? Does it invest too heavily in non-producing assets, such as lavish headquarters and Lear jets? Comparing the PP&E ratio of the firm with a few of its close competitors can frequently shed light on these questions.

Note that there are additional accounts, such as intangibles, that may cause an unusual net operating asset turnover ratio. You should identify and understand these accounts. For example, if a firm has engaged in an acquisition involving significant goodwill, this will typically drive the net operating asset turnover down relative to the company's competitors. However, this is not necessarily a bad sign, and competitors may have similar amounts of internally generated goodwill that is not recognized on their balance sheets.

Continuing our retail example, in the bottom panel of Figure 5.6 we compare Kohl's turnover ratios with the corresponding ratios for Nordstrom and Ross Stores. As we noted earlier, Kohl's net operating asset turnover is slightly slower than Nordstrom and considerably slower than Ross Stores. We might not expect Kohl's to keep up with Ross Stores, given Ross Stores' position as a discount retailer and their clearly stated strategy to quickly move inventory through sales and promotions. But why are Kohl's assets deployed less efficiently than Nordstrom? Comparing the working capital accounts reveals some interesting differences. First, Nordstrom's Days Inventory are significantly shorter than Kohl's, averaging 65 days in fiscal 2009, compared to almost 100 days at Kohl's. So Kohl's inventory stays in the stores 35 days longer than at Nordstrom. The only strategic reason for this would be that Kohl's feels they can charge a higher margin in return for holding more inventory; otherwise, it looks like Kohl's is struggling with its inventory management. Working against Nordstrom's asset turnover ratio is the fact that they offer a private label credit card and, as a consequence, carry a significant receivable balance. In fiscal 2009, customers took on average 84 days to pay their Nordstrom credit card balance. Nordstrom's investment in receivables more than offsets Kohl's slow inventory turnover, and the small difference in their Days Payable isn't large enough to make much difference. In fact, if we add the Days Inventory, the Days Receivable, and subtract the Days Payable, we get an estimate of the length of the whole operating cycle: for Kohl's it is 63 days and for Nordstrom it is 103 days. While we might question Kohl's inventory management, their overall working capital management isn't the cause of their slower net operating asset turnover. It is due to long-term operating assets.

The only other significant operating asset for Kohl's and Nordstrom is PP&E, and this is where Kohl's loses the race with Nordstrom. PP&E make up about one half of Kohl's total assets and about one third of Nordstrom's total assets, so Kohl's fiscal 2009 PP&E turnover ratio of 2.454 is drastically lower than Nordstrom's ratio of 3.866. It is hard to imagine that Kohl's stores are so much plusher than Nordstrom's stores; the opposite is almost certainly true. The obvious interpretation is that Nordstrom generates more sales dollars per dollar of PP&E investment because of a combination of good merchandising and shrewd asset investments. Without discounting this conclusion, we offer two less economic explanations. The first is that both companies sell over the Internet and these sales bear no direct relation to the size of the PP&E investment. If Nordstrom does significantly more Internet business than Kohl's, this could enhance their PP&E turnover ratio. Unfortunately, Nordstrom doesn't break out the fraction of sales derived from the Internet, so we can't investigate this explanation any further. The second potential distortion in the PP&E turnover ratio is caused by the accounting measurement of PP&E. Both companies use a mix of leased stores, owned stores, and owned buildings on leased land. Of these, only the owned land and buildings appear in PP&E; the leased assets are expensed as part of SG&A when the lease payments are made. In fiscal 2009, Nordstrom leased approximately 49% of their stores while Kohl's only leased about 38% (as always, these juicy facts are gleaned from the MD&A section of the companies' 10-K filings). This will decrease Nordstrom's PP&E and increase their SG&A relative to Kohl's. And knowing this helps to reconcile the mystery that was posed at the start of this section: if Nordstrom is pursuing a luxury retail strategy, why is their net operating margin not significantly larger than Kohl's and their asset turnover ratios significantly smaller? If we correct for the different mix of leased versus owned stores between the two companies, we get closer to the ordering of margins and turnovers that we expected to see.

# 5.9 LEVERAGE

In both the Basic and Advanced DuPont decompositions financial leverage makes the good times better and the bad times worse. As we analyze the firm's past, we can see how much leverage the firm employed, and whether it amplified superior or inferior operating performance. But leverage has a forward-looking feature that the previous ratios lacked. Leverage increases the riskiness of the expected future cash flows. Levered firms commit themselves to making fixed payments to creditors, and the common equity holders must ultimately surrender control of the firm to the creditors if these payments cannot be met. The more financial leverage a firm has, the greater the chance that unexpected poor performance will be amplified to the point that the firm cannot pay its creditors. The likelihood of defaulting on amounts owed to creditors is known as *credit risk*. Many of the ratios we discuss in this section form the basis for the debt covenants between the firm and its creditors. A firm may have great long-term potential, but if it runs into short-term liquidity problems, it may not live to see the long-term. For this reason the analysis of credit risk also includes a detailed examination of the firm's ability to meet its obligations in the next year or two. Our DuPont decompositions examined how financial leverage contributes to the level and variability of ROE; now we want to assess the amount of credit risk that the leverage imposes on the equity holders.

In this section we first discuss some summary measures of a firm's capital structure and short-term liquidity. We then discuss how these and other variables can be combined to make an explicit prediction of how likely it is that the firm will default on its debt.

## Long-Term Capital Structure

A firm's capital structure – its mix of debt and equity – is the primary long-term driver of credit risk. The most common way to represent a firm's capital structure is the ratio of total debt to total common equity:

$$Debt\ to\ Equity\ Ratio = \frac{End-of-Year\ Current\ and\ LongTerm\ Debt}{End-of-Year\ Common\ Equity}.$$

This ratio is similar to the definition of financial leverage used in the Advanced DuPont Model. It differs in that we exclude preferred stock and minority interests from the numerator, because these capital providers typically have fewer rights than debt holders in the case of a skipped payment. Because we want to assess risk at the most recent point in time, we also compute the debt-to-equity ratio based on the ending balances, rather than the average balances, as in the Advanced DuPont Model.

In the context of credit analysis, this ratio provides an overall indication of the extent of a firm's long-term credit commitments. Other things equal, higher debt-to-equity implies a higher probability of financial distress. The weakness of this ratio is that it fails to take into account the firm's ability to pay off its creditors. For example, firms with very stable and predictable cash flows, such as utilities and banks, frequently run very high debt-to-equity ratios. This is because they have a stable flow of cash flows from their customers (utility bills and interest payments) reducing the risk that they won't be able to meet their debt payments, and so a high debt-to-equity ratio is not necessarily an indication of financial distress for firms with strong and stable cash flows.

Our next ratio is funds from operations to total debt, computed as:

*Funds from Operations to Total Debt*

$$= \frac{Funds\ from\ Operations}{Average\ Total\ Debt}, where$$

Funds from Operations = Net Income + Depreciation & Amortization + Increase in Deferred Taxes + Increase in Other Liabilities + Minority Interest in Earnings + Preferred Dividends.

Funds from operations represent the amount of 'funds' or working capital created or destroyed by the firms operations. This measure directly compares the amount of debt with the flow of funds that will be used to service the debt. Thus, this measure overcomes the shortcoming described above for the debt-to-equity ratio. One benchmark for this ratio is the interest rate that the company pays on its debt. Unless funds from operations can comfortably cover interest payments, the probability of default is high. A potential shortcoming of this ratio is that working capital can be tied up in illiquid current asset accounts, such as prepayments and inventories. In reality, it will be difficult to pay creditors with these assets. Thus, a common variant of this ratio is the cash from operations to debt ratio. This ratio backs out the non-cash working capital accounts from the numerator to get Cash from Operations (CFO):

$$CFO\ to\ Total\ Debt = \frac{Cash\ from\ Operations}{Average\ Total\ Debt}.$$

This ratio is a useful check, but you should not interpret it too literally. Growth firms frequently run negative cash from operations as they invest in working capital to generate sales growth. This growth is not necessarily a bad thing, but we need to make sure that the firm has the necessary plans in place to finance this growth.

## Short-Term Liquidity

The above ratios focus on the firm's capital structure to assess the credit risk created by the firm's long-run financial obligations. The next set of ratios focus on short-term liquidity. These ratios provide an indication of the firm's ability to meet its short-term cash commitments as they come due. The first ratio is the current ratio, measured as the ratio of current assets to current liabilities:

$$Current\ Ratio = \frac{End-of-Year\ Current\ Assets}{End-of-Year\ Current\ Liabilities}.$$

Current assets represent the assets that the firm expects to convert to cash over the next 12 months. Current liabilities represent the obligations that the firm must satisfy over the next 12 months. A current ratio greater than one indicates that the company has enough current assets to meet its current liabilities. An obvious shortcoming of this measure is that, in the event of financial distress, some of the current assets may not be readily converted into cash at their book values. If no one is buying the company's inventory then it might not be worth its book value, and you can imagine the difficulty in converting prepaid rent back into cash. An alternative measure of the ability to meet current liabilities is the quick ratio:

**Quick Ratio**
$$= \frac{End - of - year\ Operating\ Cash\ and\ Marketable\ Securities + Receivables}{End - of - year\ Current\ Liabilities}.$$

This ratio restricts the numerator to cash, marketable securities and receivables, which are all likely to be converted into cash on short notice at close to their book values.

The next two ratios are called *interest coverage ratios*. These ratios provide an indication of the ability of a firm to cover its interest charges based on its ongoing operating profits. The first ratio uses EBIT (earnings before interest and taxes) in the numerator and interest expense in the denominator, while the second ratio replaces the numerator with EBITDA (earnings before interest, taxes, depreciation and amortization):

$$\textbf{\textit{EBIT Interest Coverage Ratio}} = \frac{EBIT}{Interest\ Expense}, and$$

$$\textbf{\textit{EBITDA Interest Coverage Ratio}} = \frac{EBITDA}{Interest\ Expense}.$$

The key difference between the ratios is the exclusion of depreciation and amortization expense from the numerator of the second ratio. The rationale for excluding depreciation and amortization is that they represent non-cash charges, and therefore do not reduce the amount of cash available to meet interest payments. On the other hand, a firm must ultimately replace its depreciable assets in order to stay in business, and so it can also be argued that inclusion of these charges provides a more meaningful indicator of long-term solvency.

Continuing our comparison of retail firms, at the end of fiscal 2009, Kohl's debt-to-equity ratio is 0.263 while at Nordstrom it is 1.662. The low level of debt means that Kohl's has very little credit risk. Their CFO-to-Total Debt is greater than one – they could have paid off their entire debt balance with the most recent year's operating cash flows. And Kohl's EBIT interest coverage ratio is extremely healthy. They generated enough EBIT to make their interest payments 12 times over. Compare these values to Nordstrom, who has significantly more leverage, lower CFO-to-Debt and lower interest coverage.

There is one accounting distortion that we should consider before concluding that Kohl's is financially healthy and has little credit risk. As discussed earlier, Kohl's leases about half of its stores and almost all of these leases are accounted for as operating leases, meaning that they do not show up as debt on the books. Nonetheless, these leases contractually commit Kohl's to significant fixed payments, much like interest and principal payments on debt. We can include the impact of operating leases on Kohl's credit risk by treating the operating lease payments just like interest in the coverage ratios. Specifically, we would add the payment back to EBIT in the numerator and to the interest in the denominator of the coverage ratios, creating an adjusted interest coverage ratio (often called a *Fixed Charge Coverage ratio*). Footnote 4 in Kohl's 10-K shows that the fiscal 2009 rent expense on operating leases was $498 million. Adding this back to EBIT and to Net Interest results in an adjusted ratio of 3.469. Kohl's all of a sudden doesn't look quite as safe.

## 5.10  MODELING CREDIT RISK

The analysis of leverage in the previous section gives us some interesting ratios, but it doesn't directly quantify the probability of default. Predicting the likelihood that a company will default on its debt is one of the most common uses of financial statement analysis. Every junior loan officer at every local bank requires financial statements from a commercial loan applicant and, if the loan is granted, then requires that financial statements be submitted on a regular basis in order to monitor the financial health of the company. The loan contract contains covenants that limit subsequent borrowing or equity distributions by the company and establishes periodic tests of financial health. If the company fails a health test, then the loan is declared to be in technical default and it becomes immediately due and payable in full. The idea is that, if the company starts to look sufficiently sick, the bank can rush back in and grab assets before they are all gone.

Being in technical default on a loan doesn't necessarily mean the firm will fail, or seek bankruptcy protection, but these events are highly correlated. In any case, defaulting on a loan has enormous consequences; legal fees skyrocket, vendors stop granting credit, and customers stop buying goods and services. For example, when General Motors entered bankruptcy proceedings in 2009, the United States government pledged to honor new car warranties just to keep sales from plummeting. Interestingly, they did not pledge to honor existing warranties. Regardless of whether the firm can work out the default with its lenders or is forced into liquidation, default is a situation all parties wish to avoid.

Clearly lenders and company management want to avoid default, but who beyond this cares about estimating the likelihood of default? Investors in corporate bonds also care about the probability of default. Bond rating agencies specialize in issuing credit ratings for corporate debt to help bond investors assess credit risk. More surprisingly, in certain contexts the default probability can be an important input in pricing a firm's equity. If the firm defaults, the value of the equity is approximately zero, so the expected value of the equity is really the probability that it won't default times the value of the equity given that it continues as a going concern. For most firms the probability of default is so low that we ignore default when valuing the equity. But for a firm with a high probability of default, default should not be ignored. You can think of an equity investment in a troubled firm as purchasing an option – the default probability is the likelihood that the option ends up out of the money, in which case the equity holders can abandon their claim of the firm. We refer to this option as the abandonment option, and we discuss it in more detail in chapter 12.

## Estimating the Likelihood of Default

Broadly speaking, you should approach default forecasting in the same way as any other financial statement analysis topic: use the past financial statements to get a clear understanding of the company's past financial performance and current financial position, and then forecast how you believe the firm will evolve in the future. But there are a few twists. First, for the purposes of assessing the risk of default, we don't really care how successful a firm is beyond the point where we are confident that it will avoid default. The difference between good financial performance and great financial performance matters when forecasting the cash distributions to equity holders, but makes little difference to the cash distributions to creditors. The maximum that creditors get is the agreed upon interest and principal payments. Second, we have a very specific notion of what unsuccessful is – failure to make contractual interest and principle payments or a violation of debt covenants.

The long-term capital structure and short-term liquidity ratios discussed earlier give you a qualitative feel for the firm's credit risk. In this section we attempt to attach specific probabilities of default to different levels of these and other ratios. Specifically, we introduce six ratios that have been shown to be predictive of future default. We compute these ratios in the Credit Analysis sheet in *eVal*. Below each ratio we report the historical frequency that firms with a ratio near this value defaulted on their debt during the subsequent five years. As a benchmark, over the past three decades the probability that an industrial firm will default during a five-year period has been about five percent, although this rate doubled in 2008-2009 due to the financial crisis.

Before proceeding with our model of default probability, we want to issue a word of warning. The actual covenants found in a typical loan contract are extremely detailed. They spell out exactly how each ratio will be measured, what line items will be included and excluded over what time periods, and what the consequences are for violating different hurdle rates for each ratio. By comparison, the ratios below are simple and standardized. For example, as illustrated by our discussion of Kohl's, these ratios ignore operating lease obligations that would typically be included in an actual covenant. You should consider the ratios below as a general guide for the types of ratios found in actual debt covenants, knowing that in practice the ratios are highly customized to each specific firm.

Figure 5.7 graphs each of the six ratios we use to build our model of default probability. The distribution of each ratio is computed for the entire sample of public firms between 1980 and 1999, excluding banks, insurance companies and real estate companies (because their financial characteristics are so different from the majority of firms). For each ratio we sort this data into ten equal-sized groups, called deciles, and then plot the frequency that firms in each decile defaulted over the next five years.[2] Each graph also shows the cutoffs for each decile just above the axis; for instance, the value shown above deciles 5 and 6 is the median value of the ratio for the entire sample.

---

[2] The default probabilities associated with different levels of each ratio are taken from Falkenstein, Boral and Carty (May 2000).

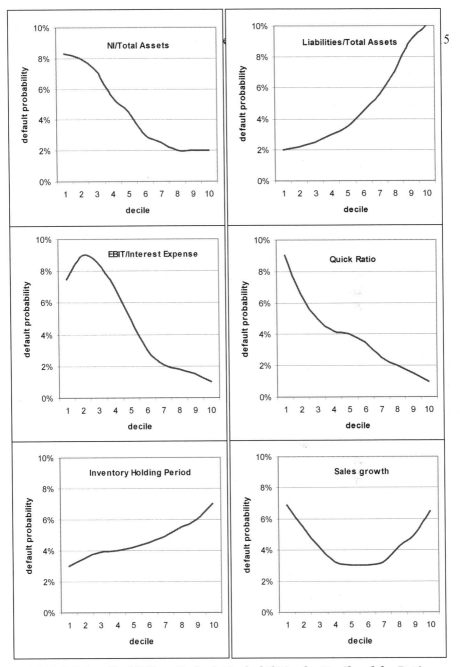

**FIGURE 5.7: Implied 5-Year Default Probabilities by Decile of the Ratio**

## Profitability

For the purposes of predicting default, we measure profitability as the return on total assets before extraordinary items: (net income – extraordinary items)/total assets. Regardless of the firm's other financial characteristics, if it is sufficiently profitable then it will generate enough cash each year to pay its creditors. But how much more likely is it for a firm to default on its debt when its profitability for the year is in the top 10 percent of all firms than if this ratio is in the bottom 10 percent? To get a feel for this, consider the top left graph in Figure 5.7. As expected, the graph slopes down – firms with higher levels of profitability are less likely to default on their debt. To quantify this, the graph shows that the median firm has a return on total assets of 2%, and an implied default probability of about 4%. However, the bottom decile of firms have return on total assets of less than –45% and the odds that they will default in the next five years jumps to over 8%, while the top decile of firms have a return on total assets of more than 12% and a default probability is only 2%. In other words, it is over four times more likely that a firm in the bottom decile will default than a firm in the top decile.

## Leverage

The greater a firm's financial leverage the less the cushion that is available if profits fail to generate the necessary cash flow to pay creditors. Because some firms have negative equity (and this would mess up our graph), Figure 5.7 plots total liabilities/total assets rather than debt/equity, which is the more traditional measure of leverage.  As a firm's leverage increases, the default rate increases steadily, starting at 2% for the firms in the lowest decile and increasing to 10% for firms in the highest decile.

## Liquidity

If you have enough cash, or assets that will soon become cash, you can surely pay your bills, hence the importance of liquidity ratios in credit analysis. As we discussed earlier, it is difficult to pay debt holders with inventory and certain other current assets, so the Quick Ratio (cash, marketable securities and receivables divided by current liabilities) is the ratio we use to predict default. As Figure 5.7 shows, the Quick Ratio is predictive across the entire distribution, but the slope is steepest for the worst firms, those in the first two deciles. The default probability is 9% for firms with a Quick Ratio less than 0.38 but drops to 5% in the third decile, where firms have Quick Ratios between 0.52 and 0.81.

## Interest Coverage

Interest coverage is typically computed in a very precise and complicated way in most debt covenants. But for our purpose, we simply graph EBIT/interest expense. Between the second and sixth decile, the slope of the interest coverage graph is very steep, showing that this ratio does a good job of discriminating winners from losers inside this region. The graph flattens out on the high end because it doesn't really make much difference if you are covering your interest eight times or ten times. On the low end the graph actually slopes up, which seems counter-intuitive. But for firms with negative EBIT, an increase in interest expense lowers the EBIT/interest ratio, which probably explains the unusual shape of the curve in the low region. As a crude benchmark, the median EBIT/interest ratio is 2.2.

## Inventory

The inventory holding period is less predictive than the previous measures, as seen by its modest slope in Figure 5.7. We include it nonetheless because it captures information that is very different from the previous default predictors. Previously we described the inventory holding period as a measure of how efficiently the company manages its inventory. All else equal, a shorter holding period is better. In the context of default prediction, if the holding period is very long then, besides suggesting inefficient inventory management, it may indicate an even more serious problem. It could be that the firm is having trouble selling its inventory and, consequently, may suffer financial distress in the future. Firms in the lowest decile of this ratio are probably service firms that have little or no inventory, so the ratio doesn't really apply to them; as a benchmark, the median inventory holding period is about 50 days.

## Sales Growth

Unlike the previous graphs, sales growth has a U-shaped relation with default probability, as seen in the bottom right graph in Figure 5.7. While this makes it more difficult to interpret, we include it because it captures information that is very different from the more traditional ratios. In the lowest deciles, sales are declining (i.e., negative sales growth), which is clearly a bad sign. But more curiously, the odds of default are high for firms with the highest sales growth. The intuition is that the set of firms with rapidly growing sales includes a greater proportion of firms with unprofitable sales. Further, such rapid sales growth is more likely to be financed by additional borrowing, further increasing the risk of default. As a benchmark, the median annual sales growth for the sample is 10%, and this corresponds to the lowest default risk. Sales declines of more than 20% or sales growth of more than 80% imply twice as high a probability of default.

## Final Thoughts on Credit Risk

We stress once again that the ratios given here capture the spirit, but not the actual details, of the financial health tests specified in an actual debt contract. Further, if your forecasts imply that a poorly performing firm will turnaround and be wildly profitable in the future, then the implied default probabilities based on its historical performance don't really mean much.

# 5.11  CONCLUSION

Ratio analysis is an indispensable part of equity valuation and analysis. Ratios are the tools that you will use to evaluate financial performance. If you make a career in financial analysis, then you'll soon be reeling off the financial jargon we've introduced in this chapter with reckless abandon. But you should always remember the important caveats of ratio analysis. First, you should make sure you know how a ratio is computed before you start interpreting it. Second, ratios don't provide answers, they only guide you in your search for answers. Unusual ratios tell you which part of a firm's Form 10-K you need to delve into to get your answers. Finally, management know that you'll be computing all these ratios, and they'll go to great lengths to make sure these ratios look nice. Be particularly skeptical of ratios that management flaunt in their press releases and be vigilant in your search for evidence of creative accounting.

# 5.12 QUIZZES, CASES, LINKS AND REFERENCES

## Quizzes
• Chipotle Mexican Grill (Problem 3)
• Pandora (Problem 3 (i), (ii) ands (iii))
• LinkedIn (Problem 3)
• Salesforce (Problem 3)

## Cases
• Analyzing Apple (Questions 8-11)
• Interpreting Margin and Turnover Ratios
• Netflix, Inc. (Questions 6-9)
• Overstock.com (Questions 7-10)
• Royal Caribbean Cruises in 2010 (Part A)
• Sirius Satellite Radio (Questions 10-14)
• High Yields at Annaly Capital (Questions 5-7)
• Has Zynga Lost Its Zing? (Questions 8-11)
• A Tale of Two Movie Theatres
• Is Tesla's Stock Price in Ludicrous Mode? (Questions 7-10)
• Buiding *eVal* (Part C)

## Links
• *eVal* Website: http://www.lundholmandsloan.com/software.html
• www.hoovers.com website: http://www.hoovers.com

## References
Falkenstein, E., A. Boral and L. Carty, (2000), "RiskCalc for Private Companies: Moody's Default Model", Moody's Investor Service Global Credit Research. Available online at:
  http://papers.ssrn.com/sol3/papers.cfm?abstract_id=236011

CHAPTER SIX

# Cash Flow Analysis

## 6.1 INTRODUCTION

One of the novel features of accrual accounting is that firms can report oodles of accounting earnings in periods when they generate very little cash. As a simple example, a firm selling its goods on credit records sales revenue but doesn't actually receive any cash until and unless the customer pays. Many other transactions can also create large gaps between accounting earnings and cash flows. This is why companies like Enron and Lehman Brothers were able to report healthy earnings one quarter, then go broke in the next. Their earnings turned out to be based on unrealistic accounting assumptions rather than actual cash flows. The fact that earnings and cash flows are different isn't, by itself, a sure sign of trouble. As we discussed in Chapter 4, the accrual accounting process was designed to generate more meaningful measures of periodic financial performance. Nonetheless, generating cash, not earnings, is the ultimate long-term goal of a business. Cash is what the firm needs to buy assets and pay creditors, and it is what standard valuation models tell us must ultimately determine the value of a firm.

This chapter describes how to create a pro forma statement of cash flows based on standardized income statements and balance sheets. We then describe how to use the information in the resulting cash flow statements to evaluate the cash consequences of the company's operating, investing, and financing activities. Is the company generating positive cash from their operations? Is it reinvesting operating cash flow? If not, where is the free cash flow going? We'll also help you to evaluate whether the cash flow implications of your forecasted financial statements make sense. There is no point in assuming that a firm will raise gobs of new cash through an equity issuance at an extremely high price if the company's stock is currently out of favor with Wall Street.

Next, we'll show you how to compute the inputs into discounted cash flow valuation models. We defer the technical development of the models to Chapter 10; here we simply describe how to compute the main inputs and discuss how they can be interpreted as measures of wealth distribution.

Finally, we'll finish with a discussion of how we can study differences between earnings and cash flows to evaluate the quality of earnings. You may recall from Chapter 4 that accounting distortions often cause earnings to temporarily deviate from cash flows, but that these distortions ultimately reverse. Examining differences between earnings and cash flows can help us to identify such distortions and forecast their reversals. But how do we distinguish legitimate accruals from illegitimate distortions? While the only sure method is to corner the company's chief accounting officer in a dark alley, we offer some less reliable but more pragmatic alternatives.


## 6.2 THE STATEMENT OF CASH FLOWS

We begin with a brief review of how to construct a statement of cash flows. If this task is completely new to you, then we recommend you consult an intermediate accounting textbook. Ultimately, the statement of cash flows reconciles the beginning and ending balances in the Cash account. The actual definition of "Cash" includes highly liquid short-term marketable securities; consequently, the line it is often labeled "Cash and Cash Equivalents."

You can intuitively think of the statement of cash flows as a categorized summary of all the transactions that ran through the company's bank account during the year. The statement of cash flows categorizes and summarizes these transactions by dividing them into operating, investing, and financing activities. To illustrate the logic behind the construction of this statement, we start with the basic accounting equation:

Assets = Liabilities + Equity

We next divide assets into cash and non-cash assets, take the annual change in each term (denoted by $\Delta$), and rearrange to get:

$\Delta$Cash = $\Delta$Liabilities + $\Delta$Equity - $\Delta$Non-cash Assets

The statement of cash flows explains the change in Cash on the left-hand side of the equation by decomposing the changes in liabilities, equity and non-cash assets on the right-hand side of the equation. The statement organizes the changes in these accounts into three familiar categories: operating, investing, and financing. We have listed common transactions summarized in each of these categories below.

| $\Delta$Cash | = -$\Delta$NonCashAssets | + $\Delta$Liabilities | + $\Delta$Equity |
|---|---|---|---|
| Operating Cash Flows | = +$\downarrow$Receivables | +$\uparrow$Payables | + Net Income |
| Investing Cash Flows | = -$\uparrow$PP&E | | |
| Financing Cash Flows | = | +$\uparrow$Debt | - Dividends |

To consider some common examples, operating cash flows increase with (i) decreases in receivables (which is reflected as a decrease in a non-cash asset in the above equation); (ii) increases in accounts payable (which is reflected as an increase in liabilities in the above equation); and (iii) net income (which is reflected as an increase in equity in the above equation). Investing cash flows and financing cash flows work similarly. Selling PP&E or issuing debt increases cash; buying PP&E or retiring debt decreases cash.

Creating a pro forma statement of cash flows from the firm's balance sheet and income statement can be intricate, but it is not fundamentally complicated. The equation above says that the change in cash equals the change in everything else on the balance sheet (taking care to subtract the changes in non-cash-assets). Start by computing the change in every line item on the balance sheet. The top line, the change in cash, is the thing you are trying to explain. Now run your finger down the balance sheet and sort the change in every line into operating, investing or financing. By the magic of algebra, the sum of the operating, investing, and financing will equal the change in cash. The only tricky thing is to remember that some line items on the balance sheet change for more than one reason. For instance, purchasing more PP&E is investing, but depreciating that PP&E is an operating expense. Thus, the change in PP&E gets allocated into two difference categories. As long as all the bits and pieces add up to the total change in PP&E on the balance sheet, everything will reconcile.

The pro forma statements of cash flows created by a spreadsheet program such as *eVal* are unlikely to exactly match the statements in the firm's Form 10-K. One reason is that our definition of cash may not match the company's definition. A second reason is that we construct the cash flow statements based only on the information from the standardized income statements and balance sheets, so our classification of items into operating, investing, and financing activities may be less accurate than those on Form 10-K. The company's published statement of cash flows is the most accurate source of information about past cash activity. It is nevertheless useful to construct pro forma statements for both the past and the forecasted future so that you can see a time series of cash flow data computed on a consistent basis.

## 6.3 EVALUATING A FIRM'S PAST CASH FLOWS

The statement of cash flows is the starting point for evaluating the firm's past cash flows. Recall from Chapter 2 that the MD&A section of Form 10-K includes a required discussion of the firm's liquidity and capital resources. It is useful to review this discussion and have it close at hand while conducting your cash flow analysis. You should then work your way through each of the three sections of the statement of cash flows.

### Evaluating Cash from Operations

The first section reports cash from operating activities. The first port of call is to see whether cash from operations is positive or negative. Positive cash from operations is generally good news. The company's operations are generating cash flow that can be either reinvested in the business or paid out to debt and equity holders. We'll find out exactly what the firm is doing with its operating cash flow in the next two sections. Negative cash from operations is a more mixed signal. One reason for negative cash from operations is that the company's operations are performing poorly. To see whether this is the case, check the company's net income. If net income is also negative, then poor operating performance is a likely explanation. In this case, you need to establish whether the company is going to be able to turn its operating performance around, and whether it has sufficient financial resources to complete the turnaround. A second reason for negative cash from operations is that the company is investing in working capital. Investments in working capital, such as receivables and inventory, reduce cash from operations but do not reduce net income. That is why they are subtracted from net income to arrive at cash from operations. Investments in working capital can be good or bad. If a company is investing in working capital to grow a business on which it is generating a healthy economic return, the increase in working capital is good. On the other hand, if the increase in working capital is not accompanied by healthy growth in the underlying business, it is more likely to be bad. For example, if a company's products are not selling, inventory will increase, and will probably have to be written down in the future. But growth in working capital without accompanying growth in operations is not always a bad signal. For example, assume that a company implements a successful new credit program for its customers. Receivables will increase even if sales are flat, as customers take advantage of the new credit program. If the interest generated by the credit plan is sufficient to provide the company with a healthy return on its incremental investment in receivables, the program is justified.

There are a couple of other things to check before moving on from the operating section. First, if there is a big gap between net income and cash from operations, you should make sure that you understand what is driving this gap. Recall from Chapter 4 that the difference between net income and cash flows represents accounting accruals, and this is where accounting distortions are most likely to lurk. We'll talk more about how to identify accounting distortions in Section 6.6. For now, you should just realize that a big gap raises a red flag about earnings quality. What is a big gap? As a rule of thumb, if the difference between net income and cash from operations is greater than 5 percent of total assets, then you should follow the advice in Section 6.6.

The second thing to check is the extent to which cash from operations is distorted by unusual one-time items. For example, a big one-off tax payment can temporarily depress operating cash flows. Or a cash receipt from the settlement of a major legal dispute can temporarily inflate cash flows. It is useful to separate these one-time items from recurring cash flows to evaluate the long-run cash-generating ability of the firm's operations.

## Evaluating Cash from Investing

The second section of the statement of cash flows reports cash from investing activities. While cash from operating activities is usually positive, cash from investing activities is usually negative. This is because most firms require ongoing capital expenditures to maintain their operating activities. For example, a trucking company must buy new trucks to replace spent ones that are taken out of service. A useful way to check whether a company is increasing or decreasing its investment base is to compare its capital expenditures in the investing section to the depreciation add-back in the operating section. If capital expenditures are greater than depreciation, then the company is growing its capital base. Growth in a company's capital base can be evaluated in much the same way as growth in working capital. If the growth in the capital base is accompanied by profitable growth in the firm's operations, all is usually well. But growth in the capital base that is not accompanied by profitable growth in the firm's operations should raise a red flag. Either the company is using its capital less efficiently or accounting distortions are inflating capital and earnings. We'll provide you with more advice for identifying such distortions in Section 6.6.

Apart from capital expenditures, you'll also find cash expenditures on investments and intangibles in this section. For investments, you should make sure you understand exactly what they are. At one extreme, they could be low-risk investments, such as treasury bonds. At the other extreme, they could represent investments in shady off-balance-sheet entities that could disappear overnight. Purchased intangibles most frequently relate to goodwill associated with the acquisition of other businesses. For acquisitions, you should follow up and make sure that the acquisitions make good economic sense. Do the earnings of the acquired company justify the price that was paid for the acquisition? All too often, companies generate healthy cash flows from their existing operations only to squander them by overpaying for acquisitions. Some managers would rather build an empire for themselves than return cash to equity holders.

As a final check on the investing section of the statement of cash flows, you should see whether the sum of operating and investing cash flows is positive or negative. The sum of operating and investing cash flows is frequently referred to as *free cash flow*. This is the cash flow that is free to be distributed to the debt and equity holders. If free cash flow is negative, then the company has to either dip into cash reserves or raise new capital to finance its operations. In this case, you should check that the company's operations have sufficient potential to warrant additional infusions of capital. If not, the company is unlikely to survive.

## Evaluating Cash from Financing

The third and final section of the statement of cash flows reports cash from financing activities. This section tells us what the firm has been doing with its free cash flow. If free cash flow is positive, then the firm is probably distributing free cash flow to debt and/or equity holders. Such cash distributions are what give debt and equity securities value in the first place, so it is a good sign to see that a company is distributing free cash flow. If free cash flow is negative, then the firm is probably funding the shortfall by issuing new debt and equity securities. If the company is primarily issuing equity, this is usually a sign that there is uncertainty about its ability to produce positive free cash flow in the near future.

Note that we qualified our statements about the relation between free cash flow and financing activities using the word *probably*. The reason for this qualification is that a firm can use its cash reserves to bridge differences between free cash flow and cash from financing activities. For example, firms with positive (negative) free cash flow can add to (subtract from) their cash reserves rather than engage in financing activities. The last few lines of the statement of cash flows indicate whether this is the case. If a firm is funding negative free cash flows by using up its cash reserves, you should determine how long it can continue to do this before it runs out of cash. The ratio of negative free cash flows to cash reserves is often termed the *burn rate;* the reciprocal of the burn rate provides an estimate of how long it will be before cash runs out. On the other hand, if a firm is squirreling away positive free cash flows as cash reserves, you should understand management's motives. Are they too selfish to pay this money back to investors? Are they empire builders who are planning value-destroying acquisitions? Is the cash trapped overseas and they fear the tax consequences of repatriating the money? Firms that try to sell themselves as "growth" stocks are particularly reluctant to pay cash back to investors, because this basically amounts to an admission that they have run out of growth opportunities. Be wary of managers who hoard free cash flow.

## 6.4 EVALUATING A FIRM'S FUTURE CASH FLOWS

After you forecast the company's future income statements and balance sheets, you get the future statements of cash flow for free in most spreadsheet programs. *eVal* constructs these pro forma statements using the procedure described in Section 6.2. You should evaluate the forecasts of future cash flows in much the same way that you evaluated the past cash flows. In addition, you should make sure that the future cash flow forecasts make economic sense. For example, it is unrealistic to think that a firm could finance a long string of negative future operating cash flows by issuing short-term debt. Creditors usually like to see a healthy stream of future cash to facilitate the timely repayment of debt.

As before, begin your evaluation with forecasted cash from operations. If it is significantly negative for the distant future, you should ask yourself whether the firm is really going to continue its operations. It doesn't make sense to continue losing money forever. Either the firm will ultimately generate positive operating cash flows or it will cease operations. You need to figure out which alternative is more likely and then adjust your forecast financial statements accordingly. Even if cash from operations is only forecast to be negative for a few years, you still need to ask yourself whether the company will be able to raise sufficient financing to keep itself afloat until positive operating cash flows arrive. While you might forecast that cash flows will be huge and positive in 10 years, other investors may disagree. Unless you are personally prepared to provide the firm's entire financing needs in the meantime, it may not survive long enough to reach that glorious day.

Your evaluation of forecasted cash from investing should ask similar questions. First, you should make sure that your capital expenditure plans are consistent with those espoused by management in the 'Liquidity and Capital Resources' section of MD&A in the most recent Form 10-K. Second, if you have forecast that the firm is going to have significant capital expenditures, you should make sure that financing is likely to be available. If the firm's operations are forecast to be unprofitable, the firm may have a tough time convincing investors to provide financing to fund additional capital expenditures.

If you are forecasting that a firm will generate positive free cash flows, what do your forecasts imply about where the money will go? Will the firm pay down debt, will it increase dividends or will it simply let its cash balance pile up? How do the implied financing cash flows compare with the firm's historical activity, and with management's plans outlined in the MD&A? It would be silly, for instance, to make forecasts that imply that the firm will pay large dividends in the near future when the firm has publicly stated that it has no intention of doing so. You should be particularly wary of firms with a record of wasting free cash flows on unsuccessful projects. Make sure that you don't inadvertently assume that such firms will stop this behavior and start graciously paying out all of their free cash flow as dividends.

# 6.5 CONSTRUCTING DCF VALUATION INPUTS

Chapter 10 covers valuation models, one of which is the standard discounted cash flow (DCF) model. Unfortunately, the cash flows reported in the statement of cash flows do not correspond exactly with the inputs to the DCF model. Recall from our discussion in Section 6.3 that the sum of cash from operations and cash from investing can be loosely referred to as *free cash flow*. The key difference between this measure of free cash flow and the measures of free cash flow used in DCF valuation models is that valuation models tailor their cash flow metrics to the stakes(s) being valued. For example, if we are valuing equity, we only want to consider free cash flow that is distributed to equity holders. The free cash flow measure computed from the statement of cash flows shows *all* free cash flow, regardless of whether it is paid to equity holders, paid to debt holders, or held in cash reserves. The stakes most commonly valued are common equity and invested capital (the sum of debt, minority interest, preferred stock and equity). We present computations for the corresponding measures of free cash flow below.

## Free Cash Flow to Common Equity

The *free cash flow to common equity* is simply the net cash distributions to common equity holders. If this amount is negative in a particular year, it means that common equity holders have contributed more cash to the firm than they have received. The DCF to common equity, which we briefly introduced in

Chapter 1, is the most basic of valuation models. We can compute this amount several different ways, and, if we do so properly, we will always get the same answer. Because different people prefer different computation methods, the *eVal* workbook computes the amount in all the common ways and demonstrates that they are, indeed, the same. Figure 6.1 shows *eVal*'s free cash flow to common equity computations for Kohl's in the year ended 1/31/2011. If you want to see these computations in *eVal* for yourself, you can load Kohl's data from the 'Case Data' sheet in *eVal*.

|  | A | F |
| --- | --- | --- |
| 1 | **Cash Flow Analysis** | |
| 4 | Company Name | |
| 6 | | Forecast |
| 7 | Fiscal Year End Date | 1/31/11 |
| 72 | Free Cash Flow to all Investors | |
| 74 | Net Operating Income | 1,132,413 |
| 75 | - Increase in Net Operating Assets | (461,255) |
| 76 | +/-Clean Surplus Plug (Ignore) | 0 |
| 77 | =Free Cash Flow to Investors | 671,158 |
| 79 | Computation based on SCF: | |
| 80 | Cash From Operations | 1,652,751 |
| 81 | -Increase in Operating Cash | (105,399) |
| 82 | +Cash from Investing | (961,720) |
| 83 | +Interest Expense | 137,049 |
| 84 | -Tax Shield on Interest | (51,523) |
| 85 | +/-Clean Surplus Plug (Ignore) | 0 |
| 86 | =Free Cash Flow to Investors | 671,158 |
| 88 | Financing Flows: | |
| 89 | +Dividends on Common Stock | 0 |
| 90 | +Interest Expense | 137,049 |
| 91 | -Tax Shield on Interest | (51,523) |
| 92 | +Dividends on Preferred Stock | 0 |
| 93 | +Dividends Paid to Minority Interest | 0 |
| 94 | -Net Issuance of Common Stock | 681,779 |
| 95 | -Net Issuance of Debt | (96,147) |
| 96 | -Net Issuance of Preferred Stock | 0 |
| 97 | =Free Cash Flow to Investors | 671,158 |
| 99 | Traditional Computation of FCF: | |
| 100 | EBIT | 1,804,138 |
| 101 | -Taxes on EBIT | (682,190) |
| 102 | +Increase in Deferred Taxes | 17,528 |
| 103 | = NOPLAT | 1,139,476 |
| 104 | +Depreciation & Amortization | 604,888 |
| 105 | +Non-Operating Income (Loss) | 10,465 |
| 106 | +Other Income (Loss) | 0 |
| 107 | +Ext. Items & Disc. Ops. | 0 |
| 108 | =Gross Cash Flow | 1,754,829 |
| 109 | -Increase in Working Capital | (144,639) |
| 110 | -Capital Expenditures | (931,174) |
| 111 | -Increase in Investments | (14,924) |
| 112 | -Purchases of Intangibles | (9,485) |
| 113 | -Increase in Other Assets | (6,137) |
| 114 | +Increase in Other Liabilities | 22,688 |
| 115 | +/-Clean Surplus Plug (Ignore) | 0 |
| 116 | =Free Cash Flow to Investors | 671,158 |

|  | A | F |
| --- | --- | --- |
| 1 | **Cash Flow Analysis** | |
| 4 | Company Name | |
| 6 | | Forecast |
| 7 | Fiscal Year End Date | 1/31/11 |
| 48 | Free Cash Flow to Common Equity | |
| 50 | Net Income | 1,046,887 |
| 51 | - Increase in Common Equity | (365,108) |
| 52 | +/-Clean Surplus Plug (Ignore) | 0 |
| 53 | =Free Cash Flow to Common Equity | 681,779 |
| 55 | Computation based on SCF: | |
| 56 | +Cash From Operations | 1,652,751 |
| 57 | -Increase in Cash | (105,399) |
| 58 | +Cash From Investing | (961,720) |
| 59 | +Increase in Debt | 96,147 |
| 60 | -Dividends Paid to Minority Interest | 0 |
| 61 | -Dividends Paid on Preferred | 0 |
| 62 | +Increase in Preferred Stock | 0 |
| 63 | +/-Clean Surplus Plug (Ignore) | 0 |
| 64 | =Free Cash Flow to Common Equity | 681,779 |
| 66 | Financing Flows: | |
| 67 | +Dividends Paid | 0 |
| 68 | -Net Issuance of Common Stock | 681,779 |
| 69 | = Free Cash Flow to Common Equity | 681,779 |

**FIGURE 6.1: Free Cash Flow to Common Equity and All Investors for Kohl's**

The first method of computation uses what is often referred to as the clean surplus relation. The clean surplus relation says that the change in book value equals net income less net cash distributions to common equity holders:

Ending Common Equity
    = Beginning Common Equity + Net Income – Net Cash Distributions

Since free cash flow to common equity is just the net cash distributions to common equity, we can rearrange the above relation to solve for free cash flows as follows:

Free Cash Flow to Common Equity = Net Income - Increase in Common Equity
        681,779                 = 1,046,887   - 365,108.

In this case, common equity holders are forecast to receive 681,779 from the company. Now we'll show you how we can arrive at the same answer using the amounts already computed in our statement of cash flows. The next method of computation in *eVal* backs into free cash flow to common equity by taking the aggregate free cash flow from the firm's operating and investing activities and then subtracting cash that is either retained in the firm or paid out to non-equity capital providers. We start with the cash from operations and then subtract the increase in the cash balance. This adjusts for any cash flow that was retained in the firm. We next add cash from investing and add (subtract) any cash that was received from (distributed to) debt, minority interests, or preferred stockholders. What's left must have been paid out to common equity holders. You will note that the answer on the Cash Flow Analysis sheet is exactly the 681,779 we computed above.

The final computation is the most intuitive. Simply look in the Financing section of the statement of cash flows and pick out the two items that are cash transactions with the common equity holders—Dividends Paid and Net Issuance of Common Stock. Once again we see that common equity holders are forecast to receive 681,779 from Kohl's during the year. We also see that the entire amount comes from a negative entry next to the 'Net Issuance of Common Stock'. This means we are forecasting that Kohl's will repurchase $81,779 of stock in fiscal 2010.

Kohl's growth rate in 2010 was slowing, but its operations were still profitable, Kohl's was forecast to generate significant free cash flow. Rearranging the clean surplus relation produces a useful heuristic for understanding whether a firm is expected to generate positive or negative free cash flow:

FCF to Common Equity      $= NI - (CE_{end} - CE_{beg})$
                          $= CE_{beg} (NI/ CE_{beg} - (CE_{end} - CE_{beg})/ CE_{beg})$
                          $= CE_{beg} (ROE - \text{Growth Rate in CE}),$

where

FCF = Free Cash Flow
NI = Net Income
CE = Common Equity at either the beginning (beg) or end of the period, and
ROE = Return on Beginning Common Stockholders Equity.

This means that free cash flows to common equity should be positive (negative) whenever ROE is greater (less) than the growth rate in common equity. In Kohl's case, ROE is around 14%, while its growth rate is only around 5%, so FCF is positive.

We have already touched on the pluses and minuses of free cash flow to common equity as a measure of firm performance and equity value. It is a measure of wealth distribution, not a measure of wealth creation. As such, in any given period it is generally a poor performance measure. In the long run, however, this is what the common equity holders actually get as a return on their investment. In this sense, it is final arbiter of equity value.

## Free Cash Flow to Investors

Free cash flow to all investors is the net amount of cash distributed by the firm to all providers of capital: debt holders, minority interests, preferred stockholders, and common equity holders. This is the primary input to the traditional DCF model. The traditional DCF model also involves another wrinkle. The cash savings from the tax deductibility of interest payments on debt are not included in *free cash flow to investors*. The reason for their exclusion is not that these tax savings don't increase free cash flow—they do. Rather, it is because there is a tradition of valuing these cash inflows by reducing the discount rate that is applied to all other cash flows. The tradition involves the computation of another beast called the *weighted average cost of capital,* which we'll get to in Chapter 9. This all seems unnecessarily convoluted to us, but who are we to argue with tradition? *eVal* reports computations using this traditional method so that you can communicate with brainwashed b-school graduates who don't know any different. But we can assure you that you would get exactly the same valuation if you instead use the more direct approach of including these cash savings in free cash flow and leaving the discount rate alone.

As with the free cash flow to common equity, we can compute free cash flow to all investors a number of different ways and always get the same answer. The right side of Figure 6.1 shows *eVal's* computations of free cash flow to investors for Kohl's. The first computation of free cash flow to investors makes use of the relation between net operating income and changes in net operating assets, and is analogous to the clean surplus relation that we used to determine the free cash flow to common equity above. We simply redefine net income as net operating income and common equity as net operating assets. Recall from Chapter 5 that the Advanced DuPont model defines net operating income and net operating assets by isolating the income statement and balance sheet items that are associated with the firm's operating and investing activities. Here, we use the same approach to calculate the free cash flow generated by the firm's operating and investing activities. We define net operating income and net operating assets exactly as given in Chapter 5. Recall that net operating income is defined before the tax savings accruing from the tax deductibility of interest on debt. We simply apply the firm's effective tax rate to earnings before interest and taxes, thus deducting how much tax the firm would have had to pay assuming it had no debt. As mentioned above, we'll incorporate any tax savings by reducing the discount rate in the valuation computation. Using Kohl's fiscal 2010 forecasts as an illustration, we can now write:

Free Cash Flow to Investors = Net Operating Income - Increase in Net Operating
                                                                    Assets
        671,158                  = 1,132,413              – 461,255.

Intuitively, this calculation starts with operating income that is available to all providers of capital and then deducts all amounts that are reinvested in the firm as opposed to being distributed to capital providers.

The next two methods of computing free cash flow to investors make use of measures already computed in the statement of cash flows. The first of these methods starts with cash from operating and investing activities, subtracts cash that is retained in the firm, adds back interest expense, and subtracts out the tax savings from interest. The reason that interest is added back is that interest is a cash flow to debt holders and not an operating expense. Accountants don't appreciate this distinction and so leave interest expense in the operating section rather than shifting it to the financing section of the statement of cash flows. The tax savings of interest are added back to conform to "the tradition." The next method takes the most direct route: it simply picks the appropriate cash flows out of the financing section of the statement of cash flows, again correcting for the misclassification of interest and the subtraction of tax savings on interest. Note that in all cases we get 671,158 of free cash flow to investors for Kohl's fiscal year 2010.

There is one more common method of computing free cash flow to investors, which we label the "traditional" approach, because it is the recipe used in most finance textbooks. This approach starts with EBIT (i.e., earnings before interest and taxes) and then replicates many of the adjustments found in the operating and investing sections of the statement of cash flows. The traditional folk derived this method long before firms were required to report a statement of cash flows, and many of them still prefer to use this method rather than using the statement of cash flows as a shortcut. The general logic behind this approach is to start with EBIT, adjust for taxes, add back noncash charges (e.g., depreciation), subtract net changes in working capital, and subtract investment expenditures. Note that we don't have to worry about adding back interest expense or subtracting tax savings on interest. This is because we started out with EBIT, which is earnings before interest and taxes, and then applied the effective tax rate to EBIT, essentially ignoring the tax savings from interest. Adding back deferred taxes to the result of the above computation gives us *NOPLAT*, which stands for *net operating profit less adjusted taxes*. If you get out a large piece of paper and pour a tall cup of coffee, you can reconcile this last method with all the other more direct methods. The pieces are all the same; the jigsaw puzzle is just put together in a different order.

Just as we did for free cash flow to equity, we can rearrange the clean surplus relation for free cash flow to all investors to yield the following heuristic.

$$FCF = NOA_{beg} (RNOA - \text{Growth Rate in NOA}),$$

where FCF is now free cash flow to all investors.

This heuristic tells us that FCF to all investors should be positive (negative) when RNOA exceeds the growth rate in NOA. Since Kohl's RNOA is around 11% and it is only growing net operating assets at around 4%, it is forecast to have positive FCF.

# 6.6 CASH FLOWS AND EARNINGS QUALITY ANALYSIS

Recall from Chapter 4 that accounting distortions arise from imperfections in the accrual accounting process. Accrual accounting involves the recognition of estimated future benefits and obligations in the financial statements. Many accrual accounting estimates are subject to measurement errors. These errors can arise from limitations of GAAP, unintentional managerial forecasting errors, and intentional managerial manipulation. The examples we constructed in Section 4.4 of Chapter 4 indicate that accounting distortions often lead to systematic patterns in accruals and earnings. For example, temporarily aggressive accounting causes accruals and earnings to be temporarily high, while temporarily conservative accounting causes accruals and earnings to be temporarily low. Recall that accruals are simply the difference between earnings and cash flows. Accruals also manifest themselves as changes in assets and liabilities on the balance sheet. Now that we are armed with a good understanding of accruals, we are in a position to use this knowledge to help us identify accounting distortions. We refer to this process as earnings quality analysis, because we are primarily concerned with identifying the impact of accounting distortions on earnings.

The main goal of earnings quality analysis is to distinguish between "good" accruals, which represent accurate estimates of expected future benefits and obligations, and "bad" accruals, which do not represent future benefits and obligations and are thus accounting distortions. There are two simple *red flags* that we can use to isolate suspect accruals. First, if a firm's accruals are unusually large, accounting distortions are more likely to be at work. Second, if the unusually large accruals relate to balance sheet accounts that typically consist of less reliable accrual estimates, accounting distortions are even more likely at work.[1] For example, a big increase in accounts payable is unlikely to be due to an accounting distortion, because accounts payable can be measured with a high degree of reliability. On the other hand, a big increase in inventory is more likely to be due to an accounting distortion, because inventory is measured with a relatively low degree of reliability. A big increase in inventory may signal a build up in obsolete inventory, meaning that inventory is overvalued and an inventory write-down is overdue.

In order to help you use these red flags more effectively, we need to give you more guidance on what represents an unusually "large" accrual and which accrual categories are measured with low reliability. As a rule of thumb, whenever any individual line item on the balance sheet changes by more than 5 percent of net operating assets, it represents a large accrual and warrants further investigation. Figure 6.2 provides guidelines on the relative reliability of different categories of accruals.

As a general rule, balance sheet items that are financial in nature are measured with a high degree of reliability, while balance sheet items that are operational in nature are measured with a lower degree of reliability. Figure 6.2 therefore begins by classifying all of the standardized balance sheet items in eVal as either operating or financial. This classification mirrors the classification we used in Chapter 5, but with one important exception. Our objective in Chapter 5 was to distinguish between balance sheet items that are used in the firm's operations versus those that are not. Our objective here is to distinguish between balance sheet items that are financial in nature versus those that are not. In Chapter 5, we classified cash and marketable securities as part of operations, because firms typically need cash and marketable securities to facilitate their operations. But for the purpose of evaluating earnings quality, cash and marketable securities are financial assets that can be measured with a high degree of reliability. We therefore classify cash and marketable securities as financial assets. This results in the following modified definition of net operating assets:

Modified Net Operating Assets (NOA*)
    = (Total Assets - Cash and Marketable Securities) – (Total Liabilities - Current Debt - Long-Term Debt).

---

[1] The technique of earnings quality analysis that we describe here is supported by extensive academic evidence. We list the most relevant academic studies as references at the end of this chapter.

| Accrual Category | Associated Balance Sheet Items in *eVal* | Reliability Assessment | Illustrative Examples |
|---|---|---|---|
| Change in Non-Cash Current Operating Assets | Receivables; Inventories; Other Current Assets | Low | Category is dominated by receivables and inventory. Receivables require the estimation of uncollectibles and are a common earnings management tool (e.g., channel stuffing). Inventory accruals entail subjective cost flow assumptions, allocations and write-downs. |
| Change in Current Operating Liabilities | Accounts Payable; Income Taxes Payable; Other Current Liabilities | Medium | Category is dominated by payables, which represent short-term financial obligations of the company that can be measured with a high degree of reliability. But can also include more subjective accruals, such as deferred revenue and warranty liabilities. |
| Change in Non-Current Operating Assets | PP&E; Investments; Intangibles; Other Assets | Low | Category is dominated by PP&E and intangibles. Both PP&E and internally generated intangibles (e.g., capitalized software development costs) involve subjective capitalization decisions. Moreover, PP&E and intangibles involve subjective amortization and write-down decisions. |
| Change in Non-Current Operating Liabilities | Other Liabilities; Deferred Taxes; Minority Interest | Medium | Category includes long-term payables, deferred taxes and postretirement benefit obligations. Best characterized as a mixture of accruals with varying degrees of reliability. |
| Change in Financial Assets and Liabilities | Cash & Marketable Securities; Current Debt; Long-Term Debt | High | Category consists of financial assets and liabilities with reliably determined book values. |

FIGURE 6.2: Accrual Reliability Assessment by Accrual Category

We reiterate that this definition of operating assets differs from the definition used in Chapter 5 only in that it excludes cash and marketable securities. We refer to this measure as $NOA^*$ to distinguish it from the NOA measure developed in Chapter 5.

We next classify the operating items based on whether they are assets versus liabilities. Operating assets are generally measured with less reliability than operating liabilities, because operating liabilities primarily relate to financial obligations that are the result of a contractual commitment (e.g., accounts payable). Thus, we classify operating assets as low reliability and operating liabilities as medium reliability. Finally, it is useful to distinguish between current and noncurrent items. Noncurrent items involve estimates in the more distant future, and hence tend to be less reliable. Figure 6.2 summarizes these reliability assessments and provides illustrative examples.

You should remember that Figure 6.2 summarizes general rules and not absolute truths. There have been some famous accounting scandals involving distortions in the measurement of supposedly high reliability accruals. For example, a well-known accounting scandal at the Italian food company Parmalat involved the overstatement of the cash balance (but it also involved Italian auditors and American bankers). Nevertheless, the vast majority of accounting manipulations involve the overstatement of operating asset accounts. Therefore, the change in operating assets provided a good summary measure of the amount of low reliability accruals that are included in earnings.

This claim is supported by the results of a research study of accounting enforcement actions undertaken by the SEC.[2] The study examines over 100 cases where the SEC alleged that firms had overstated their earnings in violation of GAAP. To examine whether these manipulations were perpetrated through the overstatement of operating assets, the researchers decomposed the return on net operating assets into a cash component and an operating accrual component:

$$RNOA = FCF / NOA^*_{beg} + (NOA^*_{end} - NOA^*_{beg}) / NOA^*_{beg}$$

where

FCF = Free cash flow to all investors,
$NOA^*$ = Modified net operating assets at either the beginning (beg) or end of the period, and
RNOA = Net operating income divided by beginning net operating assets.

---

[2] See Richardson, Sloan, Soliman and Tuna. (2006). The implications of accounting distortions and growth for accruals and profitability. The Accounting Review 81: 713-743.

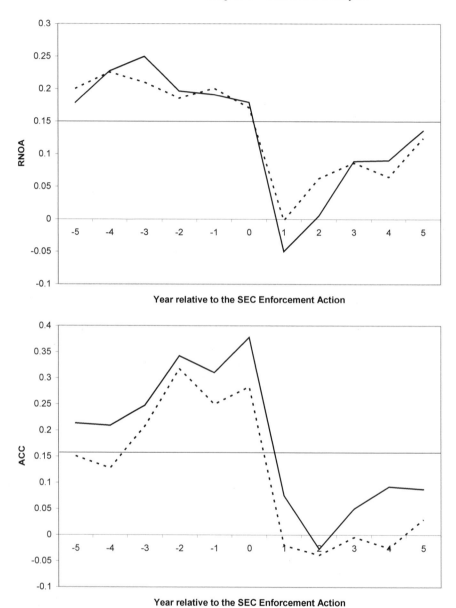

**FIGURE 6.3: Plots of RNOA and the Operating Accrual Component of RNOA (ACC) for Firms Subject to SEC Enforcement Actions.** Year 0 Represents the Year that a Firm was Subject to an SEC Enforcement Action for an Alleged Earnings Overstatement. The solid (dashed) line reflects the mean (median) of the respective variable.

They then tracked the behavior of each of the components around the year of the alleged earnings management. Figure 6.3 summarizes their results. As you can see, RNOA declines slightly in the year of the manipulation and then falls sharply thereafter. The operating accrual component of RNOA, labeled ACC on the figure, increases in the year of the alleged manipulation and then decreases sharply thereafter. The cash component (not shown in Figure 6.3) must therefore decrease in the year of the alleged manipulation and level off thereafter. The clear message emerging from the figure is that accruals and RNOA are temporarily overstated in the year of the alleged manipulation and then reverse in the following years. This is exactly the scenario we labeled as *aggressive accounting* back in Chapter 4. The increase in accruals in the year of the alleged manipulation is a clear signal that accruals are temporarily inflated in that year. This should have tipped smart investors off to the precipitous earnings declines in the following year.[3]

To assist you in identifying accounting distortions and low-quality earnings, you should compute a few different metrics. The analysis begins by calculating the current and non-current portions of the operating accrual component of RNOA, defined as follows:

$$\underbrace{\frac{(NOA^*_{end} - NOA^*_{beg})}{NOA^*_{beg}}}_{\text{Operating Accruals}} = \underbrace{\frac{(COA_{end} - COA_{beg})}{NOA^*_{beg}}}_{\text{Current Operating Accruals}} + \underbrace{\frac{(NCOA_{end} - NCOA_{beg})}{NOA^*_{beg}}}_{\substack{\text{Noncurrent Operating} \\ \text{Accruals}}}$$

where

COA
  = Current Net Operating Assets, defined as Current Assets - Cash and
    Marketable Securities - Current Liabilities + Short-Term Debt, and
NCOA
  = Noncurrent Net Operating Assets, defined as Total Assets - Current Assets
  – Total Liabilities + Current Liabilities + Long-Term Debt.

If any of these components are unusually large, you should identify the balance sheet items that are responsible for the change and look for any evidence that the change is attributable to accounting distortions. What constitutes unusually large in this context? Using data from thousands of firms over the past 50 years,

---

[3] An obvious question to ask at this point is whether stock prices act as if investors understand that high operating accruals signal low earnings quality. Academic research shows that firms with high accruals do tend to have future earnings declines but that investors don't appear to fully anticipate these earnings declines, resulting in predictably low future stock returns. For more details, see the References section at the end of this chapter.

Figure 6.4 reports the cutoffs that would place a firm above the 50th, 75th, and 90th percentiles for each of these measures. At a minimum, you should conduct a detailed investigation of the underlying accruals for any component that comes in above the 90th percentile.

| Accrual Component | 50th percentile | 75th percentile | 90th percentile |
|---|---|---|---|
| Operating Accruals | 0.08 | 0.20 | 0.38 |
| Current Operating Accruals | 0.01 | 0.05 | 0.11 |
| Non-Current Operating Accruals | 0.02 | 0.06 | 0.14 |
| % Sales Growth | 0.09 | 0.21 | 0.39 |
| Growth in NOA turnover | 0.01 | 0.09 | 0.20 |

**FIGURE 6.4: Percentile Cut-Offs for the Historical Distributions of Accrual Components**

When you see an unusually large accrual, a red flag should go up, and you should start searching for an explanation. Other than bad accounting distortions, there are two good explanations. First, recall from the examples we considered in Chapter 4 that legitimate growth in investment will lead to increased net operating assets and hence high accruals. How do we distinguish between legitimate growth in investment and illegitimate accounting distortions? Legitimate growth in investment should be accompanied by legitimate growth in sales. Thus, we should check that the sales growth rate is commensurate with the operating asset growth rate and that the sales themselves are not the product of revenue manipulation. For example, if there is a disproportionate increase in credit sales, we should make sure that the firm is not artificially inflating receivables in order to boost revenues.

The second legitimate explanation for increased accruals is a reduction in net operating asset turnover, whereby more assets are required to produce the same level of sales. An increase in operating asset turnover occurs when more operating assets produce the same level of sales. Examples include a shift to a more capital-intensive production process, offering longer credit terms to customers and insourcing operations that were previously outsourced.

Accounting distortions most often manifest themselves as reductions in operating asset turnover, so distinguishing between legitimate reductions in operating asset turnover and illegitimate accounting distortions can be tough.

Nevertheless, we can offer a couple of good pointers. First, a legitimate reduction in operating asset turnover will usually be the result of an important strategic shift in the way that management conducts business. If you see no evidence of such a shift, then accounting distortions are likely at work. Second, as discussed in Chapter 5, a successful strategic shift to lower operating asset turnover should be accompanied by higher margins. It makes no sense to sacrifice turnover unless the reward is higher margins. Perhaps the most classic signal of an accounting distortion is declining inventory turnover in conjunction with flat or declining margins. This is a strong signal that inventory is overvalued and overdue for a write-down.

In order to help you distinguish between these two alternative explanations for high accruals, you can also decompose operating accruals as follows:

$$\frac{(NOA_{end}^* - NOA_{beg}^*)}{NOA_{beg}^*} =$$

$$\frac{(Sales_{end} - Sales_{beg})}{Sales_{beg}}$$

$$- \frac{\left(\dfrac{Sales_{end}}{NOA_{end}^*} - \dfrac{Sales_{beg}}{NOA_{beg}^*}\right)}{\dfrac{Sales_{beg}}{NOA_{beg}^*}}$$

$$- interaction;$$

that is,

Operating Accruals = Sales Growth - NOA turnover growth – interaction.

This algebraic decomposition and its associated 'interaction' term are pretty nasty, and so we omit them for brevity, but we can assure you that the decomposition holds. It demonstrates that operating accruals increase one-for-one with sales growth and decrease one-for-one with NOA turnover growth. This decomposition serves two purposes. First, accounting distortions are more likely to reside in the NOA turnover growth component than the sales growth component, so a large NOA turnover growth component is an important red flag for accounting distortions. Second, as outlined above, the factors driving legitimate growth in accruals differ across the two components, so pinpointing the appropriate component will guide your search for explanations.

We refer you again to Figure 6.4 for the cutoffs for each of these accrual components. Note that this decomposition involves subtracting NOA Turnover Growth from Sales Growth, so positive (negative) values for NOA Turnover

Growth are listed as negative (positive) amounts. In other words, a positive amount for NOA Turnover Growth indicates that turnover has gone down, causing an increase in accruals.

To see these decompositions in action, let's look at Worldcom Inc. in the years leading up to the discovery of their massive accounting fraud. You may recall that WorldCom seemed to be doing just fine until early in 2002, when the firm announced it had discovered some accounting irregularities. The firm filed for bankruptcy soon thereafter and ultimately wrote down assets by $70 billion (you'll excuse us for rounding to the nearest $10 billion). Most of the write-down amount related to asset impairments. The key accounting manipulations used by the company to prop up its sagging profitability in 2000 and 2001 involved the capitalization of operating costs in PP&E. The amounts incorrectly capitalized were approximately $2 billion in 2000 and $3 billion in 2001. You'll remember that this is exactly the kind of aggressive accounting that we modeled in Chapter 4. Wall Street analysts were caught off guard by these accounting distortions. Let's see if our analysis of earnings quality could have alerted us to their presence. Below is the decomposition of Worldcom's operating accruals in 2000 (see the formulas above).

Operating Accruals = Current Operating Accruals + Noncurrent Operating
                                                                        Accruals
0.161                    =                0.018                +        0.143.

Note that 0.143 of noncurrent operating accruals (as a percent of NOA*) puts Worldcom in the top 90th percentile, as seen in Figure 6.4. Further inspection of WorldCom's financial statements reveals that the high accruals are entirely attributable to an increase in PP&E of approximately 30 percent. So why did PP&E increase by 30 percent in a year when sales increased by only 8.9 percent?

Further, in 2001 the second decomposition shows

Operating Accruals   =   Sales Growth  -  NOA Turnover Growth  -  Interaction
        0.090        =       -0.100     -       (-0.211)        -    0.021.

In 2001 sales declined 10 percent, and the NOA turnover rate declined by 21.1 percent, yet operating accruals increased by 9 percent. Inspection of WorldCom's financial statements indicates that the high accruals are primarily attributable to an increase in PP&E and Intangibles. With hindsight, we know that these unexplained increases in PP&E and Intangibles were attributable to accounting manipulations. The fact that no legitimate explanation was provided for these accruals by WorldCom's management should have provided an early warning sign that WorldCom's earnings quality was suspect. The lesson to be learned for this example is that large operating accruals lacking legitimate explanations are the calling card of accounting distortions (and, yes, the bad pun is intentional).

## 6.7 CONCLUSION

Every so often, a writer in the financial press will get upset about accrual accounting and declare that "cash is king," implying that we should use cash-based measures of financial performance over accrual-based measures. We take a more balanced view. Accrual accounting is designed to measure wealth creation in a more accurate and timely manner than simply recording cash receipts and disbursements. For most companies most of the time, these measures add information. Further, we don't have to choose between cash flows and earnings— we can have both. By using two different systems to examine a company's activities, we learn much more about what really happened in the past, and we generate more informed forecasts of the future.

## 6.8 QUIZZES, CASES, LINKS AND REFERENCES

### Quizzes
• Pandora (Problem 3 (iv))

### Cases
• Analyzing Apple (Question 12)
• Building *eVal* (Part B)
• High Yields at Annaly Capital (Question 8)

### Links
WorldCom's Form 10-Ks are available at :
https://www.sec.gov/edgar/searchedgar/companysearch.html .
Enter the CIK code 0000723527 in the box at the top right. The company was renamed MCI, but this is the one you want. The filing dated 2002-03-13 is the last one before the accounting scandal broke.

### References
• Richardson, S., M. Soliman, R. Sloan, and I. Tuna. (2006). The implications of accounting distortions and growth for accruals and profitability. *The Accounting Review* 81:713-743.

CHAPTER SEVEN

# Structured Forecasting

## 7.1 INTRODUCTION

Forecasting the future financial statements represents the ultimate goal of all the analysis we have discussed thus far. You may go on to be an All-Star analyst on Wall Street, or you may go on to manage your uncle's convenience store, but regardless of where in the business world you work, at some point you will need to forecast the future income, the future assets necessary to produce the forecasted income, and the future mix of debt and equity necessary to fund the assets. In short, while we focus on equity valuation in this text, everyone making investment decisions for a business needs to forecast future financial statements at some time. The next two chapters are aimed at teaching you how to go about this task.

From a theoretical perspective, equity valuation requires forecasts of the future cash distributions to equity holders. From a practical perspective, however, most analysts focus on forecasting net income. We begin this chapter by reconciling these two perspectives. We lay out a forecasting framework that builds forecasts of the complete set of financial statements in a systematic manner. This framework highlights the joint role of income statement and balance sheet forecasts in generating forecasts of cash distributions to equity holders.

We next discuss broad issues that arise in constructing forecasts for the purpose of valuing equity securities. Should we forecast quarterly financial statements or annual statements? How many years into the future do we need to forecast? What are reasonable 'terminal' assumptions for forecasts that are in the distant future? What balance sheet item should we use as the 'plug' that equates assets to liabilities and equity? With these preliminaries covered, Chapter 8 provides more detailed advice about forecasting each of the line items in the financial statements.

## 7.2 A SYSTEMATIC FORECASTING FRAMEWORK

The cash distributions that a firm pays to its equity holders are the result of a complex and interrelated set of operating, investing and financing activities. The only sound way to proceed is to first forecast each of these underlying activities and then aggregate their financial implications into a forecast of the ultimate distributions to equity holders. We do this by building forecasts of both the income statement and the balance sheet. By forecasting both financial statements, we can take important interactions into consideration. A good example of the interplay between balance sheet forecasts and income statement forecasts is forecasted interest expense. Your forecast of interest expense on the income statement clearly depends on the amount of debt you forecast on the balance sheet. But the amount of your debt will also depend on your forecasts of the firm's net operating assets and capital structure. And your forecast of the net operating assets clearly depends on your forecast of sales growth. If we are going to keep track of all these interactions we clearly need to develop a systematic approach to forecasting.

Figure 7.1 illustrates our solution to this forecasting puzzle. The process begins with a forecast of sales. Sales are the primary input to the forecasting process for two reasons. First, recall that the sales transaction is the trigger for the recognition of value creation under GAAP. We forecast operating income by first forecasting sales and then forecasting all of the operating expenses necessary to generate the sales. Second, the sales forecast is our basic statement about how rapidly the firm will grow. This in turn drives our forecasts of the required levels of net operating assets to generate the sales growth and the required amounts of capital to finance the purchase of the operating assets.

This two-pronged forecasting sequence is illustrated in Figure 7.1. On the left side of the figure we move from the sales forecast to the operating expense forecast by making assumptions about operating margins. On the right side of the figure we move from the sales forecast to the net operating asset forecast by making assumptions about asset and liability turnover ratios. And the right side of the figure should pay attention to what the left side is saying! For example, growth in cost of goods sold typically requires growth in inventory. More generally, you should see that the forecasting process is like applying the DuPont ratio analysis in reverse. Instead of starting with the individual line items in the financial statements and then expressing them as ratios, we forecast the ratios directly and then back into what this implies for the individual line items in the forecast financial statements.

Armed with forecasts of operating expenses, and net operating assets (i.e. operating assets less operating liabilities), the next task is to forecast the net financial obligations. Our forecast of net operating assets indicates the total amount of invested capital that is required to support the future business activities. But we still need to forecast the mix of equity and non-equity financing that the firm will use to finance the forecasted level of invested capital. That is, we need to forecast the firm's future leverage. By applying leverage assumptions to the net operating assets, we obtain the required amount of non-equity forms of financing, such as short-term debt, long-term debt, minority interest and preferred stock. At this point, you may be tempted to forecast common equity and thus complete the balance sheet. However, we have run out of degrees of freedom. We have forecast every item on the balance sheet except for common equity. Since the balance sheet must balance, we have already made an implicit forecast for common equity. Common equity is the 'plug' that is found by subtracting the liabilities from the assets. This is an important point and one to which we return later in the chapter.

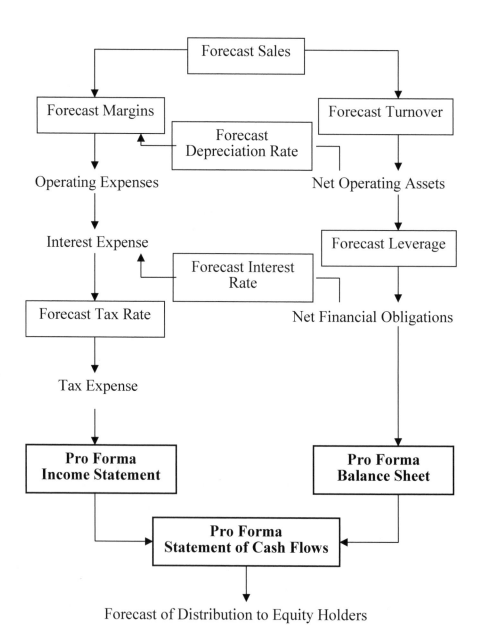

**FIGURE 7.1: A Systematic Forecasting Framework**

We have now forecasted all the line items on the balance sheet. We refer to this forecasted balance sheet as a *pro forma* balance sheet to distinguish it from the actual balance sheets that the firm reported in the past. We still have more work to do on the pro forma income statement. The three items we have omitted are depreciation expense, interest expense and tax expense. We could not forecast depreciation earlier because it clearly depends on the amount of assets on the balance sheet, so we needed to forecast the asset balance first. Similarly, we couldn't forecast interest or taxes, because interest expense clearly depends on the amount of debt financing and tax expense clearly depends on the magnitude of the interest expense tax deduction. We needed the balance sheet forecast of debt before we could construct these income statement forecasts. By applying our forecast of the interest rate to the amount of forecasted debt financing, we generate an interest expense forecast. By deducting our interest expense from our forecast of operating earnings, we generate a forecast of earnings before taxes. Applying a tax rate forecast to earnings before taxes gives our tax expense forecast.

At this point, we are pretty much done forecasting the income statement. You may note that there are still a number of income statement components that we haven't mentioned: items such as gains and losses in other income, extraordinary items and discontinued operations. Typically, by their very nature, these items are non-recurring and difficult to forecast. Therefore, ignoring them (i.e., assuming that they are zero) is often the best that we can do. One final item to consider for your income statement forecasts is preferred dividends. If preferred stock is one of the non-common-equity sources of financing represented on the balance sheet, then there will typically be a stated dividend on this stock that should be incorporated in your income statement forecasts. Recall that we are trying to value the common equity, so we must deduct cash distributions to preferred stock holders in order to derive the net cash distributions to common stock holders. The same holds true for minority interest, it typically comes with "minority interest in earnings" as shown on the income statement.

We now have both our pro forma balance sheet and our pro forma income statement. Armed with these two statements, the preparation of our pro forma statement of cash flows is a mechanical task. You should remember from your introductory accounting class that a statement of cash flows can be prepared using the information in the income statement and the beginning and ending balance sheets, so there is nothing left to forecast (if this is news to you, go back to Chapter 6). And, by referring to the financing section of the statement of cash flows, we can see how our pro forma income statements and balance sheets determine the cash distributions to common equity holders. It is worth emphasizing that we need information from both the pro forma income statement and the pro forma balance sheet to extract our forecasts of distributions to common equity holders. We can see this by recalling the clean surplus relation that we first introduced in Chapter 6:

Cash Distributions to Common Equity = Net Income – Increase in Common Equity.

We get the net income forecast from the pro forma income statement, but this alone isn't sufficient for our valuation model. To solve for cash distributions to common equity holders, we also have to deduct the increase in common equity, which is extracted from the beginning and ending balance sheets. This latter adjustment takes account of additional capital that is required to fund the net operating assets of the business. Wall Street analysts often miss this subtlety, focusing almost exclusively on net income. But the clean surplus relation makes it clear that we should be concerned with both how much income is generated *and* how much additional capital has to be invested to generate this income.

# 7.3 FORECASTING QUARTERLY VERSUS YEARLY FINANCIALS

Exchange-listed firms in the US are required to prepare financial statements on a quarterly basis. However, for the purpose of building financial forecasts for input into a valuation model, quarterly forecasting is overkill. The value of a firm is determined by its results over the next ten or twenty years, not the next few quarters. And in addition to providing unnecessary detail, quarterly forecasting requires careful consideration of seasonal effects in financial data. For example, retailers' sales and profits are usually greatest in the fourth quarter, which covers the end-of-year holiday period. A quarterly forecasting interval requires us to build these seasonal patterns into our forecasts. But given that our value estimate will be determined by many years of forecasts, detailed knowledge of the quarterly numbers has little impact on the final answer. As a consequence, most valuation models, including *eVal*, use an annual interval for building financial statement forecasts. For simplicity, this annual interval typically corresponds with the fiscal year that the company uses for financial reporting purposes.

Despite the use of an annual measurement interval in most valuation models, the quarterly financial statements are still useful. The most recent quarterly financial statements provide the most current information on a firm's performance and financial position. If we are currently in then midst of a firm's fourth fiscal quarter and we are attempting to forecast the income statement for the full fiscal year, then we should obviously use the financial statements from the first three quarters as a starting point. But it is very important to be aware of any seasonal effects in the data before extrapolating financial statement data from earlier quarters to later quarters. There are two useful techniques for incorporating seasonal patterns in income statement forecasting. The first is to sum together the most recent four quarters of financial statements. By doing so, you will be sure that any seasonal patterns are washed out over the full four quarters. The cumulative results for the four most recent fiscal quarters are often referred to as the *trailing twelve months* (TTM) or *last twelve months* (LTM) results. The second technique is to perform *year-over-year* (YOY) comparisons for the most recent quarters. This involves comparing the most recent quarters in the current fiscal year to the corresponding quarters in the previous fiscal year. For example, we compare the third fiscal quarter of the current year to the third fiscal quarter for the previous year. By doing so, we control for any seasonal patterns in the firm's performance. Similar considerations apply to forecasting the balance sheet for the end of the current fiscal year. While the most recent quarterly balance sheet is the timeliest, it may also reflect seasonal patterns in net operating asset balances. For example, most retailers build up inventory during the third fiscal quarter and run it down during the fourth fiscal quarter. If you simply extrapolate the third quarter inventory balances into the future you will overstate the inventory necessary to sustain the annual sales. Year over year comparisons of quarterly inventory changes are the best technique for controlling for such seasonal patterns.

Another role for quarterly financial statements in valuation is in assessing the ongoing performance of the company relative to your forecasting model. You may not want to wait until the end of the year to find out whether or not a company is meeting your forecasts. Indeed, quarterly earnings announcements are one of the most important catalysts for stock price revisions, which serves to confirm that market participants use information in the quarterly financial statements to update their forecasting and valuation models. For this reason, it is very useful to prepare explicit quarterly forecasts through the end of the current fiscal year.

# 7.4 FORECASTING HORIZON

Theoretically speaking, the valuation of an equity security requires us to estimate and discount all the future cash distributions for the infinite future. But, practically speaking, this would require way too many columns on our spreadsheet. Instead, we select a finite horizon over which to prepare explicit forecasts for each year and then we assume that after this point the financial statement line items settle down to a constant growth rate. In this way, we describe an infinite series of future cash distributions without having to explicitly derive an infinite number of pro forma financial statements. Oddly enough, the period at the end of the finite forecasting horizon is known as the "Terminal Period" even though the business itself is not expected to terminate. In later chapters, we will discuss how valuation formulas deal with the infinite series of future cash distributions. What we need to concern ourselves with in this chapter is the selection of an appropriate finite forecasting horizon and appropriate terminal period forecasting assumptions.

The forecasting horizon should begin with the fiscal year that we are currently in and extend out to the point where we can no longer make a better forecast than to simply assume that all the financial statement line items will grow at the same rate as sales. To be more precise, the terminal period should begin when our forecasts meet the following four conditions. First, sales must settle down to a constant growth rate. Second, margins must remain constant. This condition, combined with the constant sales growth rate, ensures that operating expenses on the income statement grow at the same constant rate as sales. Third, turnover ratios must remain constant. This condition, combined with the constant sales growth rate, ensures that the net operating assets on the balance sheet grow at the same constant rate as sales. Fourth, financial leverage ratios must remain constant. This condition, combined with the constant sales growth rate, ensures that the financial obligations on the balance sheet grow at the same constant rate at sales. Together, these four conditions ensure that all the items in the income statement and balance sheet will grow at the same constant rates as sales. As a result, cash distributions to equity holders will also grow at this same constant rate.

It is important to note that we do not expect all of these conditions to literally hold beyond the forecasting horizon. In reality, sales growth rates, margins, turnovers and leverage ratios are all constantly changing and we expect them to continue to change beyond the forecasting horizon. But what is crucial is that we don't expect them to deviate from this constant growth rate in a systematic way. In other words, our forecasts in the terminal period should be unbiased estimates of where we expect these ratios to be in the long run.

How far out do we need to build explicit financial statement forecasts before it is reasonable to assume that things will settle down to this constant long-run equilibrium? It all depends on the nature of the business and the amount of information that is available to build the forecasts. At one extreme, we could be looking at a company in a mature industry with a well-established product, stable demand, a stable production technology and stable input prices. Moreover, assume that the company offered no forward-looking information about expansion plans, there were no discernable industry trends and you generally had every reason to believe that "more of the same" is the best description of the future. In such an extreme case it is reasonable to assume that the sales growth rate, margins, turnovers and leverage ratios will remain constant at their recent levels. In this simple case, the finite forecasting period is non-existent and the first year in the forecast period is the terminal period. We generate the forecasted financial statements by naively extrapolating the past sales growth rate, margins, turnovers and leverage ratios into the infinite future. This process is called 'straight-lining', because if sales growth, margins, turnovers and leverage ratios did all stay constant at their current levels these forecasting assumptions would plot against time as a straight line. Straight lining is the default forecasting assumption built into *eVal*. We make this choice because, in the absence of additional information, it is typically the best that we can do.

In most circumstances, however, straight lining is a very naïve forecasting technique. Instead, we should use what we have learned from our analysis of the past to build more sophisticated forecasts of the future. The length of the forecast horizon depends on how far into the future we can reasonably predict variation in the sales growth rate, and the margins, turnover and leverage ratios before they settle down to their long-run expected steady-state values. Sales growth won't settle to a steady growth rate until industry-wide sales stabilizes and the firm's market share in the industry stabilizes. Thus, firms in start-up industries or firms that are gaining market share from competitors are likely to require longer forecasting horizons. Margins are a function of a firm's competitive advantage in the market place. Because it is very hard to sustain a competitive advantage for a long period of time, our forecast horizon should be long enough to capture the erosion of any competitive advantage, assuming this is what you believe will happen. Second, margins are subject to systematic accounting distortions. For example, a growing company in an R&D intensive industry will tend to have its margins temporarily depressed due to the immediate expensing of R&D. Your forecast horizon needs to be long enough to allow any temporary accounting distortions to play out.

Turnover ratios tend to be fairly stable over time, being dictated primarily by the production technology of the firm. However, rapidly growing firms often enjoy economies of scale that lead to increasing turnover ratios as they grow, so you need to anticipate when these economies will be exhausted. Leverage ratios are typically more stable. A firm's target capital structure generally balances the cost of different types of capital, taking into account the tax benefits of debt and the risk of financial distress. Various factors can cause the actual capital structure to deviate from the target capital structure in the short run, but it is typically quite straightforward for a firm to get back to its target capital structure within a few years.

The above analysis points to two key determinants of the forecast horizon. First, it must be long enough for sales growth to settle down to its steady state level. Second, it must be long enough for any anticipated erosion of any abnormal profits resulting from competitive advantage in the marketplace. In other words, the forecast horizon must be long enough for any abnormal sales growth and abnormal profits to dissipate. For this reason, the forecast horizon is sometimes referred to as the *competitive advantage period*. *eVal* gives you ten years of finite-horizon forecasting columns before the terminal period. You can start the terminal period earlier simply by straight-lining your forecasts earlier. Why no more than ten years? We have found that both students and practicing security analysts are biased toward over-estimating how long firms can sustain their competitive advantage. Typically, when a firm has a new product or new service innovation that enables it to generate abnormally high profits, analysts get excited and extrapolate the abnormally high profits far into the future, not realizing that other firms will be quick to imitate the innovation and compete away the abnormal profits. There are some rare exceptions to this rule, such as Microsoft, Coca Cola and McDonald's, but these are very unusual cases. In these exceptional cases, the firm has usually created a key proprietary asset that gives it some degree of monopoly power. If this is truly the case then it is reasonable to assume that the firm will sustain its abnormal profits indefinitely, and we can incorporate the abnormal profitability into the terminal value computation. We caution, however, that cases of indefinitely sustainable competitive advantage are rare.

# 7.5 TERMINAL PERIOD ASSUMPTIONS

Now that we are finished with the forecast horizon, we are ready to talk about the terminal period forecasting assumptions. Recall from the discussion above that the terminal period is the period in which we expect sales growth, margins, turnover ratios and leverage ratios to settle down to their constant steady state levels. The assumptions that we make about the levels of these variables will drive the terminal value computation and can have a great impact on our overall valuation results. It is therefore important that we choose plausible values for these terminal assumptions. This section provides some guidelines for plausible assumptions or, failing that, describes what assumptions might be considered ridiculous.

The first, most important, terminal value assumption is the terminal sales growth rate. We can offer you some pretty tight guidelines for this one. If a company were to grow faster than the rest of the economy forever, then it would gradually become a larger and larger proportion of the total economy. Past some point, it would basically take over the whole economy, and then the world, and then the universe! It therefore stands to reason that the terminal growth rate cannot be greater than the long-run expected economy-wide growth rate. Conversely, if a company were to grow more slowly than the economy forever, then it would gradually become a smaller and smaller proportion of the whole economy and eventually disappear. If your company produces a product that you think will eventually become obsolete, then such an assumption is reasonable. This is effectively the same as assuming the company is a finite-lived project. The most common terminal assumption is that the company will grow at the long-run expected economy-wide growth rate. This way, the company will maintain its size relative to the overall economy indefinitely.

Historically, the annual growth rate in the US economy, as measured by the nominal GDP growth rate, has averaged around 6%, composed of roughly 4% real growth and 2% price inflation. However, the financial crisis of 2007-2008 sent both real growth and inflation plummeting into negative territory, albeit briefly. As of January 2017 the Congressional Budget Office forecasts 2027 nominal GDP growth of 4 percent, with 2 percent inflation. So, in most cases, a terminal sales growth rate forecast should fall between 3% and 5%. We use 3% as the default terminal value for Sales Growth in *eVal*. If you want to think of the firm as a finite-lived project (or you are evaluating some specific finite-lived project), you can set the terminal growth rate to -100% and this will liquidate the firm (or project) in the terminal year. Finally, for reasons to be discussed in Chapter 9, your terminal Sales Growth assumption cannot exceed your cost of equity capital; if it does, you will get error messages.

Next, we must consider the terminal assumptions for margins, turnover ratios and leverage ratios. Unfortunately, it is not possible to give tight guidelines for each of these assumptions. Recall from Chapter 5 that a company can trade off these performance drivers in an infinite number of ways. For example, more outsourcing will lead to higher turnover and lower margins, while greater product differentiation will lead to lower turnover and higher margins. This makes generalized guidelines impossible. Fortunately, however, we can offer more precise guidelines on the overall combination of assumptions that you choose. As demonstrated in Chapter 5, margin, turnover and leverage combine to give return on equity (ROE). ROE is an accounting measure of the rate of return on investment, and competition tends to force rates of return toward the cost of capital. In fact, if the following two conditions are satisfied, then the terminal ROE should be identical to the cost of equity capital:

1.      the firm is operating in a long-run competitive equilibrium, and
2.      the accounting ROE provides a good measure of the economic rate of return on investment (i.e., no accounting distortions).

Under these conditions, the terminal margin, turnover and leverage assumptions must combine to give an ROE that is equal to the cost of capital.

What are plausible levels for ROE when we relax these assumptions? Let's relax the first assumption and consider a firm that has a source of competitive advantage that is sustainable indefinitely. In this case, the terminal ROE will be greater than the cost of capital. How much greater depends on how much of a competitive advantage the company is able to sustain. Here again, we caution that it is very difficult to sustain competitive advantage indefinitely. Make sure that you have a very good case for such a scenario before incorporating it into your valuation model. Finally, you should remember that a terminal economic rate of return that is more than, say, 10% above the cost of equity capital is rather implausible. Even if competition fails to drive away the abnormal return, the Federal Trade Commission and Department of Justice will prevent the abnormal return from becoming too large (as Microsoft found out).

Now let's relax the assumption that accounting ROE provides a good measure of the economic rate of return. As discussed in Chapter 4, there are many reasons why accounting rates of return can provide distorted measures of the economic rate of return. Even in steady state, these distortions can lead to systematic misstatements in common equity. For example, GAAP requires many investments that generate cash inflows over multiple future periods to be expensed in the period that they are incurred. The most common examples of such expenditures are R&D, marketing and administrative expenditures. Note that while the impact of immediate expensing 'washes out' of the income number in steady state, it still causes book value of common equity to understate invested capital. That is, the numerator of ROE is unbiased in steady state, but the denominator is systematically understated.

In the face of such accounting distortions, the best way to figure out whether your terminal ROE is reasonable is to do a 'pro-forma capitalization' of all expenditures that generate future benefits but are immediately expensed under GAAP. This requires you to identify all such expenditures, determine the period over which they are expected to generate future benefits, and then capitalize and amortize them over this period. Once you have done this, you should check that the resulting 'pro-forma' ROE is within a plausible range of the cost of capital, given any sustainable competitive advantage. An example helps illustrate the importance of making the pro-forma adjustments. Pharmaceutical companies have historically generated ROEs that average about 30%, whereas the cost of capital in this industry has only been in the range of 10-15%. Is this evidence of monopoly profits? Possibly, but first we need to consider that pharmaceutical companies' annual R&D expenditures have averaged around 25% of the book value of common equity. Now let's assume that these R&D expenditures generate benefits evenly over the next 12 years, so at any given point there is an average of 6 years worth of R&D investment missing from common equity. This means we have omitted from common equity a capitalized R&D equal to about 150% of book value (25% per year times an average of 6 years). Hence, if ROE based on as-reported numbers is

$$ROE = \frac{Net\ Income}{Common\ Equity} = 30\%,$$

then pro-forma ROE (ROE') is equal to

$$ROE' = \frac{Net\ Income}{Common\ Equity * (1 + 1.5)} = 12\%$$

which is in line with the cost of equity capital. No monopoly profits here!

## 7.6 THE BALANCE SHEET 'PLUG'

When we build a forecast of a balance sheet that contains 20 line items, we have only 19 degrees of freedom. In other words, since the balance sheet must balance, the forecasts for the first 19 line items determine the forecast for the 20th line item. More generally, regardless of the number of line items on the balance sheet, the forecast of one line item will always have to be set to make sure that the balance sheet balances. We call this line item the balance sheet *plug*. But which line item should we select for the balance sheet plug? The net operating assets are determined by the level and nature of the firm's business activities and should therefore definitely require an explicit forecast, making them unsuitable as a plug. This leaves line items relating to financing activities. These line items are more suitable as a plug, because management can generally adapt them as circumstances require. In other words, management typically decides on their desired level of operating and investing activities and then picks a set of financing activities that provide sufficient capital to fund the operating and investing activities.

While most analysts would agree that the net operating assets should be forecasted directly, there is less agreement on which particular financing line item should be used as a plug. Some analysts use cash as the plug (with a negative cash balance representing a bank overdraft). This has two shortcomings. First, it assumes that management will make no attempt to establish a financing policy that keeps their cash balance at the minimum level necessary to sustain their operating activities. This is a somewhat naïve financing policy. Second, in the case of a bank overdraft, it pre-supposes that management would be able to secure an overdraft. In the case of a financially distressed firm, this may not be a reasonable supposition.

The other common choice is to plug to common equity. The appeal of this choice is that the common stockholders are the residual claimants of the firm and are thus the natural group to soak up any surpluses or deficits in the firm's financing activities. But this approach also has two shortcomings. First, in the case of a financing surplus, plugging to common equity assumes that management will pay a big dividend or make a big stock repurchase. But many managers instead choose to either keep surplus cash or to reinvest it in new projects. Second, in the case of a financing deficit, plugging to common equity assumes that the firm will issue new equity. As with a bank overdraft, this pre-supposes that management would be able to access capital markets on acceptable terms.

There is no perfect answer to this problem. *eVal* plugs to common equity, but we warn you not to plug to equity blindly. You should look at the plug amount and ask yourself whether the implied amount of stock issued or repurchased really represents what you think management will do. If not, then you need to iterate back through the other line items in your forecasting model until you get a complete set of forecasts that you are happy with. For instance, if you really believe that management will build a large cash balance rather than make distributions to investors (like Apple has), then turn up the forecasted cash until the plug to common equity implies no cash distributions to investors.

## 7.7 FORECASTING WITH *eVal*

To illustrate how to build a comprehensive set of financial statement forecasts, we will walk you through the forecasting worksheet in our *eVal* workbook. Open *eVal* and go to the 'Forecasting Assumptions' worksheet as shown in Figure 7.2. Reading across the columns of this worksheet you will see 5 years of historical data on each of the forecasting assumptions lines and 11 years of forecast data in shaded cells. Your job is to fill in these shaded cells.

We will give you lots of detailed advice on filling in the shaded cells in the next chapter; for now we just want you to become familiar with the organization of your forecasting inputs. Reading down the rows of this worksheet you will see each of the forecasting assumptions laid out following the forecasting framework outlined in Figure 7.1. For instance, we begin with the sales growth rate assumption. If you look at the default forecasting assumptions for sales growth, you will see that it makes a smooth progression over the forecast horizon from its value in the most recent historical year to a terminal year rate of 3%. If you change the sales growth forecast for the first year of the forecast period, *eVal* automatically smoothes between this new growth rate and the terminal growth rate. The default *eVal* formula for most line items is similar, smoothing between the value in the first forecast period and value in the terminal forecast period. Therefore, one approach to quickly entering the forecasting assumptions is to forecast the first year and the terminal year and let the formulas smooth out everything in between. Or you can enter the first few years of forecasts and let the formulas smooth from the last year you entered to your terminal year forecast (play with it a bit – you'll soon get the hang of it!). Because the default forecasts for the first forecast year are based on the actual ratios for the most recent historical year, you should be particularly wary of unusual changes in the most recent year – go back and read that MD&A again!

| Fiscal Year End Date | Actual 06-01-31 | Actual 07-01-31 | Actual 08-01-31 | Actual 09-01-31 | Actual 10-01-31 | Forecast 11-01-31 | Forecast 12-01-31 |
|---|---|---|---|---|---|---|---|
| Implied Return on Equity | | 0.192 | 0.185 | 0.138 | 0.136 | 0.145 | 0.161 |
| **Income Statement Assumptions** | | | | | | | |
| Sales Growth | | 16.0% | 6.0% | -0.5% | 4.8% | 5.1% | 5.1% |
| Cost of Goods Sold/Sales | 64.7% | 63.6% | 63.5% | 63.1% | 62.2% | 62.2% | 62.2% |
| R&D/Sales | 0.0% | 0.0% | 0.0% | 0.0% | 0.0% | 0.0% | 0.0% |
| SG&A/Sales | 22.4% | 22.2% | 22.8% | 24.3% | 24.4% | 24.4% | 24.4% |
| Dep&Amort/Avge PP&E and Intang. | | 7.5% | 7.3% | 7.8% | 8.2% | 8.5% | 8.9% |
| Net Interest Expense/Avge Net Debt | | 6.7% | 6.3% | 6.8% | 6.5% | 6.5% | 6.5% |
| Non-Operating Income/Sales | 0.1% | 0.2% | 0.2% | 0.2% | 0.1% | 0.0% | 0.0% |
| Effective Tax Rate | 37.4% | 37.5% | 37.8% | 37.9% | 37.6% | 37.6% | 37.6% |
| Minority Interest/After Tax Income | 0.0% | 0.0% | 0.0% | 0.0% | 0.0% | 0.0% | 0.0% |
| Other Income/Sales | 0.0% | 0.0% | 0.0% | 0.0% | 0.0% | 0.0% | 0.0% |
| Ext. Items & Disc. Ops./Sales | 0.0% | 0.0% | 0.0% | 0.0% | 0.0% | 0.0% | 0.0% |
| Pref. Dividends/Avge Pref. Stock | | 0.0% | 0.0% | 0.0% | 0.0% | 0.0% | 0.0% |
| **Balance Sheet Assumptions** | | | | | | | |
| **Working Capital Assumptions** | | | | | | | |
| Ending Operating Cash/Sales | 2.1% | 4.0% | 4.0% | 4.1% | 13.2% | 4.0% | 4.0% |
| Ending Receivables/Sales | 12.3% | 0.0% | 0.0% | 0.0% | 0.0% | 0.0% | 0.0% |
| Ending Inventories/COGS | 25.8% | 26.2% | 27.3% | 27.1% | 27.4% | 26.8% | 26.8% |
| Ending Other Current Assets/Sales | 0.7% | 1.2% | 1.2% | 1.4% | 1.7% | 1.7% | 1.7% |
| Ending Accounts Payable/COGS | 9.6% | 9.4% | 8.0% | 8.5% | 11.1% | 12.0% | 12.0% |
| Ending Taxes Payable/Sales | 1.2% | 1.5% | 0.8% | 0.6% | 1.1% | 1.1% | 1.1% |
| Ending Other Current Liabs/Sales | 4.8% | 4.7% | 4.8% | 5.0% | 5.8% | 5.8% | 5.8% |
| **Other Operating Asset Assumptions** | | | | | | | |
| Ending Net PP&E/Sales | 33.9% | 34.4% | 39.5% | 42.6% | 40.9% | 40.4% | 40.4% |
| Ending Investments/Sales | 0.0% | 0.0% | 0.0% | 2.0% | 1.9% | 1.7% | 1.5% |
| Ending Intangibles/Sales | 1.7% | 1.5% | 1.3% | 1.3% | 1.2% | 1.1% | 1.0% |
| Ending Other Assets/Sales | 0.9% | 0.4% | 0.6% | 0.7% | 0.8% | 0.8% | 0.8% |
| **Other Operating Liability Assumptions** | | | | | | | |
| Other Liabilities/Sales | 1.4% | 1.5% | 2.3% | 2.5% | 2.8% | 2.8% | 2.8% |
| Deferred Taxes/Sales | 1.6% | 1.6% | 1.6% | 2.0% | 2.2% | 2.2% | 2.2% |
| **Financing Assumptions** | | | | | | | |
| Current Debt/Total Assets | 1.2% | 0.2% | 0.1% | 0.1% | 0.1% | 0.0% | 0.0% |
| Long-Term Debt/Total Assets | 11.4% | 11.5% | 19.4% | 18.1% | 15.6% | 17.3% | 13.3% |
| Minority Interest/Total Assets | 0.0% | 0.0% | 0.0% | 0.0% | 0.0% | 0.0% | 0.0% |
| Preferred Stock/Total Assets | 0.0% | 0.0% | 0.0% | 0.0% | 0.0% | 0.0% | 0.0% |
| Dividend Payout Ratio | 0.0% | 0.0% | 0.0% | 0.0% | 0.0% | 0.0% | 0.0% |

**FIGURE 7.2: Forecasting Assumptions Sheet in the *eVal* workbook**

The remaining income statement assumptions forecast the operating margins. The default assumption for most of the income statement items is to simply straight line their values from the most recent historical year. The exceptions to this rule are 'Other Income/Sales' and 'Extraordinary Items and Discontinued Operations/Sales'. These line items typically contain-non-recurring amounts, so a better default forecasting assumption is that they will be zero in all future periods. Of course, you should always take a close look at the exact nature of the items that have appeared here in the recent past and make your own assessment about the likelihood that they will recur in the future.

The balance sheet assumptions are listed further down the sheet and are presented in four groups. The working capital assumptions are basically forecasts of the turnover ratios, except that we put the balance sheet item in the numerator and divide by the corresponding flow variable (sales or cost of goods sold). This is basically the reciprocal of the turnover ratio. We have found that it is much more intuitive to put the balance sheet item in the numerator when we are trying to forecast the balance sheet item. Note also that we are forecasting the ending balance of the item rather than an average over the period (unlike the turnover ratios in *eVal*'s Ratio Analysis sheet which are based on average balance sheet amounts). While algebraically possible, forecasting the average balance and then backing into the implied ending balance can cause the forecasted ratios to oscillate in very disconcerting ways. Consistent with the way in which we compute turnover ratios, we express inventory and payables as a percentage of cost of goods sold and all of the other working capital accounts as a percentage of sales.

The next two groups of balance sheet forecasting assumptions are the other (noncurrent) operating asset and operating liability assumptions. As with the working capital assumptions, we forecast the ending balance of each of these line items as a percentage of sales. These assumptions fill out the asset side of the balance sheet and the operating portion of the liabilities (i.e. the net operating assets). All that is left on the balance sheet are the financial obligations and equity, which are determined by your financing assumptions. The debt, minority interest and preferred stock assumptions are statements about the firm's leverage, expressed as a proportion of total assets. Having forecasted the assets, the liabilities and the preferred stock, the common equity balance is determined – it is the *plug* that we discussed earlier.

Notice that you are allowed to forecast the dividend payout ratio. You may wonder how the ending balance in common equity can be determined if you are free to forecast any dividend you like. Doesn't a dividend reduce the common equity balance? Technically, yes, but since the common equity balance is used as the balance sheet plug, it is already determined by your other assumptions. *eVal* just adjusts the implied stock issuances or repurchases to exactly offset any dividend that you forecast. That is, your forecasted dividends reduce retained earnings, but *eVal* increases the balance in paid in capital by exactly the same amount so as to leave common equity unaffected. Play with it a bit and you will see what we mean.

*eVal* provides you with a few diagnostics to help judge the plausibility of your forecasting assumptions. First, up at the top of the 'Forecasting Assumptions' worksheet you will find the 'Implied Return on Equity.' Recall from section 7.5 that while it is difficult to provide plausible bounds for each of the individual balance sheet and income statement assumptions, they should all combine to give a return on equity figure that is within a plausible distance from the cost of capital. Second, by clicking on the Ratio Analysis and Cash Flow Analysis tabs, you can see a complete ratio and cash flow analysis implied by your assumptions. Do these forecasted ratios jibe with your views about the firm's future? One particularly important item to look at in the cash flow analysis is 'Net Issuance of Common Stock.' As we discussed earlier, this is the amount computed by *eVal* in order to make your balance sheet balance. A positive amount indicates the amount that will have to be raised through issuance of new stock; a negative amount indicates the amount that will be used to repurchase stock. You should ask yourself if the market conditions are conducive to raising new stock? Does management intend to use excess cash for stock repurchases? If not, then you need to iterate back through your forecasting assumptions until you have a more plausible scenario.

Suppose management told you they expected the balance in PP&E to be $100 million next year. To hit this amount on your forecasted balance sheet might be a bit tough – you would have to keep changing the PP&E/Sales forecast until you hit exactly $100 million on the financial statements. It might be tempting at this point to simply toggle over to the Financial Statements sheet and type in $100 million. While possible, we caution against this approach. By forecasting a balance directly, you overwrite all the checks and balances built into *eVal*. Further, even if you are sufficiently careful to keep your balance sheet balancing, it is very easy to enter individual line items that don't appear unreasonable, but together imply crazy financial statement ratios (see the Tesla Case for an example). As one small check, *eVal* will generate an error message if your balance sheet no longer balances, which is what would happen if all you did was change PP&E to $100 million.

## 7.8 FORECASTING EPS

The forecasts discussed so far are all firm-level forecasts. However, investors in public corporations rarely buy the entire firm. Instead, they buy shares representing fractional interests in the firm. For this reason, it is common practice to express certain key forecasts on a *per-share* basis. Expressing forecasts on a per-share basis allows for direct comparisons with stock prices, which are also expressed on a per-share basis. Not surprisingly, the most common component of the financial statements to be expressed on a per-share basis is earnings. Earnings is the key accounting summary measure of firm performance and so it is useful to know just how much earnings a company is generating per share of outstanding common stock. Earnings-per-share, or EPS, is the most commonly published forecast by security analysts. Moreover, the extent to which reported quarterly EPS differs from the consensus analyst forecast of EPS is probably the single most important determinant of firm-specific movements in stock price.

Given the prevalence of EPS forecasts in practice, it is useful to construct the forecasts of EPS implied by your forecast financial statements. By doing so, you can quickly evaluate whether your forecasts are more optimistic or pessimistic than the forecasts of other analysts following the firm. In theory, the computation of EPS forecasts is quite simple. We simply divide forecast earnings by the forecast weighted-average number of shares outstanding for the period. In practice, however, the forecasting of the weighted average number of shares outstanding is troublesome.

There are two distinct problems. The first is in forecasting the number of shares that will be issued and/or repurchased between now and the end of each future forecasting period. The second is in forecasting the number of common stock equivalents that will be outstanding at the end of future forecasting periods.

The first problem arises because we do not know the future prices at which any stock issuances and repurchases will take place. Our forecasted financial statements tell us how many dollars of common equity we expect to issue or repurchase in each future forecasting period. But in order to compute the associated number of shares, we need to know the prices at which these transactions will take place. This introduces a strange circularity into our computations. Remember that one of the main goals of financial statement forecasting is to figure out the value of a share of stock. But in order to forecast EPS, we first need to forecast the future price of a share of stock. If we already knew the latter, we probably wouldn't be bothered about doing the former! Fortunately, there is a pragmatic and internally consistent solution to this circularity problem. *eVal* simply assumes that your forecasts of the future financial statements of the firm are correct and appropriately incorporated in the firm's stock price. The future stock price is then computed by taking the current intrinsic stock price generated by your forecasted financial statements, compounding it at the cost of equity capital, and subtracting any cash dividends paid. The computations are mundane and automated in *eVal*, so we won't bother with a more detailed description of them here.

The above solution is fine if the current market price of the stock is close to the intrinsic price generated by your forecasting model. But what if the current market price of the stock is very different from the price implied by your model? In this case, either your forecasting model is wrong, or the market price is wrong. If you conclude that the former is the case, then you should go back to the drawing board and build a better forecasting model. If you conclude that the latter is the case, then you have identified a mispriced stock. But before computing EPS forecasts, you need to consider the possibility that the firm could issue or repurchase shares of common stock in the future at a market price that differs from intrinsic value. Firms with mispriced stock can influence their own EPS (and intrinsic share price) by engaging in strategic transactions in their own stock. Firms with overpriced stock can increase EPS (and intrinsic share price) by issuing stock, while firms with underpriced stock can increase EPS (and intrinsic share price) by repurchasing stock. This is a complicated topic, and we will defer a more complete discussion to Chapter 12.

The second problem in computing EPS concerns the fact that analysts and investors most commonly forecast <u>diluted</u> earnings per share. If you are an accounting geek, you will remember that EPS comes in two varieties – basic and diluted. Basic EPS simply involves dividing earnings by a time-weighted average of shares outstanding. Diluted EPS involves dividing earnings by a time-weighted average shares outstanding plus common stock equivalents related to potentially dilutive securities, such as employee stock options and convertible bonds. These potentially dilutive securities represent contingent claims on common equity, and incorporating them helps in figuring out what is likely to be left for the existing common stockholders. Unfortunately, the forecasting of future common stock equivalents is very complicated and difficult to do with much accuracy. We therefore focus on forecasting basic EPS. We can, however, offer you some simple practical advice if you want to forecast diluted EPS. Take a look at the firm's most recent financial statements. The income statement should report both basic and diluted EPS. If these two numbers are very similar, then potentially dilutive securities are probably not that big of a deal, and so ignoring them moving forward is reasonable. If these two numbers differ by, say 5% or more, then common stock equivalents are important and should be considered. A good 'base case' forecasting assumption is that the number of common stock equivalents related to potentially dilutive securities will remain constant in the future. But if you are looking at a firm that plans to restructure its employee stock option plan or refinance its convertible debt, you need to pull out your intermediate accounting text and burn some midnight oil.

## 7.9 CONCLUSION

Forecasting is where the rubber meets the road in equity valuation. A valuation is only as good as the forecasts that support it, and good forecasts only come from a careful synthesis of the findings from your business, accounting and financial analyses. It is important that you forecast the complete financial statements and that you use a systematic forecasting framework that maintains internal consistency in the resulting statements. It is also important that your forecasting assumptions lead to economically plausible statements about the future.

So far we have talked about forecasting from the 30,000-foot level. The next chapter gets down to the nitty-gritty of forecasting the individual line items on the financial statements.

## 7.10 QUIZZES, CASES, LINKS AND REFERENCES

Cases, links and references relating to material in this chapter are presented at the end of Chapter 8 and should be attempted after reading Chapter 8.

CHAPTER EIGHT

# Forecasting Details

## 8.1 INTRODUCTION

The last chapter described our general framework for forecasting a firm's future financial performance. In this chapter we give more specific guidance about how to come up with a reasonable forecast for each specific line item. Obviously, we can't tell you what to forecast in every circumstance; rather, we try to give you a list of things to think about.

As you proceed through the income statement and balance sheet assumptions, you may be plagued by the following two thoughts. The first is that there is always more you could do to develop a better forecast of each item. There is an endless amount of data available – maybe a little more hunting will give you the edge for the particular variable you are trying to forecast. The second doubt is that, even after all your hard work, you still feel uncertain about the resulting forecast. Both of these feelings are legitimate, but there is nothing we can do about them; the world is an uncertain place. We offer you a framework to guide you through the forecasting process and we offer you some guidance about what reasonable forecasts might be, but we don't have the crystal ball that perfectly predicts the future.

This chapter will walk you through the individual income statement and balance sheet forecasting assumptions using the standardized line items from *eVal*. In practice, you should make sure to look at the as-reported line items underlying each of these standardized line items and forecast them accordingly.

## 8.2 FORECASTING SALES GROWTH

If God offers to fill in one row of your spreadsheet, this is the one to ask for. Sales growth, or the lack of it, is a huge driver of value. You should bring everything you can to bear on this forecast. *eVal* shows the firm's past history of sales growth but this is only a starting point. Extreme levels of sales growth mean revert very quickly. Recall from Figure 5.1 that firms in the top quintile of sales growth averaged 55%, but the same firms only averaged 22% sales growth the next year. So just because sales growth has been high in the past doesn't mean that sales growth will be high in the future.

Obviously we can't give you a recipe for forecasting sales that will apply to all companies in all situations. What follows are two basic approaches along with a list of things that your should consider for most companies. One approach is to start by forecasting industry sales growth. With this as a benchmark you can then ask if the firm is likely to increase or decrease its market share. This exercise starts with macroeconomic data and works down to a firm-specific forecast. As we will see, such an approach works well when the firm is a large player in the industry. Alternatively, if the firm's industry is ill defined, or the firm is a very small part of the industry, then it might be better to start at the firm level and only look to other companies for a few key comparisons.

## Forecasting Industry Sales Growth

To build a forecast of industry sales growth, go back to chapter 2 and look over the list of available macroeconomic data. What are the key drivers of sales in your industry? More importantly, what are the key indicators of *future* sales? For example, the aging of the baby boomers is a very predictable phenomenon that has huge implications for the healthcare sector. You could study past trends in personal expenditures on healthcare as a function of the median age of the population. As another example, suppose you are studying a house-building company in the south. The demand for houses is a function of many things, including age demographics, migration patterns across geographic regions and interest rates. Governments around the world collect detailed statistics on all of these variables. You could estimate the relation between these variables and past housing demand in the south and then extrapolate from this model the demand for future housing.

Building a model of industry sales that predicts the future is no easy task. And, even if you find a set of variables that predicts industry sales very well, your particular firm may buck the trend. Nevertheless, we encourage you to spend some time on this task. Even if your work doesn't result in a great predictor of industry sales, the exercise will help you identify the key drivers of sales and this should help to keep your long-term sales forecasts reasonable. Also keep in mind that your goal is to predict future sales, not explain past sales. A macroeconomic variable that moves concurrently with industry sales will make for a beautiful graph, but unless you can generate decent forecasts of the variable, it won't be much help in forecasting future sales. For example, it turns out that the return on the S&P 500 is a great concurrent predictor of demand for cruise vacations; apparently, when the market is up, the "cruising" segment of the population splurges on a great vacation. While this observation makes for a great graph, it is completely useless for predicting future demand for cruise vacations, unless you think you can predict future movements in the S&P 500. And if you can reliably predict future movements in the S&P 500 then you really don't need this book!

Figure 8.1 illustrates how you might think about linking macroeconomic data to industry sales and firm-specific sales. For this to be a useful exercise, you need two key relationships to be very strong. You need the macroeconomic data to be predictable in the future and you need the links between the macroeconomic data, the industry sales, and the firm sales to be strong. If both of these conditions are true then you can build a sales forecast by first predicting the macroeconomic series, then forecasting industry sales from the macro prediction, and then forecasting firm sales from the industry prediction. Demographic trends, for example, are very predictable macroeconomic phenomena. It would be foolish to ignore these trends if your firm's customers come from a particular slice of the demographic pie. In addition, a number of macroeconomic trends are linked to GDP growth. While GDP growth isn't a simple series to predict, economists put so much effort into forecasting it that you can get decent forecasts from the web (check out the Congressional Budget Office or the Conference Board links at the end of the chapter). As an example, personal consumption expenditures on durable goods (e.g., washing machines) tend to grow rapidly as the economy comes out of a recession. If the GDP forecasts indicate a recession is ending, then this is a powerful indicator of a large increase in sales of durable goods in the immediate future. On the other hand, business investment in fixed goods takes much longer to start growing after a recession, so your prediction for an equipment supplier might be much more subdued.

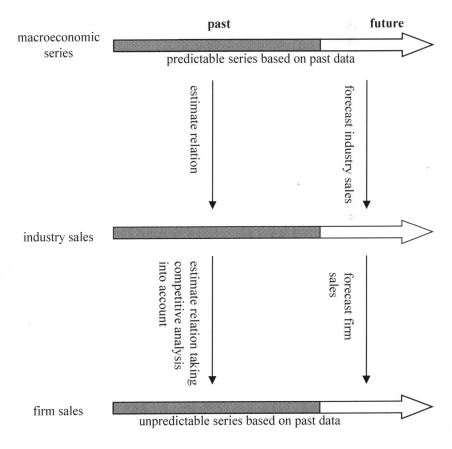

**FIGURE 8.1: Estimating Industry and Firm Sales from Macroeconomic Data**

Once you have a forecast of industry sales growth, the next task is to predict how this will relate to your particular firm's sales growth. At this step you need to consider the intensity of competition from alternative sources for the same products or services. Who are the firm's competitors and how intensely are they competing? The link between industry sales and firm sales is obviously stronger if the firm makes up a significant fraction of the industry. The link is weakest when the firm is small or when the industry is growing rapidly.

As an example, the growth in grocery store sales in the US is remarkably stable, ranging between zero and three in recent years. No matter how much advertising stores put in the local newspapers, people can only eat so much. Grocery store sales would probably mirror population growth perfectly except that grocery stores have expanded their product lines to include pharmacies and home goods. Further, the past decade saw larger grocery store chains swallow up many smaller ones. The result is that Kroger's, the largest grocer in the world, grew sales at an average rate of about 5 percent in the past five years. Over the same period the much smaller chain, Wholefoods, grew considerably faster, averaging 7.5 percent, as Americans discovered 'whole' food. Kroger's, which accounts for more than 16 percent of total grocery sales in the US, can only deviate from the industry rate by so much because it is such a large part of the industry. Wholefoods, at only two percent of the industry, is far less governed by the overall industry growth rate.

The firm-specific facts that we discuss in the next section are typically the main drivers of sales for small and growing firms. In addition, firms with winning strategies may generate unusually large sales growth in the short run by stealing market share from other firms. But in the long run even these companies can't escape the economic forces of the industry.

## Firm-Specific Influences on Sales Growth

There are many useful predictors of future sales that come from the firm itself. One significant indicator of future sales is the firm's current and future investments in operating capacity, especially in new sales locations or new products. Firms make investments to generate future income so, assuming the firm isn't making dud investments, these investments will be harbingers of future sales. As an example, you can divide retail sales growth into growth from opening new stores and growth from increased sales at existing outlets (with the latter known as same-store or comparable-store sales growth). California Pizza Kitchen can grow rapidly by opening up new restaurants all over the country but the very nature of a restaurant puts severe limits on the amount of sales growth that can be generated from the existing locations. Only so many people can squeeze into one booth. Retail companies frequently disclose their plans for new store openings over the next few years and you should use this information to estimate the contribution that new stores will make to total sales growth. You can then combine this with an estimate of the more modest contribution that same-store sales growth will make to arrive at the total sales growth rate.

This same logic extends well beyond forecasting in the retail sales business. Most investments are made to generate a sequence of future sales. When the newly invested capital goes online there is a big burst of new sales, followed by a reasonably steady stream of future sales from that investment. It is therefore useful to distinguish between the large bursts of sales growth that come from newly invested capital and the much lower growth in sales, if any, that comes from the continued operation of the previously-invested capital.

One way to separate the sales growth from new investments from the sales growth on existing investments is to use the following formula:

Sales Growth = (1 + growth rate in new assets)(1 + growth in sales per asset) – 1.

Thus, if you forecast that California Pizza Kitchen will increase their number of outlets by 12 percent, and they will increase their sales per outlet by 3 percent (maybe by increasing prices), then the formula predicts that total sales growth will be $(1 + 0.12)(1 + 0.03) - 1 = 15.4$ percent. Of course, even if the number of outlets increases by 12 percent and the prices go up 3 percent, there are reasons why the formula might not produce an accurate estimate. For instance, what if sales in the first year are unusually high as everyone in town wants to try out the new pizza place, a common occurrence in the restaurant industry. The formula would miss this "honeymoon" effect. Alternatively, what if the new outlets are smaller, or at inferior locations, than the existing outlets? The formula would miss this as well. Nonetheless, it is a useful starting point for a sales forecast whenever there are identifiable and reasonably homogeneous sales-generating units, and you have some source of information about the growth in units and the growth in sales per unit.[1]

You can frequently gain some useful information about sales-generating assets from the segment disclosure footnote in the financial statements. This footnote describes sales, profits and investments by major business units and geographic regions. This information can help focus your attention on the largest sources of sales for the firm and shows you where they are investing for the future. The firm's MD&A (capital resources section) is also a good source of information about the firm's future growth prospects.

Forecasting future sales is very important but very difficult. Take this part of the forecasting task seriously, but also be mindful that some fraction of future sales is inherently unknowable. Floods, pestilence, technological innovation and the inherent fickleness of the consumer all combine to make sale inherently difficult to forecast. Use all of your collected wisdom to make an educated guess, and to put a reasonable bound on your estimate, but then move on.

Finally, we would like to repeat the warning from the previous chapter. Do NOT make the terminal year forecast of sales growth very large; 5% might be a maximum.

---

[1] A model that incorporates these and other complications into a sales forecast is given in Curtis, Lundholm, and McVay. (2014) "Forecasting Sales: A Model and Some Evidence from the Retail Industry." *Contemporary Accounting Research*, 31: 581–608.

Think about what it would mean to forecast a large growth rate into perpetuity; as the company grows faster than the world economy it would slowly but surely take over the entire planet. So unless you mean to forecast this type of world domination, don't use a big sales growth forecast in the terminal period.


# 8.3 EXPENSE FORECASTS

Having completed the sales growth forecasts, now it is time to think about how expenses are going to eat away at those revenues.

Many expenses move directly with sales, such as Cost of Goods Sold and many Selling, General and Administrative Expenses, and so we forecast these expenses as a percentage of sales. However, just because the forecast input is a percentage of sales doesn't mean that you should forecast it as a *constant* percent of sales. Firms may enjoy economies of scale as they grow or they may implement cost management programs; both would lower these expense ratios. In addition, remember that a sales price increase has the same effect as lowering expenses when it comes to forecasting expenses as a percent of sales.

In some cases, the account balances rather than sales levels are the drivers of the income statement items. For example, there is a very strong relation between the Debt on the balance sheet and the Interest Expense on the income statement – the debt balance times the interest rate equals the interest expense. So for interest expense and some other items, the best forecast of the income statement item is based on its relation to a balance sheet item. Finally, when forecasting a firm's expense ratios, it is useful to benchmark your forecasts relative to industry peers and sell-side analysts' forecasts.


## Cost of Goods Sold

The ratio of Cost of Goods Sold (COGS) to Sales describes how much of every sales dollar is spent directly on providing the product or delivering the service. When forecasting this item think about how the firm's products or services are viewed in the product market. Can they charge a price premium over their competitors? Is this premium sustainable in the long run? The effects of competition are first seen in this line item: as a firm is forced to lower its prices in response to competitors' price reductions, this ratio will increase. Are there manufacturing efficiencies to be gained that will lower production costs? As the firm grows, do you anticipate it getting sufficiently large that it can demand lower prices from its suppliers (as Wal-Mart does)? Much of the ratio analysis of profitability that we discussed in Chapter 5 will help you forecast this item. In addition, you may find some guidance for this forecast by reading the firm's MD&A and earnings announcements. Note that the discussion in the MD&A may be pitched in terms of the Gross Profit Margin, defined as

$$Gross\ Profit\ Margin = 1 - \frac{Cost\ of\ Goods\ Sold}{Sales}.$$

Finally, remember that a pure price increase, with no other changes, will increase reduce the COGS/Sales ratio and increase the gross profit margin.

Along with the firm's own past, the COGS/Sales ratio of a few close competitors is a good place to start when forecasting this ratio. If the firm has a low COGS/Sales ratio relative to its peers then you need to think about whether or not it can sustain this advantage. If you are analyzing a young firm with no clear cost structure yet exhibited in the data, then using a more mature firm's COGS/Sales ratio in your forecasts is a good idea. If the firm has exhibited some economies to scale that have caused the COGS/Sales ratio to decline in recent years then ask yourself how much longer you expect this trend to continue. If you believe that economies of scale are a significant factor for your firm, see the discussion of estimating them in the section on Selling, General and Administrative Expenses below.

## Research and Development Expenses

While there is no necessary relation between Research and Development (R&D) Expenses and Sales, many firms budget their R&D expenditures in exactly this way. Be particularly cognizant of the stage in a firm's life cycle when forecasting this item. Start-up firms will invest a much larger fraction of their sales in R&D with the intent of bringing this percentage down over time. Also, there may be a relation between the firm's R&D spending and the price premium implied in your COGS forecast. A firm whose strategy is to continually develop new products and sell them at a premium will have a higher R&D to Sales ratio and a lower COGS to Sales ratio than a firm who copies other firms' products and sells them at a discount. For example, a hallmark of IBM is its research and development activity – it had the largest number of patents granted per year for any firm in the world over 22 year's running (as of 2015). This strategy is reflected in its ratios: IBM's ratio of R&D Expense to Sales has been between five and six percent every year for the past five years, and its gross margin hangs around 47 percent. In contrast, Lenovo Computer invests less than two percent of its revenue in R&D but its gross margin is only 14 percent – clearly a different strategy than at IBM.

Remember the Sales forecast that you made a few moments ago? If your company is engaged in R&D most likely they are doing it to increase Sales in the future. It may not happen in the next period, and it may not happen at all, but increases in R&D spending are often associated with future sales increases as the thing the firm was doing R&D on id developed into a saleable product. After all, that's why they were doing the R&D. In this sense, R&D expenditure is an investment – it is just that the investment is sufficiently uncertain that the conservative nature of accounting means that the entire expenditure is expensed in one period rather than capitalized and amortized over multiple periods. With one notable exception. Software development costs can be capitalized as an asset once the product is "technologically feasible" – whatever that means – so these expenditures will not show up in R&D expense immediately. Given the vagueness of this definition, companies have considerable flexibility when choosing whether to allocate expenditures to R&D, in which case they are expensed immediately, or to software development, in which case they are classified as an asset and then amortized to expense over a number of years.

## Selling, General and Administrative Expenses

Selling, General and Administrative (SG&A) expenses have some components that move directly with sales, such as commissions paid to the sales force, and other components that are only weakly related to sales, such as the CEO's salary. Over short horizons, many costs in this category are almost completely fixed, like rent on facilities, property taxes, or utility bills for the administrative headquarters. The fixed components will give this ratio economies of scale, so it may decline as a percentage of Sales as Sales grow. Working against this effect, however, is the fact that many of these expenditures are highly discretionary. For example, when sales are high the firm may invest in management training programs but when sales are low they may cut back on these types of discretionary expenditures. Examine how this ratio has changed in the past in response to changes in the sales growth rate for evidence of economies of scale. In addition, the MD&A discussion might give you some clues about future movements in this ratio. In particular, cost-cutting initiatives are frequently aimed at this line item.

If you believe there are significant economies of scale in SG&A or any other line item, you may want to quantify the effect more precisely. To do this, start by plotting the percentage change in SG&A on the percentage change in Sales each year and then examine the chart for two patterns. Assuming there is a discernable upward pattern, is the slope significantly less than one? If so, then your company is exhibiting economies of scale in SG&A. Second, does it appear that the slope of the line is flatter when the percentage change in Sales is negative? If so, then SG&A is exhibiting "sticky" costs. It is often harder to cut costs in bad times than it is to increase costs in good times. Consequently, when sales are declining, costs tend to decline more slowly, hence the label "sticky". Both effects are illustrated in Figure 8.2. The figure shows the result of the following estimation:

% change in SG&A
$= \alpha + \beta *$%change in Sales $+ \gamma *$Indicator if Sales declined*%change in Sales + error.

If $\beta = 1$ then there are no economies of scale and costs increase in direct proportion to sales. More commonly $\beta < 1$, meaning that the firm enjoys economies of scale. If $\gamma < 0$ then the slope of the line differs for sales increases and sales decreases, capturing the "sticky" cost phenomenon.

We tend to think of economies of scale as a good thing – when sales increase costs do not increase as rapidly. However, when sales decline the sword cuts the other way – costs do not decline as rapidly. And the "sticky cost" phenomenon shown in Figure 8.2 makes matters even worse. As the figure illustrates, a 10 percent reduction in Sales is estimated to result in only a 3.6% reduction in SG&A. It is this effect that often brings on bankruptcy, as illustrated in the "Tale of Two Movie Theaters" case.

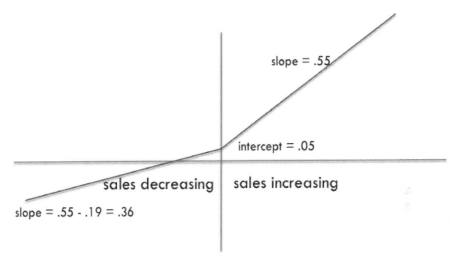

**FIGURE 8.2: Economies of Scale and "Sticky Costs" in the US Economy from 1979-1998 (adapted from Anderson, Banker and Janakiraman (*Journal of Accounting Research* 2003).** Both Scales are in Percentage Changes.

## Depreciation and Amortization

The depreciation and amortization expense forecast is based on the ratio of Depreciation and Amortization Expense from the income statement to Average (Net) Property, Plant and Equipment (PP&E) and Intangibles on the balance sheet. For firms using straight-line depreciation and replacing assets at roughly the same rate as they depreciate them, this ratio is approximately constant and equal to one over *half* the average useful life of the assets. Why half? Because in steady state, the assets are roughly half way through their useful life, so net PP&E is roughly half gross PP&E. But remember that this rule only applies for stable firms. For a growing firm, the ratio is smaller, because the existing assets are less than half way through their useful life, and hence less than half depreciated. But you should make sure that as the firm's growth rate slows, you trend this forecasting assumption to one over *half* the average useful life of the assets.

Another problem that frequently arises when forecasting Depreciation and Amortization is that the line item is not shown on the income statement and so is coded as zero by the standardized data providers. For example, Intel doesn't list depreciation/amortization expense on their income statement and so standardized data may show this ratio as 0%. If you get the actual financial statements you can typically find the depreciation and amortization amounts on the Statement of Cash Flows but this is of only limited value, because you don't know which income statement line item that the company lumped these expenses into. They could be included as part of COGS, as part of SG&A or, most likely, divided between these two line items. If you know which line item contains the depreciation and amortization expense then you can correct the financial statements in *eVal* by moving the balance to the 'depreciation and amortization' line item. Otherwise, all you can do is skip this item and pick it up implicitly in your forecasts of COGS and SG&A.

To forecast the depreciation and amortization expense ratio, you need to think about the type of assets that the firm must deploy to generate sales and how long these assets are expected to last. The footnote that describes the firm's accounting policies typically gives the useful lives of their major types of assets. If the firm primarily uses just one type of asset, then this disclosure is a great guide for your forecast (e.g. if the asset has a ten-year useful life then forecast 20% in steady state) but more commonly all you learn is that buildings have a 20-40 year life, equipment has a 5-10 year life, and computers have a 2-4 year life. In addition, the intangible asset goodwill is not amortized at all. Instead it is treated as an indefinite-lived asset (like land) and each year the accountants ask if it has been "impaired." The consequence of this accounting treatment is that it is very difficult to forecast when the consumption of goodwill will show up as an expense in the financial statements. Practically speaking, all you can do is try and match the forecast impairment of the goodwill to its expected future life.

## Interest Expense

The ratio of Interest Expense to Average Debt is the firm's average interest rate on all of its debt. The past rate at which the firm has borrowed is a good indicator of their future borrowing rate, unless you forecast a large change in either the firm's default risk or macro-level interest rates. You may also want to read the debt footnote and see what rate the firm has borrowed at most recently. As a reminder, we warned you in Chapter 5 to beware of interest income that is netted against the company's interest expense. This will make the past interest expense look extremely low when computed as a percent of average debt. If this is the case, then you should find the amount of interest income and move it into the non-operating income line item on the financial statements. Another complication arises if a firm has convertible debt. Convertible debt carries a lower interest rate because of the value of the conversion option. The easiest method of dealing with this problem is to assume that the firm will issue straight debt in future years at the going market rate of interest (see Chapter 12 for more detail on this issue).

## Non-operating Income

Non-operating Income can include such things as dividends received or interest income on investments, the write-down of assets, and other miscellaneous income. Because this item represents a mix of many things, few of which have obvious drivers, we ask you to forecast it as a percent of sales with the idea that the amounts for these items vary roughly with the firm's size. If the past amounts of non-operating income are significant then you should go back to the actual financial statements, figure out what is in this item, and update your forecast accordingly.

If the non-operating income is interest or dividends from a financial asset you need to think about whether that asset will exist in the future. For example, a firm might have an unusually large cash balance if it has recently raised capital but not yet spent it, and this cash balance will generate some interest income. If you believe that the cash will soon be invested in operating assets, then the interest income will soon disappear. Alternatively, the asset might be an investment in another company that was made for strategic reasons and is not expected to change in the near future. In this case, the dividend income or equity method income is likely to continue in the future, but will bear no relation to the level of company sales. In this case you will want to forecast the non-operating income as a dollar amount and back into what the amount is when expressed as a fraction of sales. The general point is that income rarely falls from the sky, even non-operating income; rather, it takes assets to produce it. Make sure that you know where these assets are on the balance sheet – they may be in Cash and Marketable Securities, they may be in Investments or they may be lumped in with something else – and keep track of the relation between the balance of these assets and your forecast of non-operating income.

Other items that frequently show up as part of non-operating income are asset write-downs, impairment charges and restructuring charges. While all of these charges sound like one-time events, it is actually quite common for companies to record expenses like these year after year. If you see a string of impairment and restructuring expenses in a firm's past financial statements, then it is very likely that they will continue in the future. In effect, the company is moving normal operating charges into this line item. If this is the case, then your forecasts should treat them as recurring expenses. In addition, if you anticipate a significant asset write-down in the future, possibly because you believe the company's accounting is currently too aggressive, then you should work out more precisely how the write-down will affect this ratio.

## Effective Tax Rate

A firm's Effective Tax Rate is the ratio of the Tax Expense to earnings before income taxes (EBT). As a ballpark figure, the statutory federal tax rate for most firms in the US is 35%. (The lowest corporate tax rate among the G7 nations is in Canada at 15%.) To this you add a few percentage points for state and local taxes and possibly deduct a few percentage points for the tax advantages that come from having foreign operations, if your company should be so lucky. The firm's tax footnote contains a great table that explains why the effective tax rate differs from the statutory rate. In accounting language, the items appearing in this table are called "permanent differences" to distinguish them from the "timing differences" that create deferred taxes, as discussed later. You should look through this table with an eye for things that might change in the future. For example, if a company is planning to move its operations from California, with a flat corporate tax rate of 8.84%, to

Wyoming, with no state corporate income tax, it will save 8.84% on its effective tax rate (but it will give up the ocean view).

If the firm is losing money (pretax), then its current effective tax rate may be a very poor indicator of its future tax rate. Suppose, for example, that you are examining a young company that has yet to show a profit. The company's losses create net operating loss carry-forwards, which can be used to reduce taxes in the future if it becomes profitable, but can only be booked as assets in the year of the loss under strict conditions. So our young company will probably have an effective tax rate close to zero. But if you forecast that the company will become profitable, then you need to trend the effective tax rate toward the statutory tax rate. We hate to send you there, but the only place you can learn about all this stuff is in the tax footnote.

## Minority Interest

Minority Interest, also called Non-Controlling Interest, represents the claim on the income of the consolidated firm of the shareholders in subsidiaries. For most firms this is zero because they own 100% of their subsidiaries, so there are no minority shareholders to make a claim, and you can skip to the next item. However, ignoring this line item for firms that actually have a minority interest can lead to big mistakes.

For an example, until recently Verizon owned 55% of Verizon Wireless, while Vodafone owned the 45% minority portion of the joint venture. Consequently, the consolidated Verizon after tax income included 100% of Verizon Wireless, a significant part of Verizon's total reported income. But because they didn't actually own all of Verizon Wireless, they showed the Vodafone claim as a minority interest expense. In *eVal* we ask you to forecast the minority interest amount as a percent of after-tax income. But since the size of the minority interest claim varies with the subsidiaries income and not the parent company's income, there is no necessary reason that this line item will remain constant. It is generally very difficult to get much information about the subsidiaries income, however, so this scaling variable is the best we can do. If the subsidiary's income moves roughly with the parent's income, then this percentage will be fairly constant.

## Other Income

Other income is a bit of a catch-all line item. This item differs from the "Non-Operating Income" because it is after-tax. You might find the after-tax effects of investment gains/losses or equity method investments here. If this item is non-zero then you really need to read the as-reported financial statements to figure out what the company or standardized data providers have put here and whether you believe it will continue in the future. As with non-operating income, we ask you to forecast this as a percent of Sales simply to capture the idea that these items tend to increase with the size of the firm, not because sales is really the driver of these costs. This line item is also a good place to tuck any major adjustments that you might make to the financial statements. For instance, if you want to forecast a large write-off, possibly because you think the company's accounting practices are aggressive, then you can enter the after-tax effect on this line item and keep it nicely separated from the rest of your forecasts.

## Preferred Dividends

The ratio of Preferred Dividends to Average Preferred Stock is quite similar to the ratio of Interest Expense to Debt discussed earlier. This ratio gives the preferred dividend payout percentage, which can usually be found in the financial statement footnotes, or can be inferred from the statement of shareholders' equity. For some firms you may notice that their balance sheet shows preferred stock outstanding yet shows 0% for this ratio in the past data. This occurs because some standardized data providers do not give the preferred stock dividend in their database, so our default entry is zero. If you see an historical balance of preferred stock, then you should get the firm's complete financial statements to look up the historical dividend percentage. Note that the dividend on preferred stock is distinct from the dividend on common stock, which we will discuss shortly.

## Some Final Thoughts about Forecasting the Income Statement

The results of your income statement assumptions are forecasts of the firm's entire sequence of future income statements. For each line item, you should think once again about the transition from the firm's most recent historical performance to its performance in the next few years, through its transition to your terminal year forecasts. As a rough guide, you might think of the near term performance as being driven by firm-specific activities, such as a rapid expansion plan or a cost-cutting initiative, while the long-term performance as being driven by industry-wide and economy-wide forces, such as the GDP growth rate. Do your forecasts paint a reasonable picture of how the firm might evolve? You will undoubtedly feel more confident about your near-term forecasts than your long-term forecasts; this is simply the reality of forecasting in an uncertain world.

You aren't completely done with your income statement assumptions. These assumptions combine with your balance sheet assumptions to generate implied financial ratios and cash flow forecasts, and these forecasts might be implausible. If this is the case, as it often is after just the first pass, then you need to revisit your income statement assumptions and iterate to a plausible and internally consistent set of forecasts.

## 8.4 BALANCE SHEET FORECASTS

The next set of assumptions construct the balance sheet forecasts. They are organized into assumptions about the Net Operating Assets, consisting of working capital, other operating assets and other operating liabilities; and assumptions about Financing. The Net Operating Assets are forecasted as a percent of Sales (or as a percent of COGS) because they are the assets that generate the sales. In contrast, the financial obligations are forecasted as a percent of total assets because they are determined by the capital structure of the firm.

# 8.5 WORKING CAPTIAL FORECASTS

Working Capital requirements are driven largely by the operating cycle of the firm. Consequently, all the forecast assumptions in this section are linked to either Sales or COGS. A firm's past working capital requirements, and your forecasts of its future requirements, are a statement about the firm's operating efficiency. An improvement in operating efficiency means the firm can generate the same level of sales with fewer net assets tied up in working capital.

## Operating Cash

Every firm requires some amount of Operating Cash. A typical amount might be 3% of Sales, but firms vary widely in their actual holdings of cash and cash equivalents. If your firm has traditionally held a large amount of cash relative to its peers, then it probably doesn't need all this cash for daily operations; rather, part of the balance is really an investment in financial assets. As we discussed in Chapter 5, if the past operating cash balance appears larger than you think necessary for operations, you need to get the actual financial statements and make an estimate as to how much of the line item is really operating cash and how much is an investment in financial assets. Once you have an estimate of the amount of true operating cash and the amount of financial assets, you have a few choices about how to proceed. Assuming you think the firm is going to hang onto the financial assets, you can continue to forecast a high ratio of Operating Cash to Sales and then include the interest income from the financial assets in non-operating income. Alternatively, you can reclassify the financial assets into the 'Investments' line item and forecast its balance separately.

A bolder alternative for dealing with excess cash is to effect a pro forma liquidation of it in the first forecast period. For example, assume that a firm has been recently running its cash balance at 10% of sales, but only reasonably requires cash equal to 3% of sales in order to run its operations smoothly. Within your forecasting model, you can simply choose to set the operating cash/sales assumption to 3% for all future years. This will effectively force a large cash distribution to equity holders in the first year of the forecast period, either in the form of a stock repurchase or a cash dividend (the latter requiring you to also change the dividend payout assumption). On the surface this might seem absurd since it is probably unlikely that the firm will distribute the cash next period. But, from a valuation perspective, so long as the firm is generating a competitive return on its excess cash balance, the present value of a future stream of interest income should be equivalent to the liquidation value of the cash, and so either approach should yield a similar valuation. From a pedagogical perspective, liquidating the excess cash immediately has the advantage of getting it out of the picture so that we can focus on forecasting the operating variables. For this reason, the liquidation alternative is a common choice in a traditional discounted cash flow valuation. We nevertheless caution that if the firm is not expected to generate a competitive return on its cash balance, or if it is instead expected to waste the cash buying other assets that yield a poor return (corporate jet anyone?), then the liquidation alternative will overvalue the excess cash balance.

## Receivables

The ratio of Receivables to Sales depends directly on the company's credit policy and its customers' ability to pay. A ratio of 0.25, for instance, means the average receivable was outstanding for one quarter of a year, or about 90 days. This is approximate, because sales and collections fluctuate throughout the year, but you get the idea. Insofar as receivable credit is effectively granting the customer an interest-free loan, this is an important strategic decision the firm makes, and one you should think carefully about when forecasting. If the firm's past values of this ratio are constant then this reflects a consistent collections policy that is unlikely to change in the near future. However, if the ratio is changing significantly or differs drastically from competitors' ratios, then you will need to investigate further. Ask yourself, "What is the firm's relative bargaining power with its customers?" A small firm that supplies a large firm might see a favorable Receivables to Sales ratio disappear quickly when economic times get tight.

A good example of this phenomenon is the "Can Salton Swing?" case. Salton used to be the sole maker of the famous George Foreman Grill ("it's a lean, mean grilling' machine!"). They sold the bulk of their grills to a few large retail chains, like K-Mart and Wal-Mart, who are not generally known for the generous terms they provide their suppliers. Indeed, as the George Foreman Grill became a small appliance hit between 1998 and 2001, Salton saw the average time it took to collect its receivables go from 41 days to 73 days and its inventory holding period go from 113 days to 143 days as these big customers slowly put on the squeeze.

## Inventories

The ratio of Inventories to COGS is very similar to the receivables ratio, except that both the numerator and the denominator are computed using historical costs rather than selling prices. The other principle difference is that the company can acquire inventories without selling them, which would increase the numerator without the commensurate increase in the denominator. For that reason an increasing Inventory to COGS ratio is traditionally considered to be a warning sign that the company is having trouble selling its goods. Of course, the common retort is that they are stocking up for a new product release that will send sales skyrocketing. When forecasting this ratio think about why it might differ from its historical past. Do you anticipate the company implementing a 'just-in-time' inventory handling system and thus lowering the required amount of inventory? Alternatively, do you anticipate that the firm's customers or suppliers have so much bargaining power that they will force the firm to hold the inventory for increasingly long periods? Was there some unusual event in the most recent fiscal year that caused the ratio to differ significantly from its normal level?

As discussed in Chapter 4, a firm attempting to manipulate its income upward may delay the recognition of expenses by failing to write off obsolete inventory.

Effectively they hold this expense in inventory for too long, with the result that the inventory turnover ratio falls. Later, when they write off the inventory, the ratio instantly improves. If you see evidence of this behavior in the inventory turnover ratio, you might want to investigate the firm's inventory accounting a bit further.

## Other Current Assets
Other Current Assets include tax refunds, prepaid expenses and other miscellaneous items. We ask you to forecast this item as a percent of sales because it tends to increase with the size of the firm, so this ratio should be fairly stable. However, if this is a large amount, you really need to look at the as-reported financial statements and see what is included in this line item and decide if it does indeed move with sales.

## Accounts Payable
The ratio of Accounts Payable to COGS is the mirror image of the Receivables ratio for the firm's suppliers (with respect to their accounts with the company). It reveals how quickly the firm is paying for the inventory it purchased and sold. Since this is an interest-free loan to the firm, the higher this ratio, the more free credit the company is receiving. You may forecast that the ratio will increase if you believe that the firm has sufficient power over its suppliers that it can delay paying its bills. When times get tight in the automotive industry, for example, the Big 3 automakers don't renegotiate the contract terms with their suppliers – they simply delay paying their suppliers for long periods.

## Taxes Payable and Other Current Liabilities
Taxes Payable frequently shows up as a current liability simply because the firm owes taxes as of the end of the fiscal quarter but they don't have to pay them until a later date. Other Current Liabilities includes dividends declared but not yet paid, customer deposits, unearned revenue and other miscellaneous obligations that will be met within a year. We ask you to forecast these items as a percent of sales because they tend to increase with the size of the firm, so this ratio should be fairly stable. But, as with Other Current Assets, if the amounts in these categories are significant, you should read the financial statements to see precisely what they are and decide if you think the past ratios are good predictors of the future.

# 8.6 OTHER OPERATING ASSETS AND LIABILITIES FORECASTS
The key issue for this set of assumptions is determining the size of the firm's future investment in long-lived assets necessary to produce the forecasted sales. Consequently, these items are forecasted as a percent of sales. Your forecasts of these ratios are a statement about the firm's expected production technology. If the firm out-sources much of its production, its investment in assets will be significantly smaller than the investment that is necessary for a more vertically integrated

operation. Of course, since outsourcing captures a smaller portion of the value chain, the firm should earn correspondingly smaller margins.

## PP&E

To forecast the ratio of PP&E to Sales you should consider the firm's existing capacity relative to your forecast of sales growth. Firms tend to add capacity in large lumps, so as you analyze the firm's past ratio of PP&E to Sales, be aware of whether the past ratio amounts were generated by assets operating at full or partial capacity. A good source of information for forecasting this item is the discussion of liquidity and capital resources in the MD&A; in fact, firms often give estimates of future capital expenditures here. And capital-intensive industries, such as steel or auto-making or airlines, often give capacity utilization statistics included in their Selected Data Schedule (Item 6 on Form 10-K). Finally, you can get industry-level statistics on growth rates in investments in different classes of assets from the Bureau of Economic Analysis Fixed Asset tables.

It is common for PP&E to rise rapidly during a company's early years and then remain relatively constant thereafter. But note that this pattern does not imply that the *ratio of PP&E to Sales* will rise and then flatten out. If the company's sales are also rising rapidly in the early years, this ratio could remain constant throughout the growth and maturity phases of a firm's life cycle. What you really need to think about is whether there are significant economies to scale that the firm will enjoy as it grows. As California Pizza Kitchen expands across the country its investment in PP&E will necessarily grow at the same rate as sales because there are very few scale economies in a restaurant chain (i.e. having a restaurant in Nebraska has little effect on the investment required to open a restaurant in Oregon). Alternatively, after Iridium put the necessary satellites in place for its global phone system, sales grew significantly without significant additional investment in PP&E.

Suppose you are lucky enough to have the firm tell you their planned future capital expenditures (and you believe them). Given the beginning balance of PP&E, your forecasted amount of depreciation, and the company's estimate of its capital expenditures, the ending PP&E amount is determined (equivalently, your forecast of ending PP&E determines capital expenditures).

## Investments

Investments are primarily made up of equity holdings by the firm in other companies. If this amount is significant for your company, then read the financial statements and figure out exactly what this investment represents. We default to forecasting this item as a percent of sales, but there is often no structural reason for the size of the investment to be related to sales. Consider two examples. About 20 percent of Coca Cola's total assets in 2016 are investments in other companies, primarily bottlers of Coke. We would expect that the scale of the bottling companies will rise and fall with sales of Coke, so forecasting as a percent of consolidated sales is probably a good idea. In contrast, Apple Computer holds over $170 billion in long-term marketable securities at the end of fiscal 2016, which is about half of their total assets. These investments do not play a role in supporting Apple's sales and so their ratio to sales could vary substantially over time.

## Intangibles

Intangibles are all those assets that can't be physically touched. To be recognized in the accounting system, the intangible must usually have been acquired in an arms-length transaction by the firm. So *purchased* patents, copyrights, licenses and trademarks would be included, but *internally developed* versions of the same things are not. What you really need to forecast is *purchased* intangibles but, unfortunately, companies that purchase lots of intangible assets generally develop lots of them internally as well. To make matters worse, the biggest purchased intangible is "goodwill," defined to be the excess of the purchase price in a corporate acquisition over the fair market value of the identifiable assets (tangible and intangible) received. Because it is only created by an acquisition, goodwill tends to arrive in large and unpredictable lumps. Goodwill, plus the rather arbitrary distinction between purchased and internally developed intangible assets, makes forecasting intangibles very difficult. As with investments, there is no particular reason why this item should remain a constant percent of sales; we use this ratio only because larger firms tend to have more intangibles than smaller firms.

Intangible assets indefinite lives, like goodwill, are not amortized. Rather, the firm performs periodic impairment tests to see if the fair value is less than the book value. How the firm decides when an intangible has become impaired is rather arbitrary. Basically, if the future cash flows related to the intangible look bleak, then an expense is recorded to write the asset down. These large expenses often get recorded only after everyone knows something bad has happened. For example, Quaker Oats bought Snapple at the end of 1994 for approximately $1.7 billion, and so "Snapple" remained on the Quaker Oats books for $1.7 billion at the end of 1996. Although management repeatedly mentioned the poor performance of the Snapple brand in the 1996 10-K filing, they concluded that they did not believe a write-down was necessary at that time. Nonetheless, in 1997 they recorded a $1.4 billion loss when the Snapple brand was sold for a mere $300 million.

## Other Assets and Other Liabilities

Other Assets includes many items; some examples are long-term receivables, pre-opening expenses for retail stores and pension assets. Other Liabilities include pension liabilities and other miscellaneous non-current liabilities. See the financial statement footnotes for specifics if your firm has a significant amount for these items.

## Deferred Taxes

To forecast deferred taxes you need to think about the firm's tax "timing differences." You may have noticed that when we forecasted the firm's effective tax rate, we considered "permanent differences" that caused the rate to differ from the federal statutory rate of 35%, but did not take into consideration the timing of the tax payments. Timing differences arise because the taxing authority's rules for income recognition differ from the financial accounting rules. For example, a firm might have accelerated tax deductions because of an investment in a certain type of asset. In this case, not only does the firm get to deduct the cost of the investment, but they also get to deduct most of it in the first few years of the asset's useful life. Accountants capture the net effect of these timing differences in the balance of deferred taxes, so named because accelerated deductions today mean higher taxes tomorrow when the deductions run out. The firm's specific deferred tax items are described in the footnotes to the financial statements. The principle source for deferred tax liabilities is usually the timing difference between depreciation on PP&E and the tax deductions for these investments. Early in the life of an asset this will result in deferred tax liabilities (representing the future increase in tax payments when the accelerated tax deductions for the PP&E are exhausted); later this effect will reverse and the liability will shrink back to zero. But as long as the firm is replacing its assets, this liability will remain. If the firm maintains its assets at a fixed level then the deferred taxes will remain a constant percentage of total assets; the ratio will increase slightly if the asset base is growing. But if you forecast that the firm will stop adding to its capital base, this ratio will fall dramatically. This is because, without new acquisitions of assets, new tax deductions are not generated, causing tax payments to increase and the liability to fall.

## Some Final Thoughts about Forecasting the Net Operating Assets

The key statistic coming out of the working capital, other asset and other liability assumptions is the Net Operating Asset Turnover ratio (defined as Sales over Net Operating Assets). This statistic summarizes your forecasts of the net operating assets that a firm will need to put in place in order to create the sales that you forecasted. Because a firm's asset turnover is largely determined by its production technology, this ratio does not usually change radically over short periods. Therefore, if your forecasts show this ratio changing dramatically, go back and make sure that you have good reasons for the specific forecasts you have made.

# 8.7 FINANCING FORECASTS

The main consideration for this set of assumptions is the firm's long-term capital structure. What is the mix of debt and equity that the firm will employ to support the level of net operating assets you have forecasted? The optimal capital structure for a firm takes into account the risk that debt financing brings with it, as well its tax advantages. Volumes have been written in corporate finance textbooks about optimal capital structure. When forecasting this item you should examine the firm's capital structure in the recent past, and the capital structure of other firms in the same industry. In the liquidity section of the MD&A, firms will sometimes discuss their target capital structure; if so, you should consider this in your forecasts. Each of the items in this section is forecasted as a percent of Total Assets.

## Current Debt and Long Term Debt

Current Debt is short-term borrowing plus the current portion of long-term debt that is due within a year. Long-term Debt, combined with the current debt above, is the firm's total debt financing. These liabilities, unlike the other non-current liabilities above, are represented by contractual interest-bearing claims to debt capital providers. As such, they are financing liabilities rather than operating liabilities. Details of a firm's debt contracts are given in the footnotes to the financial statements. Particularly noteworthy is the discussion of short-term borrowing, the allocation of total debt to current and non-current portions, and the schedule of future maturities of existing debt.

## Minority Interest

Minority Interest represents the claim of shareholders in a firm's partially owned subsidiaries. There is no immediate reason why this amount should remain a constant percentage of Total Assets other than larger firms tend to have larger minority interests, if they have them at all. You could make a more informed estimate of this amount if you knew that the firm intended to acquire a less-than-100% interest in another company, or if you knew the firm would not be making any more acquisitions of less than 100%. But, in all honestly, it is hard enough to forecast a firm's future acquisition activity without having to also estimate the percentage of ownership they will acquire when they acquire less than 100%.

## Preferred Stock

Preferred Stock is more like long-term debt than equity when it comes to forecasting the value of the firm's common equity. Details of the preferred stock holdings can be found in the financial statement footnotes. You may want to forecast that this item remains a constant dollar value, rather than a constant percentage of total assets, unless the firm specifically says that it intends to continue issuing preferred stock.

## Some Final Thoughts on Forecasting the Financing Ratios

The end result of this set of forecasts will be a leverage ratio, defined either as invested capital to equity or debt to equity. Like the net operating asset turnover ratio, these ratios tend to be very stable for a firm over time, probably because the optimal capital structure of a firm is driven by fairly stable economic factors. Do not fall into the trap of believing (and forecasting) that a firm will increase its return on equity simply by borrowing to increase its leverage. Remember that more debt begets more interest expense; increasing leverage only increases ROE if the return the firm earns on the new capital exceeds the after tax cost of debt. Note that the Forecasting Assumptions sheet in *eVal* automatically takes this into account – you forecast the interest rate in the income statement assumptions and this amount is applied to the forecasted debt balance.

You have now constructed the forecasted balance sheets for your company. The turnover ratio assumptions determine the net operating assets and the financing assumptions determine the financial obligations. The common equity is therefore determined: common equity = net operating assets less financial obligations.

## Dividend Payout Ratio

The Dividend Payout Ratio shown historically is the percent of net income that is paid out as cash dividends. But note that your preceding forecasts completely determine future net income and future total common equity. Hence, your forecasting assumptions already imply the net amount of new common equity that will be issued or distributed (through a dividend or stock repurchase). The dividend payout ratio assumption determines what retained earnings will be, but with a compensating adjustment to paid in common capital (net) that sets common equity to the level implied by your previous forecasting assumptions. That is, since the future equity balances are already determined, this assumption can only change the composition of the equity. Nonetheless, it is a useful item to forecast, because later, when performing a cash flow analysis, you will be asked to think about the reasonableness of the firm's implied stock issuance activity, and the more they pay out in dividends the more they need to issue in new equity to finance future growth.

# 8.8 PRO FORMA ANALYSIS OF FORECASTS

Wait! You aren't done yet! Once you complete your fast pass at your forecasting assumptions, you should do some ratio and cash flow analysis on these future financial statements to see how reasonable they really are. Use the procedures discussed in chapters 5 and 6 to determine what your forecasts imply for the future ratios and cash flows? Is this what you meant to forecast? Are the implied ROEs and margins consistent with industry norms? If the turnover or leverage ratios are changing significantly, make sure that this is what you really mean, because typically these ratios are relatively stable over time.

# 8.9 QUIZZES, CASES, LINKS AND REFERENCES

## Quizzes
• Chipotle Mexican Grill (Problem 4)
• Pandora (Problem 4)
• LinkedIn (Problem 4)
• Salesforce (Problem 4)

## Cases
• Analyzing Apple (Question 13)
• The Home Depot, Inc.

- Royal Caribbean Cruises in 2010
- Netflix, Inc. (Questions 10-12)
- Overstock.com (Questions 11-14)
- Sirius Satellite Radio (Questions 15-18)
- Building *eVal* (Part D)
- The Eighty Minute Forecast
- Has Zynga Lost Its Zing? (Question 12)
- Is Tesla's Stock Price in Ludicrous Mode? (Questions 11-13)

## Links

Congressional Budget Office: http://www.cbo.gov/
Conference Board: https://www.conference-board.org/data/
Bureau of Economic Analysis: http://www.bea.gov/

## References

Anderson, Banker, and Janakiraman. 2003. "Are Selling, General and Administrative Costs 'Sticky'?" *Journal of Accounting Research*, 41: 47-63.
Curtis, Lundholm, and McVay. 2014. "Forecasting Sales: A Model and Some Evidence from the Retail Industry." *Contemporary Accounting Research*, 31: 581–608.

CHAPTER NINE

# The Cost of Capital

## 9.1 INTRODUCTION

The forecasted financial statements describe an infinite series of future cash distribution. In order to combine all these distributions into a single estimate of present value, we need a discount rate, commonly referred to as the firm's *cost of capital*. This chapter explains what it is we are trying to estimate with the cost of capital and it gives some advice on how to go about making the estimate. But we should be truthful at the outset: there are no good answers to these questions. None of the standard finance models provide estimates that describe the actual data very well. The discount rate that you use in your valuation has a large impact on the result, yet you will rarely feel very confident that the rate you have assumed is the right one. The best we can hope for is a good understanding of what the cost of capital represents and some ballpark range for what a reasonable estimate might be.

This chapter is closely linked to the next chapter on valuation models. You can probably read either one first: your choices are to read about the discount rate used in the valuation models without yet fully understanding the models, or you can read about the models without yet fully understanding the discount rate, one of the most important inputs for the models. Computing the value of the equity only requires one valuation input: the cost of equity capital. However, if you use one of the valuation models that computes the value to all capital providers, then you will also require estimates of the cost of capital for all other non-controlling interests, such as debt capital, preferred stock and minority interests, and then weight these pieces correctly to derive a weighted average cost of capital. We begin with the cost of equity capital because it is a necessary input to any equity valuation model.

## 9.2 COST OF EQUITY CAPITAL

At its most basic level, the cost of equity capital is the expected rate of return that equity investors could earn on their next best alternative investment with an equivalent level of risk (i.e., the opportunity cost of the equity capital). The "equivalent risk" portion of this statement is where the problem lies. What is the correct measure of risk? Risk has something to do with investors' distaste for the uncertainty in future payoffs, but how should we quantify this distaste? Should we quantify risk only by reference to the volatility of the company's underlying cash flows, or should we rely on stock price volatility to infer risk? Should our measure of risk take into consideration the fact that we may or may not hold a diversified portfolio of equity securities? How we estimate the cost of equity capital—the expected return on an investment with "equivalent risk"—depends on the answers to these and other questions.

## What Is Risk?

The discount rate that we use in our valuation model serves two purposes. It must account for the time value of money and it must account for the riskiness of the investment. The time value of money, absent any risk, is a straightforward concept. It is why bank's pay interest on savings accounts and charge interest on even relatively risk-free loans. If risk was not an issue, we could use the risk-free interest rate; say the yield on a 10-year U.S. Treasury bond, as our cost of equity capital. Unfortunately, risk is very much an issue.

The forecasted financial statements are your best estimates of how the future will unfold for the company, but it is certainly possible that the actual outcomes could be better or worse. And, even if reality plays out exactly as you forecasted, the market may still not value the firm as you think it should. In short, the payoff to investing in any equity is uncertain. Further, investors generally dislike uncertainty. (What would you rather have: $1 million for sure or a 50/50 gamble between $0 and $2 million?) A fundamental measure of risk would quantify the amount of uncertainty and the investors' distaste for different levels of uncertainty, and then combine these measures in a model of investor decision-making. But, while developing a fundamental measure of risk works great on paper, in practice it is very difficult to quantify an investment's level of uncertainty and extremely difficult to quantify investors' distaste for it. Consequently, the standard approach sidesteps the issue by looking at how the market has historically compensated investors for bearing risk. We don't attempt to measure the fundamental risk directly; rather, we measure the compensation that was offered in exchange for bearing it.

Because investors dislike uncertainty, they will only hold a risky security if they are compensated for doing so. Higher-risk investments must offer higher expected returns. We measure risk as the additional expected return beyond the risk-free rate that the security offers. The idea is simply that the risk-free rate captures the time value of money, so everything else in the expected return must be compensation for risk. To measure the expected return for different levels of risk, we identify different *risk classes* or *risk factors* and then compute the average past-realized returns for firms in each class. The amount by which the average return in a risk class exceeds the risk-free rate is the *risk premium* for firms in that risk class. The trick, then, is to identify risk classes that group together firms with similar fundamental risk, even though we are punting on actually measuring the fundamental risk itself.

One issue that plays a big part in any discussion of risk is the idea of diversification. A particular equity investment may feel very risky because your estimates of the firm's future cash flows seem quite uncertain, but if the company is only one investment in a large portfolio, then even though its individual payoffs may seem risky, this risk could be diversified away in the portfolio. Consider, for instance, a small hardware store chain in Wisconsin whose cash flows are particularly susceptible to the local Wisconsin economy. Now imagine that you hold this investment in a portfolio of stocks that include hardware stores in many other states; when one state's economy is down, another state's economy may be up, so that the average of all the investments is less volatile than any one investment. Diversification lowers risk. Before you conclude that a particular company has uncertain cash flows and is therefore very risky, think about the source of the uncertainty. If the source can be diversified away in a portfolio, then the market is probably not willing to compensate investors for bearing the risk.

As a practical answer to the question "what is risk?" we offer the most famous model in the world of finance: the capital asset pricing model (CAPM).

## Capital Asset Pricing Model

Our formal pass at quantifying risk is derived from the *capital asset pricing model* (CAPM). Without diving into a semester-long class on the subject, the CAPM says that a firm's expected stock return is given as

$r_e = r_f + \beta (r_m - r_f)$, where

$r_e$ is the expected stock return for the firm; equivalently, it is the firm's cost of equity capital,
$r_f$ is the risk free rate of return,
$r_m$ is the expected return for the whole market, and
$\beta$ is "beta," the firm's sensitivity to the market's return.

One implication of the CAPM is that every investor holds a mix of the risk-free bond, which returns $r_f$, and the entire market portfolio, which is uncertain but returns $r_m$ in expectation. The only source of risk that cannot be diversified away in the market portfolio is variation in the market return and, consequently, the only thing that determines an equity security's contribution to risk is $\beta$, the sensitivity of the security's return to the market return. Firms with high $\beta$s are more risky than firms with low $\beta$s and firms with the same $\beta$ are equally risky. Putting it all together, the firm's cost of equity capital $r_e$ is the sum of compensation for the time-value of money $r_f$ and compensation for bearing risk, where the amount of risk a firm engenders is captured by $\beta$, and the amount of compensation the market is expected to deliver per unit of risk over and above the risk-free rate is $(r_m - r_f)$. This last amount is referred to as the equity market risk premium.

To use the CAPM, you need an estimate of the risk-free rate, an estimate of the equity market risk premium, and a firm-specific estimate of beta. The risk-free rate, measured by the yield on the 10-year U.S. Treasury Bond, has ranged between 1% and 3% since the financial crisis of 2008, but has been over 10% at times, as seen in Figure 9.1. To get the latest yield on 10-year Treasury Bond, go to Yahoo! Finance and search for the ticker '^TNX'.

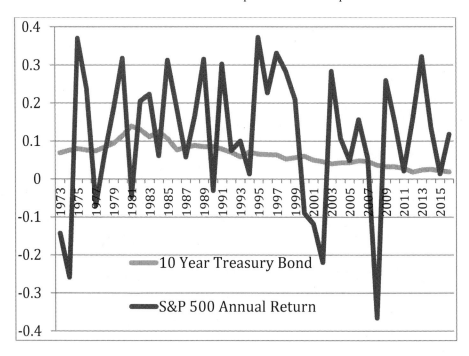

**FIGURE 9.1: Historical Stock Market Returns and Treasury Bond Yields**

The expected equity market risk premium $(r_m - r_f)$ is much more difficult to estimate. This is the amount investors expect to earn as compensation for bearing the risk of owning the market portfolio. The average of the difference between the S&P 500 return and the annual yield on the 10-year Treasury bond between 1973 and 2016 is 5.01%. But, as seen in Figure 9.1, while the risk-free rate changes very little over time, the realized returns on the S&P 500 have fluctuated wildly, ranging from 37% in 1995 to -37% in 2008, with a standard deviation of 17.4 percent. If we use the entire US stock market (rather than just the S&P 500), and set the time period to be 1929 to 2001, we get an average risk premium of 6.7%. If we average over 16 countries with historical stock return data from 1900 – 2001, we get a 5.4% average risk premium with a standard deviation of 14.6% (Dimson, Marsh and Staunton 2000). None of this should make you feel very confident about your estimate of the expected risk premium.

Estimating the firm-specific beta, $\beta$, is also fraught with difficulty. It is typically estimated by regressing the realized $r_e$ on the realized $r_m$ for the past five years of monthly returns. What we are shooting for is a measure of how closely the firm's equity price moves with the broader market. Since the market movement is the only source of risk that is priced in the CAPM, a firm with greater sensitivity to the market is a riskier investment. As a benchmark, a firm that perfectly tracked the market would have a $\beta$ of one; a $\beta$ of 0.5 would be very low and a $\beta$ of 1.5 would be very high, by historical standards. The trouble with estimates of firm-specific beta is that they change drastically over time for no apparent reason. For example, IBM's beta estimate was 1.5 in 1966 and 0.85 in 1969; it was 0.51 in 1995 and 1.2 in 1998. Surely IBM's fundamental risk didn't change this much during these two three-year periods. Because of this instability, it is not uncommon to use the average beta in the firm's industry rather than the firm-specific estimate. Figure 9.2 gives the average beta by industry for 100 industries, computed over the past five years of monthly data (as of 2017).

Another source for beta estimates, computed for individual stocks over the most recent five-year horizon, is Yahoo! Finance. Enter the company ticker symbol and look at the summary page. For example, as of May 2017, the beta for Nordstrom is given as 0.74. In contrast, Figure 9.2 lists the industry average beta for Apparel as 0.88. Is Nordstrom's significantly less risky than the average firm in the Apparel industry? When the financial crisis hit in 2008, sales plummeted at Nordstrom, as it did at many high-end retailers, while sales at the discounter Ross Stores actually increased. This suggests that Nordstrom is more risky, not less risky, than the average firm in the apparel industry. Nonetheless, as of May 2017 Ross Stores has a beta of 1.03. If we use a risk-free rate of 2%, a market premium of 5% and a beta of 0.74, we get a cost of equity capital for Nordstrom of 6.4%, but if we substitute in a beta of 1.03, a risk free rate of 3%, and a market premium of 6%, we get a cost of equity capital of 9.18%. This is a huge variation!

A more scientific reason to question the CAPM estimate is that it fits the actual data very poorly. The CAPM says that the only systematic thing causing different firms to have different stock returns is their beta. So you would think that if you estimated firms' betas at a point in time and then tracked the subsequent stock returns, you should find that firms with higher beta estimates would, on average, have higher subsequent stock returns (as compensation for the extra risk). Unfortunately, many studies have shown that this relation is very weak. Further, you may ask yourself, why are we relying on market prices to tell us about the firm's risk in the first place? The whole premise of this book is that securities can be mispriced, and we can discover the mispricing by our careful analysis. Finally, there is a difference between the realized risk premium over the past 85 years and the expected risk premium going forward. Back in 1926, it would have been difficult to know that the U.S. economy would turn out to be such a huge success story. Part of the difference between the market return and the risk-free rate over this period is simply due to good luck. For this reason, we are inclined to use something closer to a global risk premium, which was estimated at 5.4 percent in the Dimson, Marsh and Staunton study.

| Industry | # of Firms | Beta | Industry | # of Firms | Beta |
|---|---|---|---|---|---|
| Advertising | 41 | 1.36 | Insurance (Life) | 22 | 1.03 |
| Aerospace/Defense | 96 | 1.07 | Insurance (Prop/Cas.) | 50 | 0.83 |
| Air Transport | 18 | 1.12 | Investments & Asset Management | 156 | 0.90 |
| Apparel | 58 | 0.88 | Machinery | 127 | 1.06 |
| Auto & Truck | 15 | 0.85 | Metals & Mining | 97 | 1.30 |
| Auto Parts | 63 | 1.12 | Office Equipment & Services | 24 | 1.49 |
| Bank (Money Center) | 10 | 0.86 | Oil/Gas (Integrated) | 7 | 1.08 |
| Banks (Regional) | 645 | 0.47 | Oil/Gas (Production and Exploration) | 330 | 1.38 |
| Beverage (Alcoholic) | 25 | 0.79 | Oil/Gas Distribution | 78 | 1.20 |
| Beverage (Soft) | 36 | 0.91 | Oilfield Svcs/Equip. | 148 | 1.37 |
| Broadcasting | 30 | 1.22 | Packaging & Container | 26 | 0.84 |
| Brokerage & Investment Banking | 45 | 1.08 | Paper/Forest Products | 23 | 1.12 |
| Building Materials | 41 | 1.01 | Power | 68 | 0.54 |
| Business & Consumer Services | 165 | 1.07 | Precious Metals | 109 | 1.25 |
| Cable TV | 14 | 1.12 | Publishing & Newspapers | 37 | 1.32 |
| Chemical (Basic) | 45 | 1.00 | R.E.I.T. | 238 | 0.72 |
| Chemical (Diversified) | 8 | 1.52 | Real Estate (Development) | 18 | 0.68 |
| Chemical (Specialty) | 100 | 1.20 | Real Estate (General/Diversified) | 11 | 1.27 |
| Coal & Related Energy | 38 | 1.36 | Real Estate (Operations & Services) | 54 | 0.99 |
| Computer Services | 117 | 0.99 | Recreation | 66 | 0.92 |
| Computers/Peripherals | 55 | 1.06 | Reinsurance | 3 | 0.75 |
| Construction Supplies | 51 | 1.31 | Restaurant/Dining | 86 | 0.77 |
| Diversified | 24 | 0.76 | Retail (Automotive) | 25 | 0.91 |
| Drugs (Biotechnology) | 426 | 1.40 | Retail (Building Supply) | 6 | 1.30 |
| Drugs (Pharmaceutical) | 164 | 1.02 | Retail (Distributors) | 88 | 1.10 |
| Education | 36 | 1.23 | Retail (General) | 19 | 1.05 |
| Electrical Equipment | 119 | 1.14 | Retail (Grocery and Food) | 14 | 0.69 |
| Electronics (Consumer & Office) | 24 | 1.08 | Retail (Online) | 57 | 1.23 |
| Electronics (General) | 164 | 0.86 | Retail (Special Lines) | 108 | 1.02 |
| Engineering/Construction | 48 | 1.18 | Rubber& Tires | 4 | 1.35 |
| Entertainment | 79 | 1.20 | Semiconductor | 80 | 1.20 |
| Environmental & Waste Services | 89 | 0.85 | Semiconductor Equip | 45 | 1.10 |
| Farming/Agriculture | 37 | 0.92 | Shipbuilding & Marine | 11 | 1.20 |
| Financial Svcs. (Non-bank & Insurance) | 258 | 0.65 | Shoe | 10 | 0.85 |
| Food Processing | 87 | 0.75 | Software (Entertainment) | 13 | 0.98 |
| Food Wholesalers | 16 | 1.20 | Software (Internet) | 297 | 1.13 |
| Furn/Home Furnishings | 30 | 0.84 | Software (System & Application) | 236 | 1.13 |
| Green & Renewable Energy | 25 | 1.14 | Steel | 38 | 1.60 |
| Healthcare Products | 254 | 1.04 | Telecom (Wireless) | 17 | 1.12 |
| Healthcare Support Services | 121 | 0.94 | Telecom. Equipment | 107 | 0.99 |
| Heathcare Information and Technology | 125 | 0.95 | Telecom. Services | 67 | 1.04 |
| Homebuilding | 33 | 1.08 | Tobacco | 22 | 1.28 |
| Hospitals/Healthcare Facilities | 38 | 1.10 | Transportation | 17 | 1.01 |
| Hotel/Gaming | 69 | 0.96 | Transportation (Railroads) | 7 | 0.79 |
| Household Products | 129 | 0.80 | Trucking | 30 | 1.21 |
| Information Services | 64 | 0.98 | Utility (General) | 18 | 0.38 |
| Insurance (General) | 19 | 0.90 | Utility (Water) | 22 | 0.65 |
|  |  |  | Total Market | 7330 | 1.00 |

FIGURE 9.2: Industry Average Betas. Source: Damodaran Online

## What Number Do I Put in My Model?

Ultimately there is no good answer to the question "what is the cost of equity capital?" As a practical matter, we want to be able to compare the valuations of different firms on a risk-adjusted basis. If we evaluate 10 firms and then sort them based on the amount we think they are undervalued, we want this sort to reveal relative mispricing, not just differences in the riskiness across the 10 firms.

Rather than take the CAPM estimate as truth, we prefer that you use this model as a guide, combining the resulting estimate with your own intuition and some common sense. You might want to ask yourself what rate of return you would personally require on an investment with a similar level of risk. How much extra return beyond the risk-free rate seems reasonable, given the riskiness of the firm's future payoffs, and evaluated in light of the diversification you have in your portfolio and the liquidity of the security? The default value for the cost of equity capital in *eVal* is 10 percent. You can think of it as 5 percent for the risk-free rate and 5 percent for the risk premium; at least it is easy to remember!

There is one constraint on your cost of equity capital input: it must be greater than your assumed terminal growth rate in sales. If this isn't the case, then you are assuming that the firm will grow faster than the discount rate forever. This makes the perpetuity formula in the valuation models invalid; effectively, the value of such a firm is infinite.

# 9.3 COST OF NON-EQUITY CAPITAL

The only reason you need to consider the cost of non-equity capital is if you are interested in computing the value of all investors' claims on the firm, commonly referred to as the *entity value,* rather than just the equity value. It is also a necessary computation if your approach to valuing equity is to first determine entity value and then subtract the value of the non-equity claims to arrive at equity value. In this case, you need a cost of capital from debt holders, for preferred stockholders, and for minority interests (collectively called non-controlling interests). We strongly encourage you to ensure consistency between the cost of capital estimates here and the corresponding forecasting assumptions you input for the terminal period interest expense, preferred dividend, and minority interest income. For example, if your terminal period estimate of the firm's interest rate is six percent, we highly recommend inputting six percent as the cost of debt. In the short term, a firm may have debt outstanding that has a coupon interest rate different than its market interest rate. However, it would be quite odd to forecast that, forever into the future, the company will somehow manage to issue debt at a rate different than its market rate. Similarly, the cost of preferred stock and the cost of minority interests should probably match your terminal inputs for these items. Note that the value of the equity is already determined by your financial statement forecasts and your assumption about the cost of equity capital. Consequently, as you change your assumptions about the cost of non-equity capital, you will change the entity value and the value of the non-equity capital, but equity value will remain constant.

Just as with the cost of equity capital, costs of non-equity capital should not be smaller than your forecasted terminal period sales growth rate. If they are, then the perpetuity formula we use to compute the present value of the free cash flows to these capital providers is invalid. Think about what it would mean for the cost of debt to be lower than the growth rate forever. In the terminal period, the growth rate drives the growth in debt, so debt would be growing faster than it was being discounted back and the present value would be infinite.

# 9.4 WEIGHTED AVERAGE COST OF CAPITAL

To compute the *entity* value (as opposed to the *equity* value), you need a discount rate that reflects the blended cost of capital for all providers: equity, preferred stock, minority interests and debt. Another way to think about this problem is that we are trying to estimate the cost of equity capital for a hypothetical firm that has the same net operating assets of the actual firm but does not have any non-equity claims. Consequently, this rate is sometimes referred to as the cost of capital for the unlevered firm, or the expected return on invested capital. To see this, examine the basic accounting equation:

Invested Capital - Debt - Preferred Stock - Minority Interests = Common Equity,

which we can rearrange as

Invested Capital = Common Equity + Debt + Preferred Stock + Minority Interests, or

Invested Capital = Unlevered Equity.

To compute the cost of capital for this hypothetical firm, a logical approach is to take a weighted average of the cost of equity capital, the cost of preferred stock, the cost of minority interests, and the after-tax cost of debt. The *weighted-average cost of capital* (WACC), labeled $r_w$, does just this. It is computed as

$$r_w = \frac{r_e P_e + r_{ps} P_{ps} + r_{mi} P_{mi} + (1 - tax) r_d P_d}{P_e + P_{ps} + P_{mi} + P_d}, where$$

*tax* is the estimated effective tax rate,
$r_e$ is the estimated cost of equity capital,
$r_d$ is the estimated cost of debt capital,
$r_{ps}$ is the estimated cost of preferred stock capital,
$P_e$ is the estimated value of the equity,
$P_d$ is the estimated value of the debt,
$P_{ps}$ is the estimated value of the preferred stock, and
$P_{mi}$ is the estimated value of minority interest capital.

The value $r_w$ is the cost of a dollar of additional capital, holding the firm's capital structure constant. Imagine the firm raising the dollar by issuing common equity, preferred stock, minority interest claims and debt in exact proportions to their estimated values. This weighted-average cost of capital (WACC) is the natural benchmark for the firm's return on invested capital.[1]

Note that the weights used to compute $r_w$ are based on the estimated values of the equity, preferred stock, minority interests and debt, not their book values, not their current market values, and not some estimate of their future values in some future capital structure. But this raises a problem. The formula makes reference to $P_e$, the value of the common equity, yet $P_e$ is exactly what we are trying to figure out. How can we weight the different costs of capital based on their estimated values if we don't yet know the estimated value of equity? We sidestep this issue by using the estimate of $P_e$ already found when we valued the equity directly. We do the same thing for $P_d$, $P_{ps}$ and $P_{mi}$. With $P_e$, $P_d$, $P_{ps}$ and $P_{mi}$ determined, the value of the entity is then simply the sum of these four components.

Note that the thus derived estimate of the WACC is only correct if the company's capital structure and effective tax rate are not forecast to change through time. For example, the approximation employed in *eVal* uses the forecast effective tax rate in the terminal year. But if the effective tax rate is different in the earlier years of the forecast horizon, the correct WACC will reflect a time-weighted average of these different effective tax rates. Fortunately, there is a simple short-cut to computing the correct WACC in such circumstances. Since we have already estimated the individual values of $P_e$, $P_d$, $P_{ps}$ and $P_{mi}$, the correct WACC is the one that gives an entity-level value that is equal to the sum of the values $P_e$, $P_d$, $P_{ps}$ and $P_{mi}$. So you simply need to adjust the starting WACC estimate until the equity value implied using the entity-level valuation is the same as that implied by the direct equity valuation method. The general rule is that a higher (lower) WACC will give a lower (higher) valuation, so if the implied entity-level valuation is too high (low), then simply bump the WACC estimate up (down) until the two equity valuations are equal. In this way, you can solve for correct weighted-average cost of capital. This approach is completely valid, because the entity-level and equity-level valuations must ultimately yield the same equity value. You can play with this on the Valuation Parameters sheet in *eVal*.

## What Is Constant and What Is Changing?

In the previous sections, we estimated the cost of equity capital, the cost of preferred stock, the cost of minority interests, and the cost of debt as constants—a single rate

---

[1] The weighted-average cost of capital given here is "after-tax," meaning that the cost of debt has been adjusted down to account for the tax shield of interest (i.e., the (1-tax) part in the formula). By accounting for the tax deductibility of interest in the discount rate, we do not adjust the free cash flow estimates for the tax benefits of interest. An alternative approach found in some texts is to define WACC on a pre-tax basis (i.e., without the (1-tax) adjustment in the formula) and then add the tax deduction associated with interest to the free cash flows. This issue is discussed in greater detail in Chapter 10.

for each that is used to discount all future flows to each of these capital providers. We then combined these constant costs of capital to compute the associated constant WACC. However, what if you forecast that the firm's capital structure will change in the future? For instance, suppose you think that the company will drastically increase its ratio of debt to equity in the future. Based on the formula above, if you were to re-compute the WACC in the future, it could be different than the WACC based on the current capital structure. Should you base your estimate of $r_w$ on the current capital structure or on the forecasted future capital structure? Alternatively, should you use a different discount rate each period?

While the WACC formula suggests that $r_w$ should change as the capital structure changes, this is not necessarily the case. Remember that $r_w$ is essentially an estimate of the expected return on the company's invested capital. As such, it is determined by the perceived riskiness of the company's future free cash flows and not by the particular capital structure employed.[2] To see how this all washes out in our WACC formula, note that the cost of debt is typically lower than the cost of equity, since debt is typically less risky. If a company cranks up its leverage ratio, then both debt and equity should become more risky. But at the same time, the value of debt will increase relative to the value of equity. Because the WACC computation now places relatively more weight on debt, which has a relatively lower cost of capital, the overall WACC should remain about the same. So unless you are anticipating some drastic change in the company's underlying business operations, there is no need to adjust the WACC for anticipated changes in the capital structure.

# 9.5 QUIZZES, CASES, LINKS AND REFERENCES

## Links
• Yahoo!Finance: http://finance.yahoo.com

## References
Dimson, E., P. Marsh, and M. Staunton. (2000). *The Millennium Book: A Century of Investment Returns*. London: ABN-AMRO and London Business School.

---

[2] You may recall from your finance classes that the independence of the WACC from the capital structure employed is a direct implication of the well-known Miller-Modigliani theorem on capital structure.

CHAPTER TEN

# Valuation

## 10.1 INTRODUCTION

The hard work in valuation is already done. The forecasts you developed in Chapters 7 and 8 describe the future evolution of net cash distributions to equity holders. The cost of equity capital you chose in Chapter 9 determines how valuable future cash flows are today. All that remains is to combine the forecasts with the discount rate to compute the present value of the net distributions to equity holders. Why then are there so many pages in this chapter? It turns out that there are a number of different ways to compute the value of equity. While each of them leads to the same answer, each does so in a way that sheds a different light on the source of value creation. Further, different user groups have historically used different models: accounting types like the residual income models and finance types like the discounted cash flow models. If all you care about is the final answer, any of the models will do. But if you want to see the answer presented in the particular way you learned in some other class or life experience, we have a smorgasbord of models for you to choose from.

There are two features that distinguish the different valuation models. First, the flow variable, the thing that is being discounted, can be either free cash flows or accounting residual income flows (we give precise definitions below). Second, we can compute the value of the flows to equity holders directly, or we can first compute the value of the flows to all investors and then back into the value of the equity claim by subtracting the value of the flows to nonequity capital providers. If we work carefully (as does the *eVal* software), each model yields exactly the same result. Without boring you with algebraic proof, it should be obvious that each model will get the same answer if you feed each the same inputs. The forecasted financial statements and discount rate assumption *determine* the value; all we have to do is discover it.

All the models we describe allow for the possibility that the firm will live forever, so all models sum over time from the present, labeled time zero, to infinity. It takes a really long time to add up an infinite number of terms one at a time, so at some point in the future, known as the *terminal year (even though nothing terminates in the terminal year)*, we need a more succinct way of expressing the present value of the flows in the remaining years. All the models solve this problem the same way, so we defer the discussion of the present value calculations until the end of the chapter and present each model as an infinite sum of terms. Don't worry about this; there is a nifty solution to this problem.

We present all the models in algebraic notation. If you want to work through some numerical examples, the case "Four Valuation Models—One Value" is a good place to start.

# 10.2 RESIDUAL INCOME VALUATION MODELS

Although actually quite old, the residual income model has recently come back into vogue on Wall Street. Its primary advantage is that it expresses value directly in terms of the financial statements that you worked so hard to forecast, rather than translating these amounts into free cash flows. Define *residual income RI_t* in period *t* as

$$RI_t = NI_t - r_e CE_{t-1} \text{ where}$$

$NI_t$ is net income available to common equity for the period ending at date *t*,
$r_e$ is the cost of equity capital, and
$CE_{t-1}$ is common shareholders' equity at date *t-1* (i.e., the beginning of the $NI_t$ period).

Residual income is the amount by which net income exceeds the capital charge on the book value of common equity invested in the firm. If the firm could deposit its book value in a bank account at the beginning of the year and earn interest at the rate $r_e$, it would earn $r_e CE_{t-1}$ for the year. Residual income is the amount by which $NI_t$ exceeds or falls short of this benchmark. In this sense, it is *residual*.

The residual income model computes value as the sum of the initial book value plus the present value of future residual income flows. Both the book value and the net income component of residual income are accrual accounting constructs, which may make you incredulous about this model. How can the model work when we know that a firm's accounting book value is an imperfect measure of its market value and that earnings are an imperfect measure of value creation? How can these numbers be used to estimate a firm's market value? The key is to recognize that if book value is understated, then future residual income will be overstated, and by precisely enough to correct for the erroneous book value. For example, if a firm has a missing asset, one that the accounting rules don't recognize, then the asset isn't included in $CE_{t-1}$, but it produces future $NI$, making future $RI$ positive. In a later section, we will illustrate how all this adds up perfectly.

The easiest version of this model is the one that values the common equity directly.

## Residual Income to Common Equity

The algebraic statement of this model is

$$P_e = CE_0 + \sum_{t=1}^{\infty} \frac{RI_t}{(1 + r_e)^t} \text{ , where}$$

$P_e$ is the estimated market value of common equity as of the last financial statement date,

$CE_0$ is the common shareholders' equity as of the last financial statement date (i.e., time 0),

$RI_t$ is residual income, equal to $NI_t - r_eCE_{t-1}$, as defined above, and

$r_e$ is the cost of equity capital.

The model starts with the initial stock of accounting value $CE_0$ and adds to it the discounted sum of expected future residual income flows. The reason a firm's market value $P_e$ will be different than its book value is because it is forecasted to earn positive or negative residual income in the future. To get a feel for this model, imagine a savings account with $100 in it and a 10 percent interest rate. The book value of this investment, by any reasonable accounting measurement, would be $100. Further, if 10 percent is the market rate of interest on savings accounts, then the return on a similar investment with equivalent risk is probably also 10 percent, so assume $r_e$ =10 percent. In this case, regardless of deposits or withdrawals (made at the beginning of each year), the earnings each period will be 10 percent of the beginning book value, which is exactly the capital charge $r_eCE_{t-1}$, so residual income in all future periods is zero. Thus, the value of the savings account is $100. Seems pretty obvious. Now suppose that the savings account was going to pay 11 percent interest in some future years, yet the discount rate remained 10 percent. In this case the savings account would earn "residual income" in these years and its market value would exceed $100. It is as if every few years the bank manager threw some extra money into your account. If you knew this was going to happen, the account would be worth more than the $100 of book value.

In the savings account example, the key comparison was between the discount rate and the rate of interest the account paid. For a real company, the key comparison is between the forecasted ROE and the cost of equity capital $r_e$. To see this, divide and multiply $RI_t$ by $CE_{t-1}$ so that

$$RI_t = (NI_t - r_eCE_{t-1}) = (ROE_t - r_e)CE_{t-1},$$

where $ROE_t$ is computed on beginning equity.

The expression says that residual income equals the excess of $ROE_t$ over the cost of equity capital times the beginning common equity book value for the period. If you forecast that the firm's ROE will exceed its cost of equity capital, then residual income will be positive; if ROE is forecast to be less than the cost of equity capital, residual income will be negative. Stated another way, a firm is worth more than its book value only if it is expected to earn an ROE in excess of its cost of equity capital. Remembering from previous chapters that ROE was our premier measure of profitability, this equation says that profitability creates value.

This expression also demonstrates that size by itself does *not* create value. If $ROE_t = r_e$, then residual income is zero regardless of the value of $CE_{t-1}$. Similarly, growth in $CE_t$, by itself, does not create value. However, if $ROE_t$ is forecast to exceed $r_e$ in the future, then a firm wants to grow to be as big as possible. Think of it this way: if you forecast that a firm's ROE will always equal its cost of equity capital in the future, then you are really forecasting that the firm will always engage in zero net present value projects. If this is the case, then it doesn't matter how big or small those future projects are; none of them will create value. In contrast, if you forecast that $ROE_t$ will exceed $r_e$ in the future, then you are saying that the firm has positive net present value projects in the future. In this case, you want the projects to be as big as possible; in this case, growth is good. Wall Street analysts frequently confuse the value of growth with the value of profitability when assessing equity securities. Many research reports extol the huge growth potential of a company without explaining how the firm will ever turn the growth into profitability. If the company can't earn a return that is at least as great as its cost of capital, being a big firm just means that it will destroy more value than a small firm. We suspect that analysts like rapidly growing firms because such firms are likely to require investment-banking services, not because they think they are fundamentally good investment opportunities.

The residual income model has many desirable features. For one thing, it is written in terms of the accounting variables that you worked so hard to forecast. The net income and book value variables come straight from the forecasted financial statements. More fundamentally, the residual income model describes value in an economically appealing way. Value is driven by profitability and growth. Much of the previous chapters in this book have been aimed at building your intuition for how economic forces and accounting distortions will act on a firm's growth rate and especially on its ROE. By expressing value as a function of these two drivers, the residual income valuation model exploits this intuition.

Finally, because the residual income model is written in terms of accounting numbers, we will use it in the next chapter to describe some popular valuation ratios such as the market-to-book ratio, the price-to-earnings ratio, and the PEG ratio.

## Bad Accounting and the Residual Income Valuation Model

Because the residual income model is stated in terms of accounting values, you may worry that distorted accounting measurements will make the model invalid or inaccurate. But, as the next example illustrates, the model is surprisingly resilient to accounting distortions. Suppose that the sequence of forecasted common equity and net income, before any consideration of accounting distortions, is $CE_0$, $NI_1$, $CE_1$, $NI_2$, $CE_2$, $NI_3$, $CE_3$ ..., so that the residual income model yields

$$P_e = CE_0 + \frac{NI_1 - r_e CE_0}{(1 + r_e)^1} + \frac{NI_2 - r_e CE_1}{(1 + r_e)^2} + \frac{NI_3 - r_e CE_2}{(1 + r_e)^3} + \cdots$$

Now suppose that you are sure that $\$K$ of value is missing from $CE_0$, possibly due to an R&D investment that cannot be capitalized but is forecasted to payoff in $NI_1$. You could set out to correct for this error in the accounting model by adding $K$ to $CE_0$ and subtracting it from your estimate of $NI_1$; that is, you could recognize the value creation in the current book value rather than waiting for it to materialize in future earnings. In this case the valuation would be

$$P_e = CE_0 + K + \frac{NI_1 - K - r_e(CE_0 + K)}{(1 + r_e)^1} + \frac{NI_2 - r_e CE_1}{(1 + r_e)^2} + \frac{NI_3 - r_e CE_2}{(1 + r_e)^3} + \cdots$$

noting that the addition of $K$ to $CE_0$ increased book value at date 0 but that the book value at date 1 is back to normal because of the subtraction of $K$ from $NI_1$. Simple algebra demonstrates that the two valuations are equal. At first blush, this may seem impossible. Shouldn't moving $K$ to the present increase the value estimate, since money has time value? But look carefully at the second term in the second equation; not only has $K$ been deducted from date 1 earnings, but the capital charge is also higher by $r_e K$, thus perfectly correcting for the time value of this manipulation. And you don't even have to forecast *when* the $K$ of additional value will show up in future earnings. Suppose that you estimated that the additional value was going to materialize in year two rather than year one, such that your corrected forecasts yield the following value estimate:

$$P_e = CE_0 + K + \frac{NI_1 - r_e(CE_0 + K)}{(1 + r_e)^1} + \frac{NI_2 - K - r_e(CE_1 + K)}{(1 + r_e)^2} + \frac{NI_3 - r_e CE_2}{(1 + r_e)^3} + \cdots$$

With some hard work, you can show that this again equals the original amount (feeling like this is an algebra test?). By including a capital charge in the definition of residual income, the model perfectly corrects for accounting distortions. Consequently, you really don't need to get involved in correcting the historical financial statements for accounting distortions; if your forecasts anticipate the unraveling of the accounting distortion, the model will do the rest.

You *should not* conclude from this discussion that it isn't important that you understand accounting distortions. Your forecasts of the future should be based on observations of the firm's past and, if that past is distorted by poor accounting, then you need to be aware of this. For instance, if the firm has generated unusually high income by capitalizing more expenses than is appropriate, and thus deferred the recognition of these expenses on the income statement, you need to be aware that future income will be lower when these capitalized expenses eventually flow through income (as they surely must in an accrual accounting system).

## Residual Income to All Investors

This version of the model is less commonly used but reconciles nicely with the other valuation models. It computes the value of common equity by first computing the value to all capital providers combined, commonly labeled as the *entity value,* and then subtracting from this the value of the non-equity claims (debt, preferred stock and minority interests). It computes the value of each of these claims as the sum of the beginning book value and the present value of a flow of future residual amounts, just as we did for equity.[1]

To express this model algebraically, we need to remind you of some earlier notation. In Chapter 5, we defined $NOA_t$ as the net operating assets of the firm, computed as the book value of operating assets less the operating liabilities. Next, define $L_t$ as the accounting book value of the debt (current and noncurrent combined), $PS_t$ as the accounting book value of the preferred stock, and $MI_t$ as the accounting book value of the minority interest (in Chapter 5, we lumped debt, preferred stock, and minority interest together and labeled them as Net Financial Obligations, but here we will value each component separately). By the basic accounting equation, Net Operating Assets $NOA_t$ is given as

$$NOA_t = CE_t + L_t + PS_t + MI_t.$$

In Chapter 5, we also defined $NOI_t$ as the net operating income, computed after tax. It is equal to net income available to common equity holders $NI_t$ plus the after-tax interest flows to debtholders $(1- tax_t)I_t$, plus the preferred dividend flows to preferred shareholders $PD_t$, plus the minority interest in earnings $MIE_t$. That is,

$$NOI_t = NI_t + (1 - tax_t)I_t + PD_t + MIE_t,$$

where $tax_t$ is the firm's effective tax rate in year $t$. The idea behind the model is that the book value of the invested capital for all investors is $NOA_0$ and the future stream of after-tax operating income for all investors is $NOI_t$. We can therefore compute the value of the entity as the initial balance of $NOA_0$ plus the present value of the future residual $NOI_t$ stream. Denoting the weighted-average cost of capital as $r_w$, we define *residual net operating income* as:

$$RNOI_t = NOI_t - r_w NOA_{t-1}.$$

Note the similarity with residual income defined in the previous section as $RI_t = NI_t - r_e CE_{t-1}$? To compute residual net *operating* income, $NI_t$ is replaced with $NOI_t$ and $CE_{t-1}$ is replaced with $NOA_{t-1}$. With this notation in place, the *entity value $P_f$* can be

---

[1] In everything that follows, Minority Interest is treated exactly like Preferred Stock in all respects and so, if you find this source of non-equity capital a bit confusing (as at least one of the authors does), feel free to ignore it in all the formulas, remembering that it is accounted for exactly like preferred stock.

expressed as

$$P_f = NOA_0 + \sum_{t=1}^{\infty} \frac{RNOI_t}{(1+r_w)^t} .$$

All investors together own $P_f$. To find the value of the common equity holders' claim, we need to subtract from $P_f$ the value of the debt claim, the value of the preferred stock claim, and the value of the minority interest claim. And, in the spirit of residual income valuation, the value of the debt claim is computed as the initial book value of $L_0$ plus the present value of the future *residual interest expense* $I_t$ - $r_d L_{t-1}$, where $r_d$ is the cost of debt capital. Similarly, the value of the preferred stock claim is computed as the sum of the initial book value of $PS_0$ and the present value of the future *residual preferred dividends*, using the cost of preferred stock capital $r_{ps}$ as the discount rate; and the value of the minority interest claim is computed as the sum of the initial book value of $MI_0$ and the present value of the *residual minority interest in earnings*. Denoting the debt value as $P_d$, the preferred stock value as $P_{ps}$, and the minority interests value as $P_{mi}$, we get

$$P_d = L_0 + \sum_{t=1}^{\infty} \frac{I_t - r_d L_{t-1}}{(1+r_d)^t} ,$$

$$P_{ps} = PS_0 + \sum_{t=1}^{\infty} \frac{PD_t - r_{ps} PS_{t-1}}{(1+r_{ps})^t} , and$$

$$P_{mi} = MI_0 + \sum_{t=1}^{\infty} \frac{MIE_t - r_{mi} MI_{t-1}}{(1+r_{mi})^t} .$$

The entity value is the sum of the value of the common equity, the value of the debt, the value of the preferred stock, and the value of the minority interest:

$$P_f = P_e + P_d + P_{ps} + P_{mi}$$

and so we can solve for the value of common equity as

$$P_e = P_f - P_d - P_{ps} - P_{mi}.$$

This may seem like the long way around to get to a common equity valuation. The advantage of this indirect approach to valuing the equity is that it focuses your attention on the value of the net operating assets and future net operating income of the firm. The idea is that we should first work hard on valuing the entity, since this is the fundamental source of value for the firm, and then worry about how the value gets divided between the capital providers.

## The Tax Shield on Interest

If you have been following all this very carefully, you may have noticed that some money went missing. By definition,

$$NOI_t = NI_t + I_t + PD_t + MIE_t - tax_t I_t.$$

$NOI_t$ is in the income that flows to the entity. Similarly, $NI_t$ is in the income claimed by the common equity holders, $I_t$ is the income claimed by the debt holders, $PD_t$ is the income claimed by the preferred stock holders, and $MIE_t$ is the income claimed by the minority interest holders. But what about the '- $tax_t I_t$', the *tax shield on interest*? Where did it go? We could have simply left these tax savings in NOI rather than deducting them back out. While leaving them in $NOI_t$ might seem like the most logical approach, the most common 'textbook' approach is to build the value of the tax shield into the entity value by lowering the cost of debt in the weighted-average cost of capital. In other words, instead of reflecting the cash savings from the tax deductibility of interest as a higher numerator, we instead use a smaller denominator.

Recall from Chapter 9 that the weighted-average cost of capital was a mix of the cost of equity capital $r_e$, the cost of preferred stock capital $r_{ps}$, the cost of minority interests, and the *after-tax* cost of debt capital $(1 - tax_t)r_d$. Using the after-tax cost of debt lowers the weighted-average cost of capital that is used to discount the flows to the entity and therefore raises the entity value. Figure 10.1 illustrates the accounting variables and discount rates that are used to compute the value of each capital provider's claim.

If it strikes you as a bit magical that making a simple tax adjustment to the cost of debt capital is all that it takes to get the value of the tax shield on interest built into the entity value, your skepticism is justified. To be theoretically valid, we would need to add some additional assumptions; namely, that the firm's effective tax rate and leverage ratio remain constant. Incorporating the tax shield in the cost of capital is only an issue when valuing the common equity using this indirect entity approach. When valuing equity directly, interest payments and the associated tax shields are reflected in expenses, no different than marketing expenses. So if you didn't follow the discussion in this last section, you didn't really miss much.

| entity value | common equity value | | preferred stock value | | minority interest | | debt value | tax shield |
|---|---|---|---|---|---|---|---|---|
| $P_f$ = | $P_e$ | + | $P_{ps}$ | + | $P_{mi}$ | + | $P_d$ | |
| uses | uses | | uses | | uses | | uses | |
| $NOA_t$ = | $CE_t$ | + | $PS_t$ | + | $MI_t$ | + | $L_t$ | |
| $NOI_t$ = | $NI_t$ | + | $PD_t$ | + | $MIE_t$ | + | $I_t$ | $- tx_t I_t$ |
| $C_t$ = | $D_t$ | + | $PD_t - \Delta PS_t$ | | $+ MIE_t - \Delta MI_t$ | + | $I_t - \Delta L_t$ | $- tx_t I_t$ |

and discounts using

| $r_w$ = | $r_e$ | $r_{ps}$ | $r_{mi}$ | $r_d$ |
|---|---|---|---|---|

weighted average
of $r_e$, $r_{ps}$, $r_{mi}$ and $(1\text{-}tx)r_d$ ◄——— value of $tx_t I_t$ is incorporated into entity value by using $(1\text{-}tx)r_d$ in $r_w$ computation.

**FIGURE 10.1: The Variables in Valuation Equations**

# 10.3 DISCOUNTED CASH FLOW VALUATION MODELS

The discounted cash flow (DCF) model focuses on free cash flows rather than residual income flows. We compute the DCF model two ways: based on the free cash flows directly to common equity holders and based on the free cash flows to all investors. With the "all investor" approach, the common equity is valued indirectly as the entity value less the value of the debt, the value of the preferred stock claims and the value of the minority interest claims (just like the residual income to all investors model given in the previous section). The valuation attribute that drives the DCF model, in either form, is free cash flow. Chapter 6 describes in detail how this amount can be computed in several different, yet equivalent, ways. We will give a few formulas for free cash flows here, but we refer you back to Chapter 6 for the details.

## DCF to Common Equity

The *free cash flow to common equity* is the primary building block for all our valuation models. It is the net cash distributions to equity holders, labeled $D_t$. We can compute this amount directly as cash dividends plus stock repurchases less equity issuances. Alternatively, we can use the clean surplus relation and compute $D_t$ based on net income and the change in common equity. That is, the clean surplus relation in accrual accounting requires that

$CE_t = CE_{t-1} + NI_t - D_t.$

Rearranging this expression gives

$D_t = NI_t - (CE_t - CE_{t-1}).$

This is the cash flow that ultimately determines the value of a common equity claim. Discounting these flows at the cost of equity capital gives us the mother of all valuation models, the *DCF to Common Equity Model,* shown formally as

$$P_e = \sum_{t=1}^{\infty} \frac{D_t}{(1 + r_e)^t}, where$$

$P_e$ is the value of the common equity,
$D_t$ is the net cash distributions to common equity holders, and
$r_e$ is the cost of equity capital.

Your forecasted financial statements describe net income and common equity forever into the future. From these amounts, we compute $D_t$ and discount these flows at rate $r_e$. Nothing could be simpler, really. The knock on this model is that it is hard to develop much intuition for future $D_t$ flows. $D_t$ is the distribution of wealth to equity holders, which typically happens much later than the actual creation of wealth. Further, past $D_t$ is a poor predictor of future $D_t$, so you really need to rely on a good set of forecast financial statements to derive forecasts of future $D_t$. Extrapolation alone won't get you very far.

Since all four of the valuation models we discuss in this chapter are algebraically equivalent, it is hard to argue which of the models is the "original version." Nonetheless, this model is probably the first, most basic, expression of the value of an equity security. The formal derivations of the other models typically start here.[2]

---

[2] It takes little work to derive the residual income model from the DCF to common equity model. Start with the DCF model and write $D_t$ as $NI_t - (CE_t - CE_{t-1})$. For each future date, substitute for $NI_t$ the value $RI_t + r_e CE_{t-1}$. The first term in the summation (when t=1) is $(1+r_e)^{-1}[RI_1 + r_e CE_0 - CE_1 + CE_0] = CE_0 + (1+r_e)^{-1}RI_1 - (1+r_e)^{-1}CE_1$. The second term in the summation (when t=2) is $(1+r_e)^{-2}[RI_2 + r_e CE_1 - CE_2 + CE_1] = (1+r_e)^{-2}RI_2 + (1+r_e)^{-1}CE_1 - (1+r_e)^{-2}CE_2$. Adding these two terms together gives $CE_0 + (1+r_e)^{-1}RI_1 + (1+r_e)^{-2}RI_2 - (1+r_e)^{-2}CE_2$. As you can see, we are building the residual income model term by term. Every time we add another term in the summation we add in the appropriately discounted $RI_t$ term and cancel the last term in the previous sum. Since the summation is infinite, the last term is pushed out infinitely far into the future, and hence has zero present value.

## DCF to All Investors

When someone in practice says "the DCF model," this is the model they typically have in mind. This model is the warhorse of MBA programs. Unfortunately, because the computation of the *free cash flow to all investors* is rather involved, and because "all investors" models require a weighted-average cost of capital that anticipates future tax rates and leverage ratios, it is the rare user who can successfully compute the DCF to all investors model without error. Because of the long history this model has enjoyed, a number of different ways to compute the free cash flow to all investors have emerged. We summarize two methods here; we refer you to Chapter 6 for more detailed explanations. The free cash flow to all investors, denoted here as $C_t$, is computed most directly as

$$C_t = NOI_t - (NOA_t - NOA_{t-1}).$$

In words, the free cash flow to all investors equals the net operating income less the increase in net operating assets. This should feel right. All investors together claim the cash flows that emanate from the use of the net operating assets. Free cash flow differs from $NOI_t$ because accrual accounting recognizes some $NOI_t$ dollars that are not yet cash dollars, which necessarily means they are still in $NOA_t$. Subtracting the increase in $NOA_t$ from $NOI_t$ leaves us with the cash that the entity generated from its operations over the period.

You can also compute the free cash flows directly from data given on the statement of cash flows. Just ask yourself, what cash went to each investor group? The company sent equity holders the net distribution $D_t$ (i.e., common dividends plus stock repurchases less equity issuances). The firm sent debt holders interest, and less any increase in principle, denoted $\Delta L_t$. Similarly, the firm sent preferred stockholders preferred dividends $PD_t$ less any new issuances, denoted $\Delta PS_t$; and the firm sent the minority interests $MIE_t$ less any increase in the minority interest balance, denoted $\Delta MI_t$. Finally, recall that convention dictates that we exclude the cash taxes saved from the tax deductibility of interest from $C_t$ (instead, reflecting these cash flows in the form of a lower after tax cost of debt).  Putting it all together, we have:

$$C_t = D_t + I_t - \Delta L + PD_t - \Delta PS_t + MIE_t - \Delta MI_t - tax_t I_t.$$

If you suffer from insomnia and enjoy the finger exercises that only algebra can provide, you can show that this expression for $C_t$ equals the previous one.[3]

Armed with the free cash flow to all investors $C_t$, we can now compute the *entity value*—the value of the operations to all investors before distinguishing between claimants. Denoting the weighted-average cost of capital as $r_w$ and the entity value as $P_f$, we have

---

[3] Here is the proof.  By definition $NOI_t = NI_t + I_t(1-tax_t) + PD_t + MIE_t$ and $\Delta NOA_t = \Delta CE_t + \Delta L_t + \Delta PS_t + \Delta MI_t$.  Substitute these expressions for $NOI_t$ and $(NOA_t - NOA_{t-1})$ in the first $C_t$ expression.  Next, note that by the clean surplus relation $NI_t = D_t + \Delta CE_t$.  Substitute this in for $NI_t$, cancel the plus and minus $\Delta CE_t$ and you have the second expression for $C_t$.

$$P_f = \sum_{t=1}^{\infty} \frac{C_t}{(1+r_w)^t}$$

and, yes, this version of $P_f$ is exactly equal to the $P_f$ computed using the residual income to all investors model shown in the previous section. To compute the value of the common equity claim, we subtract from $P_f$ the value of the debt $P_d$, the preferred stock claim $P_{ps}$ and the minority interest claim $P_{mi}$. In the spirit of discounting cash flows, each of these non-common-equity claims is itself valued based on the cash flows it receives. Denoting the pretax cost of debt as $r_d$, the cost of preferred stock as $r_{ps}$, and the cost of minority interests as $r_{mi}$, we have

$$P_d = \sum_{t=1}^{\infty} \frac{I_t - \Delta L_t}{(1+r_d)^t},$$

$$P_{ps} = \sum_{t=1}^{\infty} \frac{PD_t - \Delta PS_t}{(1+r_{ps})^t}, and$$

$$P_{mi} = \sum_{t=1}^{\infty} \frac{MIE_t - \Delta MI_t}{(1+r_{mi})^t}.$$

The values of $P_d$, $P_{ps}$ and $P_{mi}$ computed based on their respective future cash flows are exactly the same as their values computed in the previous section based on residual income flows. Putting it all together, we compute the value of the common equity as:

$$P_e = P_f - P_d - P_{ps} - P_{mi},$$

just as in the previous section. Finally, we can mix and match between the residual income model and the discounted cash flow model. For instance, it is not uncommon to compute the value of the debt $P_d$ or the value of the preferred stock using a residual income model, with the added assumption that all future residual flows to these claimants are zero. In other words, the value of the debt and the value of the preferred stock are simply assumed to equal their current book values, $L_0$ and $PS_0$, respectively.

## Tax Shield on Interest
Just as in the residual income to all investors model, the DCF to all investors reflects the cash tax savings from the tax deductibility of interest through a lower cost of

debt. Free cash flow to all investors, $C_t$, is computed as:

$$C_t = D_t + I_t - \Delta L + PD_t - \Delta PS_t + MIE_t - \Delta MI_t - tax_t I_t.$$

Notice that $tax_t I_t$, **the tax shield on interest**, is explicitly backed out of $C_t$. Figure 10.1 shows the cash flows that are being discounted to compute $P_e$, $P_{ps}$, $P_{mi}$ and $P_d$. Looking at this figure, you might wonder how the sum of $P_e$, $P_{ps}$, $P_{mi}$ and $P_d$ can equal the entity value $P_f$, which excludes the tax shield? The answer is that the value of the tax shield is incorporated into the entity value through the lower discount rate $r_w$. Recall from Chapter 9 that the weighted average cost of capital is a mix of the cost of equity $r_e$, the cost of preferred stock $r_{ps}$, the cost of minority interests $r_{mi}$, and the *after-tax* cost of debt $(1-tx)r_d$. Using the after-tax cost of debt lowers the weighted average cost of capital, which raises the present value of the $C_t$ flows in the $P_f$ formula. For more information, see the associated discussion on the tax shield on interest in section 10.2.

Figure 10.2 summarizes all four valuation models. To fit everything on one page, we have assumed there is no minority interest. As you may have noticed by now, minority interests get treated exactly like preferred stock in all respects and so, at this point, you should be able to add them to the table yourself. Or refer to the precise formulas given above. The columns in Figure 10.2 describe what is being valued—the equity, the debt, or the preferred stock—and the rows describe which valuation attribute is being used—free cash flow or residual income. To compute the infinite sum of flows, each expression makes use of the perpetuity formula discussed in the next section.

| | | Cash Flows | Residual Income Flows |
|---|---|---|---|
| *Equity Valued Directly as $P_e$* | Value of Common Equity $P_e$ | $\sum_{t=1}^{\infty} \dfrac{D_t}{(1+r_e)^t}$ | $CE_0 + \sum_{t=1}^{\infty} \dfrac{RI_t}{(1+r_e)^t}$ <br> where $RI_t = NI_t - r_e CE_{t-1}$. |
| *Equity Valued Indirectly as $P_e = P_f - P_d - P_{ps}$* | Value of Whole Entity $P_f$ | $\sum_{t=1}^{\infty} \dfrac{C_t}{(1+r_w)^t}$ | $NOA_0 + \sum_{t=1}^{\infty} \dfrac{RNOI_t}{(1+r_w)^t}$ <br> where $ROI_t = NOI_t - r_w NOA_{t-1}$. |
| | Value of Debt $P_d$ | $\sum_{t=1}^{\infty} \dfrac{I_t - \Delta L_t}{(1+r_d)^t}$ | $L_0 + \sum_{t=1}^{\infty} \dfrac{I_t - r_d L_{t-1}}{(1+r_d)^t}$ |
| | Value of Preferred Stock $P_{ps}$ | $\sum_{t=1}^{\infty} \dfrac{PD_t - \Delta PS_t}{(1+r_{ps})^t}$ | $PS_0 + \sum_{t=1}^{\infty} \dfrac{PD_t - r_{ps} PS_{t-1}}{(1+r_{ps})^t}$ |

$D_t$ is cash flow to common equity; $CE_t = CE_{t-1} + NI_t - D_t$

$C_t$ is cash flow to all investors; $C_t = NOI_t - \Delta NOA_t$

$L_t$ is the debt balance at time t

$CE_t$ is the common shareholders' equity at time t; $CE_t = NOA_t - L_t - PS_t$

$NOI_t$ is the operating income for the period ending at t, net of tax

$I_t$ is the interest expense for the period ending at t

$NI_t$ is the net income for the period ended at t; $NI_t = NOI_t - (1-tax)I_t - PD_t$

$NOA_t$ is the net operating asset balance for the period ended at t

$PD_t$ is the preferred dividend for the period ending at t

$PS_t$ is the preferred stock balance for the period ended at t

$r_e$ is the cost of equity capital

$r_d$ is the cost of debt capital

$r_{ps}$ is the cost of preferred stock capital

$r_w$ is the weighted average cost of capital: $r_w = \dfrac{r_e P_e + (1-tax) r_d P_d + r_{ps} P_{ps}}{P_e + P_d + P_{ps}}$.

**FIGURE 10.2: Summary of Valuation Equations**

## 10.4 PRESENT VALUE COMPUTATIONS

All four valuation models given above compute value as the present value of an infinite series of flows of the valuation attribute, either residual income or free cash flow. Since it is impossibly time consuming to compute the present value of an infinite series on a term by term basis, all valuation models compute the present value term by term up to the *terminal year* and then compute the present value beyond the terminal year using the formula for a growing perpetuity. In case you have forgotten, the present value of a growing perpetuity of payments, starting with $K$ after one year and growing at rate $g$ forever after, discounted at rate $r$, is given by the following formula

$$\frac{K}{(1+r)^1} + \frac{(1+g)K}{(1+r)^2} + \frac{(1+g)^2 K}{(1+r)^3} + \frac{(1+g)^3 K}{(1+r)^4} + \cdots = \frac{K}{r-g}.$$

The left-hand side of the formula shows the sequence of terms that continue in perpetuity in the present value computation and the right-hand side of the formula shows the simplified result.

Before the terminal year, your forecasts can be as erratic as you like. Each year's forecasts will imply a flow of valuation attributes, however unusual, and the model will compute the present value of each year's flow. However, starting with the terminal year, your forecasts are constrained to behave in a more predictable manner. Sales growth is fixed at the rate you set in the terminal year and this becomes the $g$ in the perpetuity formula. Profit margins, asset turnovers, and leverage ratios also are assumed to remain constant after the terminal year. These forecasts imply well-defined financial statements forever into the future, and they are financial statements that will generate residual income flows and free cash flows that will grow forever at rate $g$. Once everything is safely growing at this known rate, we can compute the present value of the subsequent flows using the formula given above.

In previous chapters, we noted that your terminal growth forecast should not exceed the discount rate; otherwise, the present value is infinite. In terms of the formula given above, if $g$ is greater than $r$, then the result is negative, but you shouldn't try to attach any meaning to this. The formula is simply undefined when $g$ exceeds $r$.

Let's use the growing perpetuity formula to rewrite the residual income to common equity model. The model given earlier is

$$P_e = CE_0 + \sum_{t=1}^{\infty} \frac{RI_t}{(1+r_e)^t}.$$

Now suppose that, starting in year $T$, the financial statement forecasts imply that residual income will be $RI_T$ and then grow at rate $g$ forever after. We can now compute the present value as

$$P_e = CE_0 + \sum_{t=1}^{T-1} \frac{RI_t}{(1 + r_e)^t} + \frac{RI_T}{(r_e - g)(1 + r_e)^{T-1}}.$$

The first two terms are the present value for years 1 through $T$-$1$ and the last term is the present value for years $T$ and forever after. To apply the formula for a growing perpetuity in this setting, you need to think carefully about when the different residual income flows take place. The residual income in year $T$ is $RI_T$; it is $RI_T$ $(1+g)$ in year $T+1$, and so on, growing forever at rate $g$. If we were standing in year $T$-$1$ and wanted to compute the present value of this growing perpetuity, we would apply the formula and get

$$\frac{RI_T}{(r_e - g)}.$$

But we want the present value at time 0, not time $T$-$1$, so we need to discount back $T$-$1$ more years.  To do this we divide by $(1+r_e)^{T-1}$, as shown in the denominator of the last term of our modified formula.

All of the other valuation models handle the present value computations exactly the same way.  After the financial statement forecasts become sufficiently stable, insofar as they imply a constant growth rate in future free cash flows and residual income flows, the perpetuity formula kicks in to compute the remaining present value.

So in which period should you compute the terminal value? The terminal period seems like the obvious choice. This is the period that the sales growth rate and the margin, turnover and leverage ratios stabilize. It turns out that we have to wait one more year. This is because it takes one more period for the growth rates in the cash flow variables to settle down to the terminal sales growth rate. We encourage you to take a look at the valuation sheets in our *eVal* software for examples of these computations. You will see that the terminal value formula is applied to the residual income or cash flow in the year *after* the terminal year. Also, if you compute the growth rate in free cash flow from the terminal year to the year after the terminal year, you will find that it is not generally equal to the terminal sales growth rate. But in the very next year, it will always settle down to the terminal sales growth rate.

## Adjusting the Present Value to the Present

Figure 10.3 illustrates *eVal's* present value computations for the DCF to common equity and the residual income to common equity models. The amounts are from Kohl's, valued as of January 31, 2010 using the default forecasting settings. Consider the DCF to common equity, shown in the top panel. *eVal* adds the present value of first 10 years and present value beyond 10 years to arrive at the forecast equity value before time adjustment. Comparing the two amounts shows that a little less than half of the total value of the cash flows arrives in the first 10 years. But now compare this to the residual income model shown directly below. The residual income model also shows values for the first 10 years and beyond 10 years, but they aren't the same as for the DCF model. In particular, the value beyond 10 years is much smaller and, if we consider the value of common equity as of January 31, 2010 as part of the value during the first 10 years, then the residual income model shows a significantly greater portion of value arriving much earlier than the DCF model. Both models arrive at the same forecast equity value before time adjustment, but why do they allocate the value differently across time? The answer reveals a fundamental difference in the way the two models characterize value creation. The residual income model counts the balance of common equity as value already earned and counts net income as value created, regardless of the actual cash flow. The DCF model, in contrast, waits for the actual cash to arrive. Another way to say this is that the DCF treats investment as a consumption of value (cash is leaving the firm) while the residual income model treats investment as a store of value (assets are put on the books). The two models ultimately get to the same total value because they are based on the same underlying financial statement forecasts, but they differ drastically on when they count value as created.

| Valuation to Common Equity | |
|---|---|
| Free Cash Flow to Common Equity | 681,779 |
| Present Value of FCF | 619,799 |
| Present Value Beyond 10 Years | 6,392,730 |
| Present Value of First 10 Years | 5,241,733 |
| Forecast Equity Value Before Time Adj. | 11,634,463 |
| Forecasted Value as of Valuation Date | 12,216,186 |
| Less Value of Contingent Equity Claims | 0 |
| Value Attributable to Common Equity | 12,216,186 |
| Common Shares Outstanding at BS Date | 307,000 |
| Equivalent Shares at Valuation Date | 307,000 |
| Forecast Price/Share | $39.79 |

**FIGURE 10.3: Kohl's Present Value Computations**
(valuation based on *eVal* defaults as of January 31, 2010)

| Valuation to Common Equity | |
|---|---|
| Net Income | 1,046,887 |
| Common Equity at Beginning of Year | 7,853,000 |
| Residual Income | 261,587 |
| Present Value of Residual Income | 237,806 |
| Present Value Beyond 10 Years | 1,951,370 |
| Present Value of First 10 Years | 1,830,093 |
| Common Equity as of | |
| 10-01-31 | 7,853,000 |
| Forecast Equity Value Before Time Adj. | 11,634,463 |
| Forecasted Value as of Valuation Date | 12,216,186 |
| Less Value of Contingent Equity Claims | 0 |
| Value Attributable to Common Equity | 12,216,186 |
| Common Shares Outstanding at BS Date | 307,000 |
| Equivalent Shares at Valuation Date | 307,000 |
| Forecast Price/Share | $39.79 |

**FIGURE 10.3 Continued**

Regardless of which model you are working with, it is useful to think about when the model says that value is being created. In most cases, you are probably more confident about your forecasts during the first 10 years than you are about your forecasts beyond 10 years, so if most of the value is concentrated more than 10 years away, then you might be less confident in your valuation. Are we more confident in the residual income model than in the DCF model because it records valuation creation sooner? The answer is *absolutely not*! One model can be derived algebraically from the other and so it would be silly to be more confident of the left-hand side of an equation than the right-hand side. Whatever uncertainty you have in your forecasts about book value and net income translate into exactly the same amount of uncertainty in future net distributions to common equity holders.[4]

So far we have discussed the present value calculations as of the end of the fiscal year for the most recent financial statements, which is January 31, 2010 in the Kohl's example, and have worked our way down Figure 10.3 to the line labeled 'Forecast Equity Value Before Time Adjustment.' There are two more present value adjustments that take us to the next line, labeled 'Forecasted Value as of Valuation Date.' First, the present value computation treats the cash flows and residual income flows as though they are realized on the last day of each fiscal year. In reality, wealth

---

[4] Lundholm and O'Keefe (2001) provide careful discussion of this issue, along with a list of common errors in the implementation of each model that generate apparent, but not real, differences between the residual income model and DCF models.

is created and distributed somewhat more evenly throughout the year. To correct for this, we multiply the value estimate by $(1+ r_e/2)$. This effectively moves the flows forward six months in time. Second, you will typically want to compute the value as of the day you are considering the stock, not the last day of the last fiscal year. To move the valuation date, compute the fraction of the year between the entered date and the fiscal year end and adjust the value estimate by this fraction times $(1+ r_e)$ to get the present value as of the valuation date. This adjusts your valuation estimate for the passage of time between the last set of financial statements and the date selected. As time passes, you get closer to the estimated future values, so the present value increases. In the Kohl's example shown in Figure 10.3 we set the valuation date to be the same as the fiscal year end.  Consequently the only time value adjustment is to multiply 11,634,463 by (1+.10/2) to get 12,216,186 as the 'Forecasted Value as of Valuation Date.'   If you go to the Valuation Parameters Sheet and change the valuation date to a later date, say November 11, 2010, then this is 78.056 percent of the way through the next fiscal year, so the value increases further to 12,216,186*(1+.10*(.78056))=13,169,728.

## Solving for the Implied Cost of Equity Capital

So far we have input our estimate of the cost of equity capital and then solved for the value of the equity by discounting the cash flows or residual income flows using this estimate. But we can change the order of things.  We could ask what discount rate equates the present value of our forecasts with the currently observed stock price. For example, if we start with the default forecasts for Kohl's and a valuation date of January 31, 2010, and discount at 10 percent, we get the $39.79/share value as shown in Figure 10.3. But Kohl's stock price at close on January 31, 2010 was $50.37. What discount rate would reconcile with this price? A bit of guesswork on the Valuation Parameter's sheet shows that setting the discount rate to 8.548 percent would produce $50.37 in estimated value.  (Go ahead, try it yourself!)  This means that if investors' expectations at January 31, 2010 are the same as the default *eVal* forecasts, and the market is efficient (meaning that the price of $50.37 per share is "correct"), then investors should expect to earn an 8.548 percent return on their Kohl's investment. They may not earn this return every year—in fact, even if the future cash flows materialize exactly as the *eVal* forecasts predict, all the model says for sure is that the internal rate of return over the life of the firm will be 8.548 percent. If 8.548 percent strikes you as an unreasonably low return for an investment as risky as Kohl's, then effectively you are saying that investors' beliefs are more optimistic than the *eVal* defaults or the market price for Kohl's stock is too high.

There is one cautionary note we need to offer before turning you loose with the implied cost of capital. If your forecasts imply that the future net cash distributions to equity alternate between positive and negative, then it is possible for there to be more than one discount rate that equates the value of the future cash flows with the price. Without getting into the algebra behind this claim, the 'correct' value is typically the one closest to whatever you believe the true cost of equity capital to be.  As with all things in equity analysis and valuation, if the result looks unreasonable, then it probably is.

# 10.5 VALUING CONTINGENT CLAIMS AND OTHER ADJUSTMENTS

The value of *contingent claims* represents your estimate of the value of other potential claims on the future net cash distributions to equity holders that have not yet been considered in our valuation model. These can include outstanding stock warrants, conversion options in debt issues and outstanding employee stock options. They all give their holders the option to purchase shares of stockholders' equity at a price that may be less than intrinsic value. These contingent claims therefore have value, and this value must be deducted from the value of stockholders equity that we have already computed in order to figure out what is left for the existing stockholders. Intuitively, these contingent claims give their holders the opportunity to get a share of the future net cash distributions to equity if the future works out well, but allows the holders to walk away if things turn out badly. Estimating the value of these contingent claims can be quite complicated. We will describe how to compute a lower bound for this value, how to approximate it more accurately using the Black-Scholes option pricing model, and then discuss some limitations to both of these approaches.

At this point, we are trying to estimate the value of existing contingent claims; Chapter 12 confronts the related issue of forecasting the expected future consequences of contingent claims that we expect to be issued in the future. We will focus on estimating the value of existing employee stock options; the other types of contingent claims can be estimated in similar fashion. Start by reading the firm's financial statement footnote on employee stock options. Here they tell you the number of options outstanding in different ranges of option exercise prices. If any options exercise prices are lower than the current market price of the stock, then each of these options is worth *at least* the difference between these two amounts. In other words, the holder could hypothetically buy shares at the exercise price, and then turn around and sell them at the current market price. That is, the option is *in the money* by the difference between these two amounts. But this only represents a lower bound on the value of the option, because it doesn't account for the possibility that the stock price might increase even more before the option expires. How likely this is to occur depends on the remaining time before expiry of the option, the volatility in the stock price and a few other details. There are a number of models for valuing options. The most popular is the Black-Scholes Option Pricing Model, which requires the following inputs:

$S$ = Current stock price,
$K$ = Exercise or "strike" price,
$y$ = Long-term forecasted annual dividend yield,
$r$ = Annual risk-free interest rate,
$t$ = Number of years before the option expires,
$\sigma$ = Standard deviation of the log of the value of the stock price, and
$N(\bullet)$ = Cumulative standard normal distribution function.

The Black-Scholes formula is then:

$$OptionValue = Se^{-yt}N(d_1) - Ke^{-rt}N(d_2), where$$

$$d_1 = \frac{\ln\left(\frac{S}{K}\right) + \left(r - y + \frac{\sigma^2}{2}\right)t}{\sigma\sqrt{t}} \quad and \quad d_2 = d_1 - \sigma\sqrt{t}.$$

Without attempting to derive the specific form of this model, we offer some observations about it. First, note that the option's value increases with the gap between the current stock price $S$ and the option's exercise price $K$. The deeper the option is in the money, the more valuable it is. Second, the option's value increases with $t$, the number of years remaining before the option expires, and with $\sigma$, the stock price volatility. Third, the option value decreases with the dividend yield $y$ because future dividends decrease the future stock price, all else equal. Actually evaluating this formula by hand would be quite difficult because the function $N(\bullet)$ is itself quite complicated. Instead, we need a calculator. Fortunately, such calculators are readily available on the Internet; we recommend the ones available at <u>Money-Zine</u> or <u>Maxi-Pedia</u>.

Most of the inputs to the contingent claims calculator are straightforward, but the one that you may not have a good feel for is the annual standard deviation of the log of the stock price. A good source for this data item is the employee stock option footnote. Companies provide an estimate of this amount because they are required to estimate the value of options issued to employees during the current fiscal year. A ballpark figure is 30 percent, but it can range from 20% for a large stable company to over 50% for a small growth company.

A problem with using the Black-Scholes option valuation model is that real world contingent claims may not conform to its restrictive assumptions. In particular, it has been shown that employees overwhelmingly exercise their options well before expiration. This doesn't make sense, from the model's point of view, because the option still has additional value right up to the expiration date. But an employee may exercise early to lock in existing gains and eliminate risk. This means that the Black-Scholes estimates might be too high. This particular problem can be mitigated by reducing the time to expiration, $t$, to approximate the anticipated exercise date.

## Adjusting for Stock Splits and Stock Dividends

In order to estimate intrinsic value per share, we use the number of shares outstanding at the most recent balance sheet date. If the firm has undertaken a stock split or a *stock* dividend (as opposed to a *cash* dividend) between the date of the most recent balance sheet and your valuation date, then you need to adjust the number of shares outstanding. The adjustment factor is simply the ratio of the number of shares outstanding immediately after the split/dividend to the number of shares outstanding immediately before the split/dividend. For example, if your firm does a two-for-one stock split, then the number of shares outstanding doubles, resulting in a dilution factor of two. If we failed to account for the split, then our per-share valuation estimate would be twice what they should be. Imagine the embarrassment from such a mistake! You only have to adjust for splits/dividends between the date of the most recent balance sheet and your valuation date; don't adjust for any splits made before the most recent balance sheet date or after your valuation date.

What if the firm issues new shares for cash, or as part of the acquisition of another company after the last balance sheet date? Interestingly, you do not need to adjust for these *if* you believe the shares were issued at their true intrinsic value. In a stock split or stock dividend, the number of shares increases but nothing of economic value is added to the firm, so adjusting the number of shares completely captures the effect of this event. However, if the firm receives something of economic value in exchange for the shares, then the value of the firm increases along with the number of shares. If the new shares are issued at a price equal to their intrinsic value, then the increase in firm value exactly offsets the dilution caused by the increase in the number of shares. To make this perfectly clear, imagine a firm that consists of $100 in a bank account and has one share outstanding, so its intrinsic value is $100 per share. If the firm issues another share for $100 and deposits it in the bank, the firm is now worth $200 and has two shares, so it is still worth $100 per share. Complications arise, however, if the firm issues the stock at $90 or $110. We address these complications in Chapter 12.

## Putting It All Together

The valuation formulas given in the first part of the chapter compute the present value as of the most recent fiscal year end, assuming that all cash flows and residual income flows happen on the last day of each year. We then adjusted this value up by a half-year's-worth of time value, because the flows typically happen evenly throughout the year, not on the last day. We also adjusted the value up to the date that we are actually doing the valuation (or whatever date we want), rather than the end of the most recent fiscal year. We then subtract the value of any contingent claims and adjust the number of shares for any stock splits or stock dividends that occurred between the fiscal year end and the valuation date. The final result is our forecast of the intrinsic price per share. This is what we think the stock is really worth.

If the value estimate is ridiculously far from the current market price and you feel reasonably confident in your forecasts, here are a few things to check. First, are you sure you have the correct number of shares outstanding? If there was a stock split after the fiscal year end, then you may be way off in your estimate. In this respect, remember that firms sometimes do reverse splits, whereby each stockholder has to give back their shares, getting fewer in return. So make sure that what you first thought was a 10:1 stock split was not a 1:10 reverse split. Second, what if the estimated price is negative? Literally, a negative price means that you would pay this amount to *not* have to own the stock. If the estimated price is negative, it means that the present value of the cash flows that the equity holders are forecasted to send *to* the firm is greater than the present value of the cash flows that the equity holders are forecasted to receive *from* the firm. If this was literally true, then an equity holder might indeed be willing to pay to not have to own the stock. But since the firm can't force the equity holders to keep sending it money, and since equity holders are not liable to third parties for the firm's losses, the real lower bound on price is zero. If you really think the firm has positive value, you need to revise your forecasts accordingly. Negative stock prices are discussed in more detail in Chapter 12.

# 10.6 QUIZZES, CASES, LINKS AND REFERENCES

## Quizzes
• Chipotle Mexican Grill (Problem 5)
• Pandora (Problem 5)
• LinkedIn (Problem 5)
• Salesforce (Problem 5)

## Cases
• Analyzing Apple (Questions 14-16)
• Apple and the iFad (Questions 11-12)
• EnCom Corporation (Stage 3)
• Four Valuation Models - One Value
• Evaluating Intel's Earnings Torpedo
• Netflix, Inc. (Questions 13-15)
• Overstock.com (Questions 14-17)
• Can Salton Swing? (Questions 5 and 6)
• Sirius Satellite Radio (Questions 19-21)
• Building *eVal* (Part E)
• Has Zynga Lost Its Zing? (Questions 13-14)
• Is Tesla's Stock Price in Ludicrous Mode? (Question 14)

## Links
• Money-zine option calculator: http://www.money-zine.com/calculators/investment-calculators/black-scholes-calculator/

• <u>Maxi-pedia</u> option calculator: <u>http://www.maxi-pedia.com/Black+Scholes+formula+option+value+calculator</u>

# References

• Lundholm, R., and T. O'Keefe. (2001). Reconciling value estimates from the discounted cash flow model and the residual income model. *Contemporary Accounting Research* 18: 311–35.

CHAPTER ELEVEN

# Valuation Ratios

## 11.1 INTRODUCTION

In Chapter 5 we converted the financial statement data into ratios in order to reveal underlying economic properties and to make the data comparable across companies and over time. For the same reason, we can more easily compare the valuation of different companies by scaling market values by financial statement data. In this section we analyze the *price-to-book ratio*, the *price-to-earnings ratio* and the *price-to-earnings-to-growth (or PEG) ratio*, and we discuss what each ratio reveals about the market's expectations for the company's future. These ratios are commonly used summary statistics for a firm's valuation and each can be found on financial information portals, such as <u>Morningstar</u> or <u>Yahoo!Finance</u>. After we discuss each ratio we will give some historical and current benchmarks to get you grounded.

We offer a word of caution before proceeding. As we found in the last chapter, a valuation depends on an comprehensive set of forecasted financial data. Only in very special cases is it possible to value a firm based on one or two numbers from its recent financial statements. Consequently, it is unlikely that you will be able to take a quick look at the price-to-earnings ratio or price-to-book ratio and know if a firm is mispriced. Do you really think that finding mispriced stocks is as easy as dividing one readily available number by another readily available number? Tempting as such shortcuts can be, there is no substitute for the hard work of building a comprehensive set of forecasts. We recommend that you use these ratios as a way to make a quick assessment of the expectations built into a firm's current market price, but not as the sole basis for an investment strategy.

## 11.2 THE PRICE-TO-BOOK RATIO

This ratio divides the current market value of equity $P_e$ by the book value of equity from the most recent financial statements $CE_0$. If we start with the residual income to common equity model and divide everything by $CE_0$ we get

$$\frac{P_e}{CE_0} = 1 + \sum_{t=1}^{\infty} \frac{(ROE_t - r_e)\frac{CE_{t-1}}{CE_0}}{(1 + r_e)^t} \, ,$$

where $ROE_t$ is defined relative to beginning equity: $ROE_t = NI_t/CE_{t-1}$.

The first thing to note from this formula is that if you forecast that $ROE_t = r_e$ every period in the future then the price-to-book ratio is one. This is like a savings account; every period it pays interest at exactly its discount rate and so every period it is worth exactly the balance in the account. When firms have a price-to-book ratio greater than one, the market expects that, on average, they will earn a $ROE_t$ higher than $r_e$ in the future.

Note that the $(CE_{t-1}/CE_0)$ term in the numerator is the *cumulative* growth in common equity over the last t-1 periods. In other words, in year one it equals one, in year two it equals $CE_1/CE_0$, in year three it equals $CE_2/CE_0$ and so on. The numerator in our expression for the market to book ratio is therefore the firm's abnormal profitability $(ROE_t - r_e)$ times its cumulative growth in beginning book value $(CE_{t-1}/CE_0)$. This simple observation speaks volumes about the source of value in a firm. A firm is worth more than its book value only if it is expected to have an $ROE_t$ greater than $r_e$ (as we keep repeating). Assuming the firm is expected to meet this profitability threshold, growth and profitability are multiplicative. This means that really high valuations come about when firms have both high profitability *and* high growth.

To give you a few reference points, suppose that ROE is forecasted to be constant forever, and equity is forecasted to grow at rate g forever. In this case the price-to-book ratio can be simplified to

$$\frac{P_e}{CE_0} = 1 + \frac{ROE - r_e}{r_e - g}.$$

Suppose the firm has a 10% cost of equity capital, a forecasted constant ROE of 20% and a perpetual growth rate of 5%. By historical standards, these would be very rosy forecasts. Using the preceding formula gives a $P_e/CE_0$ ratio of three. We will give lots of historical statistics later in the chapter, but as a first benchmark, the median price-to-book ratio between 1962 and 2016 for all publicly-traded companies was 1.6; the bottom 25% were below 0.99 and the top 25% were above 2.6.

The price-to-book ratio is a very useful summary measure. It gives you a quick sense of what the market must think about the future growth and profitability of the firm. Of course, like everything else in valuation, our intuition can be thwarted by distortions in accounting. A good example of this is Kellogg, the maker of breakfast cereals (Tony the Tiger says "they're great!"). You may not think of Kellogg as a high flying, fast growing stock. And it isn't; annualized growth over the past five years is roughly 0 percent. Nonetheless, its price-to-book ratio has been greater than nine for the past five years! The story behind this is relatively simple. The great value of Kellogg is in its huge inventory of brands (think Rice Krispies, Cheez-its, Pop-tarts), yet none of this value is on Kellogg's balance sheet. Most of their brands have been developed internally over many years, and GAAP accounting doesn't capitalize internally developed intangible assets. Consequently, Kellogg's book value vastly understates its economic value, causing its ROE to bounce between 30 percent and 60 percent. If we plug a constant 60% ROE and a perpetual 3% growth rate into our simplified $P_e/CE_0$ model, assuming a 10% cost of equity capital, we get a price-to-book ratio of 8.1.

## 11.3 THE PRICE-TO-EARNINGS RATIO

This ratio divides the current market price per share by the past annual earnings per share, computed either as the most recent annual figure or as the sum of the past four quarters of earnings. It takes a fair bit of algebra, but you can derive the following expression from the residual income model:

$$\frac{P_e}{NI_0} = \frac{1 + r_e}{r_e}\left(1 + \sum_{t=1}^{\infty} \frac{\Delta RI_t}{(1 + r_e)^t NI_0}\right) - \frac{D_0}{NI_0},$$

where $\Delta RI_t$ is the *change in* residual income between date t and date t-1, $D_0$ is the net distribution to common equity holders for period 0 and $NI_0$ is the net income for period *zero* (i.e. so that $CE_0 = CE_{-1} + NI_0 - D_0$).

To understand what this ratio measures, ignore the $D_0/NI_0$ term for the time being; this is the dividend payout ratio for the current year, and it is typically less than one. If $\Delta RI_t = 0$ forever (e.g., residual income is a constant) and $r_e = 10\%$ then the price-to-earnings expression is $(1 + r_e)/r_e = 11$. The reason the price-to-earnings ratio often differs from 11 is because of the summation term inside the brackets. Look carefully at the summation term. It is the sum of the *changes* in residual income, scaled by the current period's net income (as opposed to the sum of the levels of residual income that you saw in the residual income model). So the price-to-earnings ratio will be greater than 11 if the market expects residual income to *grow* and it will be less than 11 if the market expects residual income to shrink. It doesn't matter whether the *level* of residual income is positive or negative, only the direction and size of the expected change. This is very different from the price-to-book ratio, which is large only if the expected *level* of residual income is both positive and large relative to $CE_0$.

What will cause residual income to grow? Obviously, growth in net income will contribute to growth in residual income, but the relation is subtler than this. For *residual* income to grow, net income must grow at a *faster rate* than book value. This is much tougher than simply growing net income. We can better illustrate this point by stating the change in residual income in relative terms. Divide $\Delta RI_t$ by common equity at time t-1 to get

$$\Delta RI_t/CE_{t-1} = (ROE_t - ROE_{t-1}) + g_{t-1}(ROE - r_e),$$

where $ROE_t$ is defined as $NI_t/CE_{t-1}$ and $g_{t-1}$ is the percentage growth in common equity from date t-2 to t-1. Suppose that $g_{t-1} = 0$, so that book value has not grown and the second term is zero. In this case, if the firm can deploy the existing book value more profitably, $(ROE_t - ROE_{t-1})$ will be positive and $\Delta RI_t$ will be positive. Alternatively, suppose that $ROE_t$ is greater than $r_e$ by a constant amount each period and that $g_{t-1}$ is positive for all periods. In this case, the first term in brackets is zero, while the second term will be positive, reflecting the increasing scale of positive profitable investments. So the price-to-earnings ratio is increasing in the expected future change in ROE and, given that $ROE_t$ is greater than $r_e$, it is also increasing in the expected growth rate in equity.

One logical benchmark for the price-to-earnings ratio that we have already discussed is to assume that residual income is a constant in perpetuity, and that the current dividend payout ($D_0/NI_0$) is zero, so that

$$\frac{P_e}{NI_0} = \frac{1 + r_e}{r_e}.$$

If $r_e = 10\%$ then this gives a price-to-earnings ratio of 11, as discussed above. Note that this is simply the capitalization factor for an up-front annuity. In other words, a regular cash payment of $NI_0$ received starting today and continuing at the end of every subsequent year would be worth 11 times $NI_0$.

A related benchmark is the "forward price-to-earnings ratio," defined as $P_e$ divided by the forecasted net income for next year, $NI_1$. In this case, assuming subsequent residual income is a constant perpetuity (i.e., $\Delta RI_t = 0$ for t > 1), we get

$$P_e = CE_0 + \frac{RI_1}{r_e} = CE_0 + \frac{NI_1 - r_e CE_0}{r_e} = \frac{NI_1}{r_e}, or$$

$$\frac{P_e}{NI_1} = \frac{1}{r_e}.$$

If $r_e = 10\%$, then we get a price-to-forward-earnings ratio of 10.

For all companies between 1962 and 2016, the median price-to-earnings ratio was 14 and the bottom 25 percent were below 9. These statistics only apply to first with positive earnings because, when $NI_0$ is negative, the price-to-earnings ratio isn't particularly meaningful. Investors either expect earnings to grow or the firm to shut down. However, we can say that these firms have 'really high' price-to-earnings ratios. Imagine two firms, each with a price of $10, but one has earnings of one cent and the other has earnings of minus one cent. Which has more price per unit of earnings? While we can't quantify it, certainly the firm with the same price but less earnings has a higher relative value. On average, for all publicly traded firms between 1962 and 2016, approximately 25 percent of the firms had negative earnings, so we can loosely think of these firms as the top quartile of the price-to-earnings ratio. We will give more values for the distribution of price-to-earnings ratios in different industries in the next section.

# 11.4 THE PEG RATIO

We have one more valuation ratio to discuss, the PEG ratio, which stands for Price-Earnings-Growth. It is defined as follows:

$$PEG\ Ratio = \frac{price - to - earnings\ ratio}{earnings\ growth\ X\ 100} = \frac{P_e/NI_1}{\left(\frac{NI_2 - NI_1}{NI_1}\right)X100}.$$

Note that the price-to-earnings ratio in the numerator is the forward ratio (i.e. the denominator is the forecast of next year's net income) and the forecast earnings growth rate is from one year ahead to two years ahead. The earnings growth rate may be defined over a longer period, say three to five years, but it still must be an annualized percentage. As we will explain shortly, the benchmark for the PEG ratio is one. Stocks with a PEG under one are considered undervalued and those with a PEG greater than one are considered overvalued.[1]

This ratio is a rough heuristic. The idea is that the price-to-earnings ratio measures the amount of earnings growth that is reflected in the market price so, if we compare this ratio with forecasted earnings growth, we can see whether the market price correctly reflects the forecasted growth and thus determine whether a stock is under-priced or over-priced. This seems reasonable, but why is one the magic benchmark? Academics have searched for special cases of a more general valuation model that will make this formula true, but with only limited success. Here is one such case.

Define the forecasted *abnormal earnings* at time t+1 as

$$ae_{t+1} = NI_{t+1} - [NI_t + r_e(NI_t - D_t)].$$

This amount is "abnormal" in the following sense. At time t+1 you may reasonably expect to earn the same net income as you did at time t, plus a 'normal' amount of earnings on any net income that you didn't distribute to equity holders, $r_e\ (NI_t - D_t)$. The amount that $NI_{t+1}$ exceeds or falls short of this amount is therefore abnormal.

The PEG ratio follows from a valid valuation model when two conditions hold. First, net distributions to equity holders are forecasted to be zero one-year ahead (i.e. $D_1 = 0$). This implies that forecasted abnormal earnings in year two are

$$ae_2 = NI_2 - (1 + r_e)NI_1.$$

Second, forecasted net income and net dividends from year three forward are such that abnormal earnings is constant, and equal to the abnormal earnings in year two, computed assuming $D_1 = 0$. That is,

$$ae_t = ae_2 \text{ for } t \geq 2.$$

If these assumptions are met, then one can show that

---

[1] See, Wikipedia for details and supporting references.

$$P_e = \frac{NI_2 - NI_1}{r_e^2}.$$

Constructing the PEG ratio from this simple valuation model gives

$$\frac{P_e/NI_1}{\left(\frac{NI_2 - NI_1}{NI_1}\right) X100} = \frac{1}{r_e^2 \, X \, 100}.$$

If $r_e$ is 10%, then this gives a PEG ratio of one. And if all these assumptions hold then stocks with a PEG ratio less than one are undervalued and stocks with a PEG ratio greater than one are overvalued.

As you can see, with some work we can beat the PEG ratio back into our world of theoretically valid valuation models. But the real question is, how reasonable are the assumptions that were necessary to get the job done? We had to assume that abnormal earnings are constant forever in the future, and equal to the abnormal earnings computed based on the forecasted earnings for the next two years. We also had to assume that net distributions to equity holders are forecasted to be zero next year. Finally, for the ratio to be benchmarked at one, we needed to assume the cost of equity capital is 10%.

To put the underlying model that supports the PEG ratio into perspective, we can rewrite price in this special case as

$$P_e = \frac{NI_1}{r_e} + \frac{NI_2 - (1 + r_e)NI_1}{r_e^2}.$$

Note that the first term is the price we would get if we capitalized forward earnings in perpetuity (i.e. $P_e = NI_1/r_e$). In the previous section we showed that such a valuation model is appropriate when residual income is constant in perpetuity (i.e. $NI_t - r_e CE_{t-1}$ is constant for all t). The model supporting the PEG ratio adds to this a bonus for abnormal earnings between year two and year one. In this sense the model behind the PEG ratio is more flexible at incorporating future growth than the forward price-to-earnings ratio, which is exactly what the PEG ratio was intended to do. If you were an analyst trying to "sell" investors on a stock with high forecasted growth in the near term, the PEG ratio is a good tool because it makes such stocks look more reasonably valued. However, such stocks are not necessarily undervalued, they may just look this way when evaluated using the PEG ratio.

## 11.5   PUTTING SOME VALUATION RATIOS TOGETHER

The price-to-book ratio is simply a scaled version of the residual income model and is therefore clearly related to the expected level of residual income. Because the price-to-earnings ratio scales by earnings in the most recent year, it is much more focused on expected growth in residual income. It is driven by how much residual income is expected to increase in the future relative to earnings today. And, to wrap all of this up into a neat package, note that

$$\frac{P_e}{CE_0} = \frac{NI_0}{CE_0} \; X \; \frac{P_e}{NI_0} \quad or$$

*price-to-book ratio = ROE$_0$ x price-to-earnings ratio,*

here defining *ROE$_0$* as the return on *ending* equity.

Remember how we hammered away on the idea that value is created by a combination of profitability and growth? Here we see this once again. The price-to-book ratio is the product of profitability, measured as ROE$_0$, and expected growth, as summarized by the price-to-earnings ratio.

The price-to-book and price-to-earnings ratios together give you a great snapshot of the market's expectations about the firm. To help you develop a feel for what a big or small ratio is, we have plotted the median price-to-book and median price-to-earnings ratios each year from 1974 to 2016 in Figure 11.1.

Two observations are immediately clear from the figure. First, valuations relative to fundamentals (i.e. net income and common equity) have been drifting steadily up over the past thirty years. This may be due to steadily declining interest rates over the same period, increasingly optimistic estimates about future growth and profitability, or a steady decline in the ability of accounting measures to capture true value. Which interpretation is correct is unclear; scholars and practitioners have championed each. The second observation is that the Internet boom and bust cycle, and the more recent financial crisis, are clearly present in the trend of valuation ratios. In both cases the median price-to-book ratio drifted above 2 and the median price-to-earnings ratio drifted to almost 20. That is, over half the firms in the economy were priced with very rosy expectations about the future. But even if you were sure that the market was overvalued in 2004, notice that it wasn't until 2008 that these ratios came back down. Bubbles are always easier to see in the rear-view mirror.

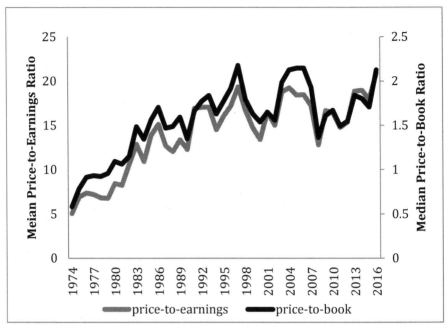

**FIGURE 11.1: Valuation Ratios through Time**

The valuation ratios not only change over time, they also vary greatly across different sectors of the economy. Figure 11.2 plots the median price-to-book and median price-to-earnings ratios as of the end of 2016 for ten economic sectors. Note the huge difference between the Energy sector and the Healthcare sector. Not surprisingly, the market sees more growth potential and greater future profitability in Healthcare than it sees in Energy as of 2016. Zooming in on Energy, recall that in 2016 there remained a world-wide glut of oil and so the prospect for increasing prices or increasing production seemed very low, thus the low ratios for the Energy sector. Right next to Energy is the Financial Sector. Most of the assets in this sector are marked-to-market, and so their accounting book values are near their market value, thus driving the price-to-book ratio close to one and the price-to-earnings ratio to the reciprocal of return on equity. The low ratios in the Energy and Financial sectors doesn't mean that stocks in these sectors are bad investments, and the high ratios in Healthcare doesn't mean that stocks in this sector are good investments. In fact, it may well mean that the market is over-pricing healthcare stocks and underpricing energy and financial stocks. We will return to the issue of picking stocks based on these simple valuation ratios in the next section.

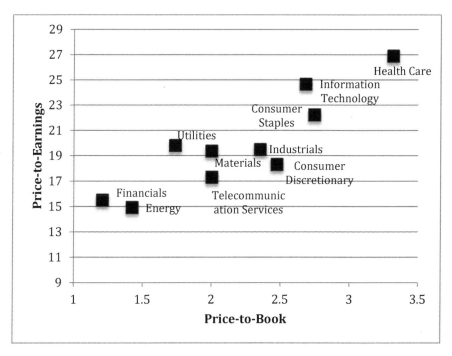

**FIGURE 11.2: Aggregate Sector Valuation Ratios in 2016**

We can use the price-to-book ratio and the price-to-earnings ratio together to see how the market views different firms in the consumer discretionary sector. Figure 11.3 plots the valuation ratios for some representative firms. The figure is divided loosely into four regions. Firms that are low on both dimensions are labeled as *Value,* and firms that are high on both dimensions are labeled as *Glamour*. The off-diagonal categories identify more unusual firms. Firms that have very high price-to-earnings ratios, but relatively low price-to-book ratios are labeled *Turnarounds*. They currently have very little earnings but, based on a big restructuring, a new CEO, or blind faith, the market expects that they will have lots more earnings in the future. The future earnings growth may not coincide with a high ROE however, so while the price-to-earnings ratio is very high, the price-to-book ratio is still low. At the other extreme we have *Harvesters*. Imagine a firm that has lots of profitability but very little, if any, growth. Without much anticipated growth, the price-to-earnings ratio is relatively low, while the high ROE generates a high price-to-book ratio. Figure 11.3 plots the valuation ratios for some different firms to illustrate the four quadrants. The Value firms are Kohl's and Dillard's; both are mid-range department stores with a price-to-book ratio around one and a price-to-earnings ratio between 10 and 12. Clearly the stock market does not see much excess profitability or growth in these two companies. Contrast this with the representative Turnaround firm – JC Penney. While Penney also has a price-to-book ratio of one, it has a price-to-earnings ratio of 1500! (shown on the graph as 40, so that it would fit). While the market does not see much difference in the long-term level of profitability for these three department stores, it sees enormous potential for Penney to increase profitability from its current level. Why such optimism? The end of 2016 saw Penney's earn its first profit in the past five years – a lowly $1 million. Starting from such a small base, if Penney were to grow income to the $169 million at Dillard's, it would represent 16,800 percent growth! While this seems unlikely, it does illustrate the power of a small denominator in any ratio.

On the other side of the price-to-book spectrum, Figure 11.3 shows Estee Lauder (selling high-end fragrance and beauty products) as the representative Glamour stock, sporting a price-to-book ratio greater than 8 and a price-to-earnings ratio of about 31. The market sees significant growth and profit potential as Millennials age into makeup-wearing adults. In contrast to the glamour of Estee Lauder, the representative Harvester stock is Altria Group – owners of the Marlboro tobacco brand. Altria has a price-to-book ratio of 10 but its price-to-earnings ratio is only 9. While selling cigarettes remains very profitable, the market doesn't see much growth potential. Our two other department stores, Nordstrom and Ross Stores, ring in with price-to-book ratios between 8 and 9, and price-to-earnings ratios between 20 and 22. The market sees continued growth and profitability at these two successful companies.

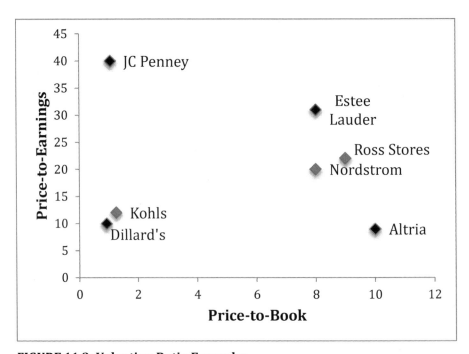

**FIGURE 11.3: Valuation Ratio Examples**

## Can You Make Money with these Ratios?

The market-to-book and price-to-earnings ratios both compare the current market price to an accounting measure of fundamental value. It is natural to ask whether or not firms that are extreme on either of these measures tend to move back to an average value. Do these statistics mean revert? And further, if they do mean revert, is it because the price corrects itself or is it because price predicts a future movement in the accounting fundamentals? If the correction is due to future price changes then it may be possible to form a profitable investment strategy based on these ratios.

Before giving you the answers to these titillating questions, we want to stress that the whole point of this book is to teach you how to develop a detailed forecast of the firm's future financial statements and then translate these forecasts into a value estimate. We expect you to arrive at a value estimate that is far superior to what you could get simply by looking at the company's earnings or book value. But with that thought in mind, the short answer is a qualified "yes". Historically, stocks with low market-to-book and price-to-earnings ratios and generated higher returns than those with much higher ratios.

Figure 11.4 gives the details of three different investment strategies based only on accounting book value, earnings and price.

| Next Year's Return | Price-to-Book Ratio | Price-to-Earnings Ratio | Book Value + 1.3 Residual Income |
|---|---|---|---|
| Return on Bottom 10% of Ratio | 19.1% | 20.7% | 21.0% |
| Return on Top 10% of Ratio | 11.8% | 11.8% | 11.1% |
| Hedge Return | 7.3% | 8.9% | 9.9% |

**Figure 11.4 Portfolio Returns to Different Price-to-Fundamental Investment Strategies.** Returns are for investments in the top or bottom 10% of the indicated ratio for all publicly-traded firms between 1976-1995. The portfolio position is taken three months after the fiscal year end and held for 12 months. See Dechow, Hutton and Sloan (1999) for details

Each strategy sorts the firms on their price-to-fundamental ratio, where the fundamental is either book value, earnings, or a combination of the two, and then buys firms with the lowest ratios and sells firms with the highest ratios. The portfolios are formed three months after the fiscal year end (to be sure that the book value and earnings data are publicly available) and are held for one year. The tests are conducted over a large sample of firms from 1976-1995. The first column of the table shows that the decile of firms with the lowest market-to-book ratio earned an average return of 19.1% while the decile of firms with the highest market-to-book earned an average return of only 11.8%. The hedge return is just the difference between these two portfolio returns. Our hedge portfolio has little exposure to market-wide risk, because it is equally long and short in the same dollar value of stocks, yet it would have returned 7.3% (i.e. it made 19.1% on the long position and lost 11.8% on the short position). The second column of the table shows a similar result for portfolios based on the price-to-earnings ratio. The hedge return to this strategy is 8.9%. The third column computes a crude "value" measure based on a weighted combination of book value and residual income. It is defined as

$$V_e = CE_0 + 1.3RI_0,$$

where the residual income weight of 1.3 is based on an estimate of the average rate at which residual income mean reverts across all firms. The strategy then computes the $P_e/V_e$ ratio and forms portfolios. As shown in the table, the hedge return to this portfolio is 9.9%.

These hedge returns are quite large by Wall Street standards. A hedge return is equally long and short in the same dollar amounts, so it is zero net investment, at least in theory. Of course, you can't walk into a brokerage house and open an account with zero dollars. But imagine that you invested your wealth in a fund that tracked the entire market and, in addition, you took the zero net position in the hedge portfolio described above. This combined strategy would beat the market return by almost 10%. A money manager who consistently beat the market by 10% would be a god on Wall Street, so is it really this easy? Not really. First, the actual transaction costs of taking a long position in 10% of the market and a short position in a different 10% of the market would be very costly. A less costly strategy would have to limit itself to a much smaller set of larger and more liquid firms, and this smaller set of firms do not have nearly the same returns as those documented in Figure 11.4. Further, while the hedge portfolio has no exposure to market-wide price movements, it still may have a significant exposure to other types of risk. What if all the short positions are in technology stocks and all the long positions are in utilities? If the techs finally discover a cheap and reliable source of green energy, you would lose your shirt. The hedge portfolio is market-neutral but it certainly isn't without risk. In fact, the return to the market-to-book strategy is so thoroughly documented that many finance professors refer to it as a *risk factor*, although it isn't clear exactly what fundamental risk such a strategy exposes one to. This is always the debate – is it mispricing or is it compensation for bearing risk? Finally, even if this profitable strategy was available in the past, there is no guarantee that it will be available in the future. If enough investors notice this pattern in the data and invest to profit on it, they will push the price of low price-to-fundamental stocks up and push the price of high price-to-fundamental stocks down, eliminating the hedge returns in the process.

# 11.6 QUIZZES, CASES, LINKS AND REFERENCES

## Cases

• The Restaurant Industry

## Links

• *eVal* Website: http://www.lundholmandsloan.com/software.html
• Morningstar: http://www.morningstar.com
• Yahoo!Finance: https://finance.yahoo.com/
• Wikipedia on the PEG ratio: https://en.wikipedia.org/wiki/PEG_ratio

## References

• Dechow, P., A. Hutton and R. Sloan. "An Empirical Assessment of the Residual Income Valuation Model." *Journal of Accounting and Economics* 26 (1999).

CHAPTER TWELVE

# Some Complications

## 12.1 INTRODUCTION

Up until this point, the valuation step has been quite straightforward. Given a series of forecast financial statements and the key valuation parameters, we just let a computer crank out the valuation. Unfortunately, life is not always this simple. In this chapter, we discuss some of the most common complications that arise in the valuation step. We stress that there are no "quick fix" solutions to these complications. Instead, it is up to you, to make sure that you anticipate and adjust for these complications. Remember, as we have stated many times before, the maxim "garbage-in, garbage out" is the order of the day.

There are two primary categories of complications. The first category relates to negative values and the abandonment option. If you forecast that a company will lose money forever, you will typically find that your valuation model yields a negative valuation. What does this mean? Stock prices are not negative in real life. This category of complications is the subject of Section 12.2.

The second category of complications relates to value creation and destruction through financing transactions. Up to this point, we have focused on computing the intrinsic value of the company to the existing stockholders, essentially assuming that they will be the sole claimants on all future net cash distributions. But what if the existing stockholders let some new stockholders invest in the company at a price that is different from intrinsic value? Whenever a company issues or repurchases shares of common stock at a price other than intrinsic value, it creates or destroys value for the existing stockholders. This category of complications is the subject of Section 12.3.

## 12.2 NEGATIVE VALUES AND THE ABANDONMENT OPTION

### Negative Values

In Chapter 10, we touched on the possibility that your valuation model could return a negative valuation. In this section, we revisit this issue and offer some advice about how to deal with this unusual situation. A negative stock valuation is actually not an uncommon occurrence for a valuation model if you simply use forecasting assumptions that extrapolate the past on a company that has been making losses. Yet in the real world, we never see negative stock prices. To understand why valuation models can provide negative stock prices, let's look at a specific example. Figure 12.1 provides a Valuation Summary sheet for Tesla, Inc. as of early 2017.

# Model Summary

| Historical Data For: | |
|---|---|
| TESLA INC | |
| Most Recent Fiscal Year End: | 2016/12/31 |
| Average ROE (last five years) | -41.97% |
| Sales Growth (last five years) | 102.87% |
| | |
| **Forecast Data:** | |
| Forecast Horizon | 10 years |
| This Year's ROE | -23.17% |
| Terminal Year's ROE | -25.17% |
| This Year's Sales Growth | 66.65% |
| Terminal Year's Sales Growth | 3.00% |
| This Year's Forecast EPS | -$9.15 |
| Forecast 5 Year EPS Growth | 56.00% |
| | |
| **Valuation Data:** | |
| Cost of Equity Capital | 10.00% |
| Valuation Date | 2017/05/17 |
| Estimated Price/Share | **-$1,941.31** |
| Estimated Price/Earnings Ratio | 212.15 |
| Estimated Market/Book Ratio | -65.99 |

FIGURE 12.1: *eVal* Model Summary for Tesla, Inc.

In case you have been in hibernation for the last ten years, Tesla is a manufacturer and retailer of all-electric cars. At the end of 2016, Tesla had introduced three luxury car models and was ramping up for the release of its first truly mass-production car, the Model 3. Consequently, Tesla had reported substantial losses for the last several years. The valuation in Figure 12.1 was obtained using the default forecasting assumptions in our *eVal* valuation workbook. Note that the estimated price per share is –$1,941.31. The summary of the forecast data indicates a forecast of ROE for the current year of -23 percent and a terminal ROE of -25 percent. If we were to look into the details of the forecasted financials, we would see that Tesla is forecast to have negative earnings, residual income, and cash flows for every future period— clearly a bleak future. We also see that sales grew at 103 percent over the past 5 years, and are forecast to trend to 67 percent this year and then gradually down to a terminal rate of 3%. When we combine the recent negative earnings, cash flows, and residual income with the rapid sales growth, we get even larger forecasted negative earnings, cash flows and residual income in the future. According to our forecasts, Tesla has a money-losing business model and plans to grow and operate the money losing business indefinitely, thereby losing even more money in the future. This all leads to a large negative valuation.

Next, look at Tesla's forecasted future free cash flows on *eVal*'s DCF Valuation sheet, which is reproduced in Figure 12.2. In 2017, Tesla is forecast to have free cash flow to common equity of -$4.6 billion. By 2020, the amount of negative free cash flow is forecast grow to -$15.0 billion. This means that, in order to keep operating the business consistent with our forecasts, enormous amounts of new common equity will have to be issued. If the existing stockholders act as forecast in our valuation model, then they will have to provide huge amounts of new equity injections into Tesla, even though they will never receive a positive cash distribution in return. Under this scenario, the value of the company to the existing stockholders is clearly negative because of the negative present value of the additional cash infusions that they plan to make.

## DCF Valuations                          ($000)

| Company Name | TESLA INC | | | |
|---|---|---|---|---|
| Most Recent Fiscal Year End | 12/31/2016 | | | |
| Date of Valuation | 5/17/2017 | | | |
| Cost of Common Equity | 10.00% | | | |
| Terminal Growth Rate | 3.00% | | | |
| | | | | |
| Fiscal Year of Forecast | 2017/12/31 | 2018/12/31 | 2019/12/31 | 2020/12/31 |
| Valuation to Common Equity | | | | |
| Free Cash Flow to Common Equity | (4,635,841) | (7,179,049) | (10,630,886) | (15,014,687) |
| Present Value of FCF | (4,214,401) | (5,933,098) | (7,987,142) | (10,255,233) |
| Present Value Beyond 10 Years | (171,279,111) | | | |
| Present Value of First 10 Years | (116,474,977) | | | |
| Forecast Equity Value Before Time Adj. | (287,754,088) | | | |
| Forecasted Value as of Valuation Date | (313,639,966) | | | |
| Less Value of Contingent Equity Claims | 0 | | | |
| Value Attributable to Common Equity | (313,639,966) | | | |
| Common Shares Outstanding at BS Date | 161,561 | | | |
| Equivalent Shares at Valuation Date | 161,561 | | | |
| Forecast Price/Share | -$1,941.31 | | | |

**FIGURE 12.2:** *eVal* **DCF Valuation for Tesla, Inc.**

Why then do we never observe negative stock prices in reality? The reason is that stockholders have limited liability. Management and creditors can never force the existing stockholders to pay more cash into the company, so the least that a stock can ever be worth is zero. This is where our valuation model doesn't jibe with reality. We have forecast that stockholders will be willing to pay in additional cash indefinitely, and our valuation model took the present value of those negative cash flows paid by common equity holders. But, in reality, either the company will develop successful products and generate profits, or stockholders will abandon the company and it will cease operations. The most obvious limitation of our forecasting model is that we have extrapolated Tesla's past losses into the indefinite future. But in reality, the stockholders of Tesla hope that the company will turn profitable when the Model 3 production cycle matures.

Given that we never observe negative stock prices in the real world, why don't we just have our valuation model default to zero when the model value is less than zero? The reason is to see how bad the hypothetical investment in the company would be. How much value are you forecasting that the company can destroy as investors send good money chasing after bad? We know that the quoted stock price will never actually be negative. Interpret the negative value estimate as how much worse of investors would be if they did continue to invest in the company as predicted by your forecasts. While real world stock prices are never negative, it is certainly true that real world investors have poured new money into loss-making businesses that never made a profit. But in the real world, a stage ultimately arrives when investors figure out that they should simply abandon the investment. Different investors reach that conclusion at different times, so in the case of Tesla, some investors may view any new equity infusions as money down the drain, while others may see them as a necessary step to making positive profits and free cash flows in the future. If you are in the first camp, your valuation model tells you how much value you expect the investors in the second camp to lose!

## The Abandonment Option

We have now established that equity cannot have a negative value in practice because stockholders have limited liability. They are free to walk away from the company and cannot be forced to provide additional capital to fund money-losing operations or pay creditors. This stockholder right is sometimes referred to as the *abandonment option*. As with many options, the abandonment option can have considerable value. In this section, we will examine the abandonment option in more detail.

The forecasting assumptions we discussed in Chapter 8 are our 'best guesses' as to what we think will happen in the future. They are point estimates of the most likely outcome rather than a range of possible outcomes. But, in reality, any number of possible outcomes could arise for most of our forecasting assumptions. Moreover, situations may arise where we know that our point estimates are imprecise and there is great uncertainty as to the ultimate outcome. As long as the range of possible outcomes is symmetric around our most likely estimate, and all the valuations are positive, then our 'best guess' valuation is a reasonably unbiased estimate of expected value. Unfortunately, when some of the possible outcomes result in a negative valuation, the abandonment option will introduce significant asymmetries into the range of possible valuations. In particular, since equity holders can choose to abandon the firm in the case of poor outcomes, the left tail of the possible range of valuation outcomes is truncated at zero. The result is that the 'best guess' valuation can seriously underestimate the expected valuation after taking the abandonment option into consideration. We illustrate the effect of the abandonment option in Figure 12.3.

Figure 12.3 charts the probability distribution of possible valuation outcomes for three different scenarios. In each of the three scenarios, the most likely point estimate of value, represented by the peak of the valuation distribution, is $100. Sensitivity analysis reveals the range of other possible valuation outcomes. The first chart represents a low-variance scenario, where the range in possible valuation outcomes is quite closely clustered around the most likely estimate of $100. Note also that the range of possible outcomes is symmetric and all values are positive. This first scenario represents the typical case, where the range of possible valuation outcomes is symmetric around the most likely point estimate valuation, all reasonably likely valuations are positive, and so the most likely point estimate valuation is our best estimate of the expected valuation.

The second chart represents a high-variance scenario, where the range of possible valuation outcomes varies widely around the most likely point estimate of $100. As with the first chart, the range of possible outcomes continues to be symmetric around the most likely valuation estimate of $100, so the expected value is still $100, but a significant range of the possible valuation outcomes in the second chart falls below zero. As discussed above, all the negative valuations are unreasonable because the existing stockholders will not indefinitely continue to invest good money after bad; rather they will exercise their abandonment option and refuse to contribute additional capital.

The range of possible valuation outcomes, assuming that stockholders optimally exercise their abandonment option, is shown in the third chart of Figure 12.3. In this chart, the distribution of possible valuation outcomes is truncated at zero. All of the possible negative valuation outcomes in the second chart are now concentrated at zero. Note that stockholders still keep all of the upside in the case of very positive valuation outcomes, but they avoid the downside in the case of negative valuation outcomes. As a result, the expected valuation of the investment is now greater than the most likely point estimate of $100. In the particular case shown in the third chart, the expected value works out to be about $110. Thus, by using the most likely point estimate valuation, we would have undervalued the stock by about 10 percent.

Probability Distribution of Valuation Outcomes for Low Variance Firm

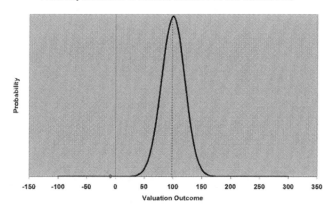

Probability Distribution of Valuation Outcomes for High Variance Firm
Ignoring the Abandonment Option

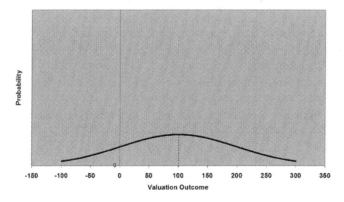

Probability Distribution of Valuation Outcomes for High Variance Firm
Incorporating the Abandonment Option

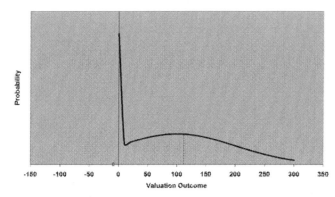

FIGURE 12.3:  Probability Distributions of Valuation Outcomes

What determines the value of the abandonment option? The third chart in Figure 12.3 should make it clear. The lower the most likely point estimate valuation and the greater the variance of possible valuation outcomes, the greater the probability of a negative outcome, and the greater the value of the abandonment option. Thus, the abandonment option tends to be the greatest in money-losing companies with great uncertainty in future outcomes. A company such as Tesla is a good example. Owning a share in this company is like owning an option on the small chance that they will become a leading and highly profitable vehicle manufacturer.

To determine whether there is an abandonment option in play, you should always conduct sensitivity analysis for a plausible *worst-case* scenario. If this scenario yields a negative valuation, then the abandonment option has positive value. To make the analysis tractable, this worst-case valuation scenario should represent a plausible outcome—assumptions that you feel are in the bottom 25% tail of likely outcomes. You also should think about a representative *best-case* valuation scenario. By assigning probabilities to each of these scenarios and assigning a value of zero to the negative valuation outcomes, you can compute the expected value of the stock *after* incorporating the abandonment option. Figure 12.4 provides some representative computations assuming that the most likely outcome has a probability of 50 percent and the best- and worst-case scenarios each has a probability of 25 percent.

The figure provides four representative cases. The first two cases represent a "healthy" firm, with a most likely valuation outcome of $100. The second two cases represent a "distressed" firm, with a most likely valuation outcome of $0. The first and third cases represent a "low-variance" firm, with the best and worst case scenarios deviating from the most likely case by $50. The second and fourth cases represent a "high-variance" firm, with the best and worst case scenarios deviating from the most likely case by $150. We compute the value without the abandonment option by summing the products of each of the valuation outcomes with their respective probabilities. We compute the value with the abandonment option using the same procedure, but after assigning a value of $0 to all negative valuation outcomes.

| | Worst Case (25% prob.) | Most Likely Case (50% prob.) | Best Case (25% prob.) | Value Without Abandonment Option | Value With Abandonment Option |
|---|---|---|---|---|---|
| Healthy Low Variance Firm | $50 | $100 | $150 | $100 | $100 |
| Healthy High Variance Firm | -$50 | $100 | $250 | $100 | $112.5 |
| Distressed Low Variance Firm | -$50 | $0 | $50 | $0 | $12.5 |
| Distressed High Variance Firm | -$150 | $0 | $150 | $0 | $37.5 |

**FIGURE 12.4:  Value of the Abandonment Option**

For the first case, of the healthy, low-variance firm, even the worst-case valuation outcome is positive, so the abandonment option has no value. In the second case, of the healthy, high-variance firm, the worst-case outcome has a negative value, giving value to the abandonment option. The value without the abandonment option is $100 and with the abandonment option is $112.5, so the value of the abandonment option is $12.5. Higher variance results in a greater value for the abandonment option. In the third case, that of the distressed, low-variance firm, the worst-case valuation outcome is again negative, giving a value of $12.5 to the abandonment option. In the fourth case, of the distressed, high-variance firm, the worst-case valuation outcome is very negative, resulting in an abandonment value of $37.5. Financial distress combines with high variance to give great value to the abandonment option. Note that in this fourth case, the value of the company with the abandonment option is $37.5, even though the most likely valuation outcome is zero. Ignoring the abandonment option can result in serious undervaluation.

# 12.3 CREATING AND DESTROYING VALUE THROUGH FINANCING

## Common Equity Transactions

Our valuation computations thus far assume that all future net cash distributions to common stockholders will accrue to the current common stockholders. This is equivalent to assuming that if the firm does sell additional shares to new investors, they do so at the share's intrinsic value. In reality, this is often not the case. Companies frequently issue new shares of stock to new stockholders and repurchase shares of stock from existing stockholders, and do so at values that are arguably wildly different from the stock's intrinsic valuation. An obvious question that arises is therefore whether these transactions can create or destroy value for existing stockholders. The answer is a resounding yes, and there have been numerous spectacular cases where companies have created or destroyed value for stockholders through transactions in their own common stock. This is exactly the stuff that keeps the fat checks coming to investment bankers.

To keep things simple, we will start by assuming that we have built a valuation model that correctly forecasts the future net cash distributions to common stockholders; that is, it captures equity's intrinsic value. By discounting these future cash distributions, we arrive at the value of common equity to the existing stockholders as a group. We then divide by the number of common shares outstanding to arrive at an estimate of intrinsic value per share. As long as all of the current stockholders continue to hold their stock and no new stock is sold, then the current stockholders will realize this intrinsic value.

But what if some existing stockholders sell their stock to new stockholders? Well, as long as these transactions take place at intrinsic value, no wealth is transferred between the selling stockholders and the buying stockholders. However, if these transactions take place at a price that differs from the intrinsic value, there is a wealth transfer between the old selling stockholders and the new buying stockholders. If trades take place above intrinsic value, the selling stockholders gain at the expense of the buying stockholders. Conversely, if trades take place below intrinsic value, the selling stockholders gain at the expense of the buying stockholders. These results should come as no surprise. After all, one of the key goals of this book is to help you identify undervalued and overvalued securities. The important point to emphasize at this juncture is that the value of the stock to ongoing stockholders continues to be the intrinsic value computed by your valuation model, regardless of the price at which trades take place between old and new stockholders.

But what if the company itself trades in its own stock? Well, as long as these trades take place at intrinsic value, again there are no wealth transfers. But if these trades take place at a price different from intrinsic value, then there are wealth transfers between the existing stockholders and the stockholders transacting with the company. Figure 12.5 summarizes the direction of the wealth transfers. The important point is that the ultimate value of a stock to an ongoing stockholder is determined not only by the intrinsic value of the stock, but also by the extent to which the company transacts in its own stock at a price differing from intrinsic value. This means that the market value of a stock is a potentially important determinant of the value of the stock even to a stockholder with no plans to trade the stock.

| | Company repurchases stock from existing stockholders | Company sells stock to new stockholders |
|---|---|---|
| **Transaction takes place at a price above intrinsic value** | Wealth is transferred from ongoing stockholders to selling stockholders | Wealth is transferred from buying stockholders to ongoing stockholders |
| **Transaction takes place at a price below intrinsic value** | Wealth is transferred from selling stockholders to ongoing stockholders | Wealth is transferred from ongoing stockholders to buying stockholders |

**FIGURE 12.5: Wealth Transfers in Stock Transactions**

A couple of examples should help to illustrate the situation. First, consider the case of a company with an intrinsic value of common equity of $1,000 and 10 shares outstanding. The intrinsic value per share is $100. Next assume that this company is able to issue an additional 10 shares at $300 per share. The company has a revised intrinsic value of $4,000 ($1,000 of original intrinsic value plus $3,000 of cash proceeds) and 20 shares outstanding, giving an intrinsic value of $200 per share. By issuing new shares at a price that exceeds intrinsic value, the company has created additional intrinsic value for ongoing stockholders at the expense of the new stockholders.

As a second example, begin again with a company that has intrinsic value of common equity of $1,000 and 10 shares outstanding. But now assume that this company's stock is only trading at $50 per share. If this company repurchases six shares of its own stock at the market price of $50, it will have a revised intrinsic value of $700 and four shares outstanding, giving an intrinsic value per share of $175. By repurchasing shares at a price below intrinsic value, the company has created additional intrinsic value for ongoing stockholders.

These opportunities to create value for existing stockholders have important implications for the valuation of an equity security. If the market value of the security differs from its intrinsic value, then we must consider the potential for the company to engage in transactions in its own stock to take advantage of this misvaluation. You can probably see that this argument has an element of circularity to it. If a company's market price is an important determinant of its intrinsic value, then how should we determine the appropriate market price? This is one reason why stock prices can get caught up in speculative bubbles. But, at the end of the day, these speculative bubbles simply transfer wealth from one set of stockholders to another. The intrinsic value of a firm's total common equity is still determined only by the present value of its future net cash distributions.

It is difficult to identify airtight examples of firms issuing or repurchasing equity at prices different from the intrinsic value because we never really know the intrinsic value for sure. Nonetheless, we offer AOL's acquisition of Time Warner as a likely illustration. In January 2000, AOL was trading at a total market value of $164 billion, a value that was difficult to justify based on forecasts of their future cash flows. AOL's management cashed in on its high stock price by issuing shares of AOL stock in exchange for all of Time Warner's stock. Whereas AOL had mostly Internet assets and a customer base with fading loyalty, Time Warner had hard assets, including magazines, cable networks, and recording studios. The acquisition transformed AOL's overvalued business into assets that had real value. In this way, they created value for the original AOL shareholders, but at the expense of the Time Warner shareholders. It didn't take long for the market to find its way back to intrinsic value. Prior to the merger announcement, Time Warner had a market value of about $84 billion, giving the combined entity a pre-merger valuation of $248 billion. By the time the deal closed a year later, the value of the combined entity had fallen to approximately $109 billion, not much more than the original value of Time Warner all by itself. Absent the acquisition, the original AOL shareholders may have had nothing in terms of future cash flows. But after this transaction, they owned over 50 percent of the new entity—and the original Time Warner shareholders, who used to own 100 percent of the valuable part of the new entity, now owned less than 50 percent. By 2003, the merged AOL Time Warner had a market value of only about $50 billion, much to the chagrin of the original Time Warner owners.[1]

From a practical perspective, how can we address the issue of potential wealth transfers resulting from a company trading in its own stock? Well, we should always be aware of significant deviations between the current market value of a stock and our estimate of its intrinsic value. If a company's market price exceeds its intrinsic value, we should consider whether the company is likely to issue new shares of stock. These issuances can take the form of seasoned equity offerings or stock-for-stock acquisitions of other companies. If

---

[1] For a more comprehensive investigation of wealth transfers via equity transactions, see Sloan, Richard G., and Haifeng You. "Wealth transfers via equity transactions." *Journal of financial economics* 118, no. 1 (2015): 93-112.

such issuances are likely, then we should try to quantify their impact on stock values for ongoing stockholders. If a company's market price is below its intrinsic value, we should consider whether management is likely to undertake stock repurchases. If repurchases are likely, then we should try to quantify their impact on stock values for ongoing stockholders. You may have noticed that our guidance is somewhat vague on this issue. This is no coincidence. A company's ability to create and destroy value for ongoing stockholders by transacting in its own stock is one of the most difficult valuation issues to grapple with. Trying to forecast how much value will be created or destroyed is a bit like trying to forecast when a Ponzi scheme will collapse.

The creation and destruction of value through financing activities is not restricted to transactions in a company's common stock. If companies are able to issue debt or preferred stock at inflated values, then they will likewise create value for existing stockholders. But there is one key difference in the case of these non-equity forms of financing. We explicitly forecast the cash flows to and from these capital providers in our valuation model. Hence, as long as we correctly forecast the favorable or unfavorable terms of issuance for non-equity capital, the resulting impact on the value of common equity will be incorporated in our valuation.

## Contingent Equity Claims

Issuing contingent equity claims is another way to create or destroy value through financing transactions. Contingent equity claims take many forms, including company-issued warrants, employee stock options, and conversion options embedded in bonds. These contingent equity claims give their holders the right to purchase shares of common stock at prices that may differ from intrinsic value, and are in many cases well below intrinsic value. If such rights are exercised, then wealth is transferred between the ongoing stockholders and the new stockholders exercising their contingent equity claims. The accounting for contingent equity claims varies depending on the form the claim takes, but none of the existing accounting rules fully reflect the impact of contingent equity claims on the intrinsic value of a share of common stock.

We can give you a simple (but admittedly crude) procedure for dealing with contingent equity claims. To the extent that a company has *existing* outstanding contingent equity claims, you should value those claims using an option calculator and incorporate them into your valuation, along the lines described in Chapter 10. To the extent that you forecast a company will issue contingent equity claims in the *future*, you can capture the economic effect of this by forecasting that the company will instead engage in a "plain vanilla" transaction of similar economic value. For instance, if you expect a company to issue warrants, you should simply assume that the company will issue common stock of equivalent value. For employee stock options, simply assume that the company will pay cash compensation of equivalent value. The accounting rules for stock compensation changed beginning in 2006, so financial statements now provide an estimate of the value of options issued to employees, which should help you forecast the future compensation value. For the issuance of convertible bonds, simply assume that the company will issue plain bonds at the corresponding market interest rate. Note that these alternative transactions are not exactly economically equivalent to issuing contingent equity claims. But the key differences hinge on changes in the future stock price of the company. And if we knew how the future stock price was going to change, we wouldn't need to do a valuation in the first place. By replacing the contingent claim transactions with their plain-vanilla counterparts, we obtain an estimate of intrinsic value that abstracts from the circularity of trying to determine a firm's current value with reference to its future market price.

We close with some words of warning. Many professional analysts value companies by ignoring stock-based compensation and related stock-based expenses. These expenses are added back to earnings on the grounds that they are 'non-cash' charges and they never hit free cash flows because they don't ever have to be paid in cash (apart from some tax-related issues). Does this mean that a firm can give away stock without any cost to existing stockholders? The answer is, of course not. The cost should enter the valuation model through the increased number of shares that will be outstanding in future periods and will reduce the amount of earnings and free cash flow that belongs to existing stockholders. This means that we can't just divide intrinsic value by the number of shares outstanding today, but we instead have to divide each future period's free cash flow by the new number of shares that we expect to be outstanding after accounting for stock-based compensation. This would be very cumbersome. A more practical alternative is to follow our advice from the previous paragraph. Include a forecast of stock-based compensation expense in earnings and make a corresponding 'pro forma' adjustment to free cash flow, essentially pretending that these expenses will instead be paid in cash. By doing so, you can still value the firm by computing the intrinsic value to all stockholders and dividing by the number of shares outstanding at the valuation date.

## 12.4 CONCLUDING REMARKS

If you have made it this far, then congratulations! By now, you should have realized that equity valuation and analysis involves a lot of hard work. There are no magic formulas that will make you rich quickly. Instead, the key to success is to have better forecasts of future cash flows than other investors. But it is the hard work of you and people like you in coming up with these forecasts that is the life-blood of the capitalist economic system. By forecasting future fundamentals, estimating intrinsic values and investing capital accordingly, you will be helping with the efficient allocation of economic resources. And if you are like us and find all of this to be an exhilarating challenge, you will have an enjoyable and productive career ahead of you.

# 12.5 QUIZZES, CASES, LINKS AND REFERENCES

## Cases
• The AOL Time Warner Merger
• The Valuation of Amazon.com in June 2001

## References
• Sloan, Richard G., and Haifeng You. "Wealth transfers via equity transactions." *Journal of Financial Economics* 118, no. 1 (2015): 93-112.

# Index

24384420R00141

Made in the USA
Columbia, SC
26 August 2018